D1713262

Personal Financial Planning for Divorce

REAL-WORLD STRATEGY FOR SUCCESS

Personal Financial Planning for Divorce

REAL-WORLD STRATEGY FOR SUCCESS

Jeffrey H. Rattiner

WILEY

John Wiley & Sons, Inc.

For general information on our other products and services, or technical support,
please contact our Customer Care Department within the United States at
800-762-2974, outside the United States at 317-572-3993 or fax 317-572-4002.

Wiley also publishes its books in a variety of electronic formats. Some content that
appears in print may not be available in electronic books.

For more information about Wiley products, visit our Web site at
http://www.wiley.com.

Library of Congress Cataloging-in-Publication Data:
Rattiner, Jeffrey H., 1960-
Personal financial planning for divorce : real-world strategy for success / Jeffrey H.
Rattiner.
      p. cm.
   Includes index.
   ISBN 978-0-470-48204-9 (cloth)
   1. Divorced people–Finance, Personal. I. Title.
   HG179.R3284 2009
   332.0240086'53–dc22

                                                            2009019193

Printed in the United States of America
10 9 8 7 6 5 4 3 2 1

To my children, Brandon, Keri, and Matthew.
Just because we don't all live together doesn't mean
for a second that I will ever stop loving you.
You are my inspiration.

To my parents, Ronald and Esther, and to
my brothers and their spouses, Steven and Vicki,
and Robert and Terri, who were lucky enough to
be blessed with wonderful marriages and children.

To my best friend, Michelle E. Boyer, who has
taught me how to love life again. Thank you for
your comments on the manuscript.

To all the divorced spouses, I know what you
went through . . . been there, done that.

To all the soon-to-be-divorced spouses, may
you learn enough from this book to help you
understand the process and determine whether
divorce makes sense for you.

To many of my Financial Planning Fast
Track students, who have asked me to write a book
on this subject.

But most of all, to the millions of happy marriages
out there—you all were rewarded with life's
number one blessing.

Contents

Preface

When Wiley asked me to write this book, I wanted it to be different from the two previous books I had authored for John Wiley & Sons, books I have written for Bloomberg Press, Harcourt Brace, Commerce Clearing House, Aspen Publishing, American Management Association, and the others I have worked on or helped co-write.

I wanted to go outside my normal writing style and provide a different twist to the numerous divorce books in the marketplace. This book focuses on the personal financial planning side of the divorce and the other issues you need to be well aware of, before, during, and after the divorce. Having recently gone through a divorce, I had a lot I wanted to say about things I had experienced and learned in the process from myself and others whom I interviewed while writing this book. This is not a book about my divorce. Rather, it is a book that incorporates some of the things I went through and many other things that friends, business associates, and acquaintances have gone through. As they say, been there, done that!

When you go through anything in life, you encounter many different perspectives on how things really work and are supposed to work. Those things then become part of the learning process. Your measure of success is how well you come through the process and overcome the situation, whatever life has to throw at you. Divorce is one of the ultimate curveballs found in life. Hopefully you will come through it unscathed.

This book presented a unique challenge: to put many of the key issues surrounding divorce into one comprehensive, practical, and user-friendly guide. The book is written to focus on many key issues that present themselves during the divorce process. It is not written in a drab style, stating important topics one after the other, but rather as a friend helping others become comfortable with the divorce process so that readers can learn ahead of time what they can expect, before experiencing undue hardship if that's not what they really want.

There is humor mixed throughout the book, not because I don't take this subject seriously, but because in any difficult situation that life presents, you need to maintain your sense of humor. Otherwise, the process can really become depressing—you begin to lose hope and faith, and you end up not seeing the light at the end of the tunnel.

And there *is* a light at the end of the tunnel. Everyone told me there would be. I didn't believe it at first, but now I definitely do. What you learn is that this nightmare will eventually end and it will be back to life as close to normal as possible. Time heals all wounds. And as my mother would say, "This too shall pass!" Of course, it's easier to say that now after the fact, but that phrase helped me throughout the process. So please don't be offended by any jokes or humorous stories you read throughout. They're intended to keep the mood light throughout this read.

I want to express my gratitude to Sheryl Garrett, CFP, founder of the Garrett Planning Network, who authored Chapter 11 on divorcing for same-sex couples. This is an often overlooked and unrepresented topic in most divorce books. Thanks, Sheryl, for being one of the true cornerstones in the financial planning industry and a great friend.

Best of luck to all our readers on whatever path you ultimately choose.

JEFFREY H. RATTINER, CPA, CFP, MBA, RFC
Scottsdale, Arizona
September 2009

CHAPTER 1

The Unthinkable

You dreaded this day. You never thought it would happen to you. And then—boom! It hits you like a ton of bricks. Papers are served on you. You can't run and you can't hide. You stand there in dumb amazement, wondering if this is all part of a bad dream.

Well, I have been there, done that! From this moment forward, your life begins to change. The once close relationship changed from adversary to enemy, and you need to adjust and determine what to do from the first day of your new life—the beginning of chapter two.

Many things run through your mind, some rational, some not so rational. You end up back at square one, wondering how to proceed. It is time to step outside the box and look in, but emotions will not let you do that so quickly. You think you need to be victorious but it is not possible in this situation.

In short, there are no winners, only losers. No matter what deal you strike (agreement you come to), you will never come out ahead. Let me correct that. There *are* winners—the attorneys and their support team (i.e., valuation experts, expert witnesses, and others who hang around for the money), who make out like bandits.

Even if you think you know what is likely to transpire, you really do not. As a highly skilled and effective educator, MBA, CPA, and CFP® who works with clients and teaches financial planning, tax, divorce, and a variety of other subjects to many financial experts, trade groups, and consumers nationwide for over 20 years, I was nevertheless naïve during my divorce process. There is no substitute for actually going through the process. As educated as I am, I still learned ten times more than I thought I knew. There is no substitute for experiencing it yourself, learning the proper way to approach the necessary steps, and wishing you could undo mistakes created during the process.

This book is not about my divorce. Rather, it is a book I believe will help others get a better grasp of the issues involved with a divorce and ensure that they are comfortable doing what they can to survive the process, minimize the damage, and save unnecessary costs. After intensive study of the many possible scenarios that can occur both during and after a divorce, I have tried to put together in one book all of the issues that can arise over many different spectrums and that are pertinent to the many types of divorces people go through. My purpose in writing this book is to assist you, in a simple, easy-to-understand format, through the entire divorce process, starting from the time you begin seriously contemplating divorce, through the start of the legal process, to the issuance of the final divorce decree. My hope is that I can help you manage the process and your expectations, inform you of the key financial consequences, provide guidance on how to negotiate and structure a settlement, provide a plan of attack and ultimate retreat, assist you in getting through a tough time, and finalize this horrible episode of your life.

Divorce from a Personal Financial Planning Perspective

All marriages are financial contracts. It's a business deal. Society just glamorizes the emotional connection to the legal contract that binds two people to each other. It reminds me of the song by Elvin Bishop, "Fooled Around and Fell in Love." The intentions are correct from the start and then it's all downhill from there!

When entering into a business deal, you should begin knowing the outcome you are willing to accept and where you want to end up. When entering the sanctity of marriage, the reasonable objective is to do so for your entire lifetime. Otherwise there is no point in entering into this legal binding contract. Every contract has pros and cons and you must be aware of the flip side.

In the event the marriage doesn't work, you will need to strive for a bottom-line financial outcome. That means ending up with a fair amount of dollars and cents so you can begin anew. Having a sense of the bottom line is sort of like a lawyer asking questions while knowing in advance what the answers will be. You need to know what to walk away with if all systems are a no-go. To help you get there, you will need to do an honest self-examination of who you really are and what you really want. Keep your attention on the things that really count. As I tell my students, "Focus!"

There is a big strategic picture (macro perspective) as well as a small tactical picture (micro approach) to a divorce. If you can gain a handle on your emotions, you will know whether it is worth sweating the small stuff! Not everything will be a catastrophe. Pick and choose your battles carefully. Determine what you value and why. That approach will help you in dividing the marital property. In other words, you need to be rationale and fully functional in order to split marital property. For example, is it worth fighting over this minuscule asset in the grand scheme of things? Is it worth getting into a frenzy over something you won't even care about one month from now? More often than not, it won't be. Therefore, the proper tactic is to punt regarding the disposition of that nonessential asset.

From a personal financial planning perspective, divorce starts off with the division of property. For the most part, it's a 50/50 split. Other factors are then worked into the equation. Included as part of the property split are the couple's assets, debt, and support (future income). It then expands to custody issues and other relevant factors.

As a result, from a business perspective you need to do the right thing to minimize your damage. That means not letting your emotions get the best of you and complicate the process by having you do things for all the wrong reasons. It's easy to do that because divorce itself isn't rational. After all, you had agreed (hopefully not under duress!) to marry this individual for love, a reason that made sense at the time, and now you are divorcing that spouse for a completely different reason. The relationship ultimately changes course through the marriage. Divorce represents the end of one relationship (with your ex) and encourages the entry into another relationship (the one with yourself). Therefore, stay focused on the settlement, and not on revenge or on intentionally hurting the ex-spouse. Keep control over your emotions. A well thought out business decision will mitigate the emotional issues and help you try to remain financially secure after it is all over.

Top Ten Master Financial Checklist

Here are ten things you need to ponder during the divorce process:

1. What do we own (assets)?
2. What do we owe (debt)?
3. What have our budgeted revenue and expense numbers looked like based on previous experience (planning)?
4. What sources of income do we expect to have going forward (support)?
5. What is the total marital estate worth now (assets minus debt)?
6. Has everything from the two of us been factored into account (future contingencies, compensation, unforeseen issues, etc.)?
7. Do I have all the paperwork necessary to begin (all the legal documents necessary for transferring title, verifying information, etc.)?
8. Can we negotiate a split ourselves in order to help us keep the cost down or do we each need representation to make it happen?
9. Which type of divorce makes the most sense (with the goal of minimizing the damage)?
10. How do we negotiate to encourage a win-win scenario for each spouse (fair division of assets, debt, and income), knowing that the ultimate conclusion will turn into a lose-lose proposition?

To accomplish this, you will need to learn the intricacies of your personal finances. You will need to develop and adhere to a budget, and investigate future discrepancies that may arise from the creation of that budget. Then you will determine what property and debt needs to be split. That will help you figure out what you need to live on, what you expect to receive income-wise, how you can manage your debt load on one income going forward, and what you need to have to maintain your lifestyle as best as you can. It won't be an exact science but you can do things to make the outcome more efficient.

Divorce Etiquette

So you are seriously thinking about taking the big step—getting a divorce. Do you have a moral obligation to tell the other party you intend to file for divorce? I am frequently asked that question. The answer is, I am not sure. If you come from a trusting and respectful marriage, the answer should be yes. This will give both parties the time to get organized, develop a game plan, and talk with each other about what you each want to accomplish. That would be the right thing to do.

However, if you have reason to believe your soon-to-be ex is not being fair to you, perhaps stealing, planning in advance, or plotting to be the first to file, then I am not sure. You would think that after so many years of marriage, that would play a factor in deciding what to do, but it really does not. Anger and emotion supersede all thoughts of rational behavior and one of you will start off the divorce process on a bad note.

Divorce etiquette should be practiced to alert your spouse of your intentions. Perhaps both of you want the divorce. Bringing everything out in the open would benefit both parties, if each of you wants a smooth divorce. It is cheaper, healthier, and beneficial to any children you may have. But, as nice and easy as that may sound, I am not sure that there can ever really be a smooth divorce.

One thing to remember as you are going through the process is that the person you married is not the same person you are divorcing. You may discover aspects of your spouse's personality that you never knew existed. Once again, that is because divorce is not an intellectual event—it is, almost always, an emotional event. If both parties can take a step back and downplay the raw emotions, great benefit will come to all parties involved. That being said, it is rare for any of us to be able to do that. However, it is best to keep in mind that the person you will be dealing with will be almost like a stranger to you.

Should You File?

"In sickness and in health, during good times and bad times . . . " Yes, we all know the words. But do they hold true today? Should you stay in a marriage for the sake of these words? Or for the sake of the children? Or because it seems to be the right thing to do? Many people get divorced simply because they grow apart from one another. It can be as simple as that. When two people are young and in love and decide to get married, their perception of life and their view of the world is very different than it is 20 or 30 years later. The objectives of young couples are easier to satisfy. Even with less money to accomplish those objectives, things often just seem to work out and, in general, couples are happier because they are working together toward the same objectives. Then children enter the picture; you take on mortgages, car payments, and other debts; and all of a sudden the rules tend to shift and your viewpoints are no longer quite so naïve. The question I hear is, when did things really change? One day you wake up and look at your spouse and say, "I don't know you anymore," or "Who are you?"

Many spouses hope that they can change the other spouse and thus delay the inevitable.

Deciding whether to file for divorce should depend on how unhappy you are. It reminds me of a song from Sheryl Crow, "If It Makes You Happy." That should be your ultimate deciding point. Are you down-and-out miserable? Are you willing to risk opening door number two, already knowing full well what you are leaving behind from door number one? Of course, there may be extenuating circumstances such as physical or emotional abuse, extreme financial situations, and other issues which will all play an important part in this big decision. The question you need to ultimately ask yourself is, "Is my marriage worth saving?"

It may be best to confront your spouse and find out what his or her thoughts are with respect to taking the plunge. Perhaps you should draw up a list of pros and cons of remaining married versus separating versus divorcing. In any event, it is better to work through it with your spouse if you can, rather than to go it alone. The rationale here is that if you both can agree on a course of action, even if it is ultimately getting a divorce, it will make the transition that much smoother.

Should You Separate or Divorce?

This is the next big step. If the answer to the earlier question is that the marriage is not salvageable, then you need to figure out the best way to go forward. Either you do want to follow through with the divorce right away or you need to reassess your thought process and contemplate your actions by perhaps taking it a little more slowly. I recommend that if you are not sure, you should not act at all. It never pays to act hastily and rash if you have not drawn closure in your mind. You have to totally accept the fact. You have to be 100 percent sold (before you act) that you are comfortable in progressing with this decision. Take the extra time you need to come to the right decision. Better safe than sorry. Ask your spouse to provide you with more time if it can help you see the entire picture clearly. Because once you start the process, it begins to snowball. It will start off slowly and gain momentum down the hill at speeds you will not be able to control, and it will ultimately get out of hand.

Separation essentially means you go into a time-out and ponder whether you wish to pursue a divorce. Until you get that final expensive piece of paper, you are still considered legally married by all accounts. There are three ways to approach separation.

Trial separation is pursued because you need a break from your spouse. In this situation, you are living apart from your spouse for a shorter period of time. The goal here is to contemplate pulling the plug or getting back together (reconciling). Ownership of property, income, and debt issues are still treated as if you are both married and acting jointly.

If you decide not to reconcile, it turns into a *permanent separation*. Permanent separation shows that you are leaning toward divorce and are not considering reconciliation. After the separation date, income earned and debts incurred are segregated to the respective spouse. The date of the permanent separation is critical because it affects property and money splits.

Legal separation is done for a variety of reasons, mainly to avoid the stigma of divorce and to keep the financial considerations alive as if you are legally married. Examples include issues due to religious beliefs, keeping the spouse on your health insurance plan, or just keeping the family together.

Types of Divorce

If you make the decision to proceed with the divorce, it makes sense early on to determine the type of divorce that can work best for you and your ex. Some types are easier than others if you both get along; other types will put you through the mill and take you down a path you do not want to go. The method you ultimately choose should be the one that is easiest on you and cheapest for both of you, keeping in mind that your health should be the primary factor in selecting which type of divorce to pursue. The other factor to keep in mind is the follow-through (after-effects) of the divorce. This could give you a preview of how you and your ex will work together on a variety of issues in the future.

The following are eight options to consider.

Arbitration

This type of settlement allows you and your ex to get down to business right away. You each agree to select an arbitrator, who is typically a former judge, who in turn rules on your case in a manner similar to a courtroom judge. Your attorney still prepares for the case in the same way as if it were going to trial, except here you will be able to schedule an arbitration session sooner than waiting for courtroom time. Hopefully the outcome should be cheaper for both of you. And unlike a trial, it is all private and therefore not open to the public.

If the arbitration is binding, then both spouses have to live with the final decision regardless of whether they agree with it.

Collaborative Divorce

This is a new wave of divorce settlements whereby lawyers take on a cooperative role of working through the process together in order to avoid having to go to court. Lawyers therefore work in a nontraditional role. Instead of representing the ex or you as a ruthless, heartless bully, the lawyer works with the ex as a peaceful, tranquil dove (I know it doesn't sound like it can work, but it can if you each hire the right attorney). If the lawyers can work it out, the result is picture perfect. But each attorney agrees in advance that if they cannot work it out, they will withdraw from the engagement. Essentially, you would then need to start over by hiring a new attorney.

Collaborative divorce works like the financial planning process in that the lawyer is the quarterback and works with a team of people to help drive an acceptable solution for all parties involved. Ideally, it should make for a faster, smoother, and cheaper solution.

You should know your boundaries for a compromise in advance. If this process doesn't work out, it could be more costly for you since you will be starting at square one again.

Contested Divorce

This type, unfortunately, is the most common and occurs when you and your ex can't agree on property, debt, support, and/or custody issues. As a result, your lawyer represents you in front of a judge to try to sell your position. What you'll find are two selfish, motivated people looking to hurt the other during the process, only to realize in most cases that it was definitely the wrong way to go, when replaying the situation after the process.

Default Divorce

This type of divorce occurs when you file and your ex doesn't respond. Since your spouse is *not* participating, you'll end up receiving the divorce due to your ex's nonhandling of this issue.

Mediated Divorce

This type of divorce involves a third-party mediator who acts as a neutral party in helping the two individuals work toward an acceptable settlement. It can be worthwhile since it should help you improve your future relationship with your ex. Each party can still employ an attorney to ensure that what they agreed to is what in fact will happen when everything is put down in writing.

No-Fault Divorce

This type of divorce works like no-fault automobile insurance. In this situation, fault is not finger-pointed and neither party is blamed. Rather, you go and inform the court either that the marriage broke down due to "irreconcilable differences" or that there was an "immediate breakdown" of the relationship.

No-fault differs from fault divorce (which was the primary method of divorce in the old days and is minimally used by a handful of states today), in which one spouse is blamed for the breakdown of the marriage. The most common reasons here include abandonment, adultery, abuse, and extreme cruelty. Generally, there's no reason to go with fault divorce unless you don't want to wait out the separation period, or you expect a fight over property and debt, settlement, and custody issues.

Simplified Divorce

This type of divorce is designed for short-term marriages, defined as five years or less, where there are no kids and minimal property issues. Because of its streamlined nature, you can probably complete this divorce with little to no help from an attorney.

Uncontested Divorce

This type of divorce is what you strive for because you and your ex can essentially work out most or all of the glitches in a divorce. The three main things you need to focus on here are:

1. Dividing your property (assets and debts) between the two of you.
2. Ongoing support payments from one spouse to the other (the responsibility and amount are usually dependent on future income sources).
3. Children's custody and overall welfare issues.

You'll agree to a settlement based on capturing these three big issues, and it should hold up under a judge's scrutiny as long as you and your ex do not

- Sign under duress.
- Clearly favor one spouse over the other.

The judge should approve your state's settlement agreement once the mandatory state waiting period is over.

What Will Others Think?

Even though the issue of whether to obtain a divorce rests with you, many people find it necessary either to seek other people's approval or to see what a divorce will do to their reputation in the community. Do not rely on what others think to make your decision. Instead, base it on your own gut. In other words, does it make sense to end the marriage and begin anew? It is human nature to worry about how a decision to divorce will affect what other people think of you. Some people will be shocked at what you are doing while others will say it is about time.

The way others view your divorce, including its impact on your children, is based in large part on how you handle it. Divorce ultimately begins when one spouse leaves or announces his or her intentions to do so. Leaving without any explanation is not the right thing to do unless there are extreme circumstances such as fear of physical retribution; there will be too many unanswered questions and it will have a negative effect on the overall communication between you and your spouse, as well as your children or others. Managing the legal process in a hostile or underhanded way is also not a smart thing to do. While you duke it out up front, the loss of money, goodwill, and the ability to peacefully coexist with your ex will be shattered and gone forever. Although these things may bring you satisfaction in the short run, they do nothing for the long haul.

What to Do First: Looking at the Big Picture

The first thing you need to do is not panic. And above all, do not do anything rash. Many people (and I was one) want to go on an all-out attack and begin the bombing of the soon-to-be ex-spouse. But that is not constructive, nor desirable. In reality, that's not what you want. You just want the process to be over as quickly and painlessly as possible so you can move on with your new life.

If you can take a step back from the situation, you'll realize that right away. Just as you would in finance and business, you need to step away and think outside the box as to what the best way to handle any difficult situation would be.

When evaluating what your life will be like over the next several months, or perhaps years, keep in mind that divorce typically takes longer than it needs to or what people think it should. That is because many parties connected to the divorce are trying to drag the process out because it brings in nice retainers to all those involved. This is not always true of all parties. My attorney did not handle it that way as she worked hard to try to settle things, but my business valuation people kept dragging their feet at every turn. In researching this book, I found many divorced people who complained bitterly about their attorneys going and going until the monies were no longer available to pay them. I would include my ex-wife's attorney among that group.

As with any difficult period in one's life, you try to minimize the pain and move forward as quickly as you can. Forget about the money issues for a moment—health issues are equally or even more important. When going through the motions to expedite the situation, people tend to make many foolish decisions by agreeing with property settlements or parenting plans that are not the most workable options. Unless the relationship is violent or has the possibility of turning into something that can blow up out of proportion, you are better off taking the time necessary to work out an agreement that suits you.

Ideally, the best course of action is to develop a pseudo winwin scenario for both parties. You may feel like sticking it to the other party, but, as I mentioned before, during the divorce process both parties ultimately lose. You can try to work it out where you both make the best of a bad situation, especially when children are involved. Engaging any of the children, at whatever age, by trying to turn them against the other parent or spreading lies does not help either parent in the long run. Unfortunately, I have seen that in my own situation. Providing for the spouse to have as little money as you can get away with is also not constructive and is in no one's best interests. Lastly, cutting off all communication with the ex, especially when there are children involved, is not in anyone's best interests either. This is a fine line to walk as you both have to act like mature adults and put the children's interests first. Again, this may require stepping back from the situation, putting emotions aside, and at least dealing civilly with each other when the children are involved. I have seen cases where the exes have remained quite friendly and everyone concerned is obviously better for it.

Taking the High Road

As much as you're tempted to do what you can for your ultimate survival, you may need to rethink your strategy. I have had many friends counsel me to "take the high road" and not worry because ultimately "it all comes out in the wash." Use this approach for your children, co-workers, friends, and others who may be a part of the process. Unfortunately, it is very easy not to do this and to go for blood instead.

Telling your children that your ex-spouse is to blame for the divorce is not the way to go about it. Unfortunately, I have had that happen to me. Your children should not be privy to any details as to whose fault the divorce is or who gets the ultimate blame. Obviously, both parties agreed to stay married when they did and to get divorced now. It is not a one-way street.

Cheating your ex by understating your finances and overstating your needs, so that you can walk away with more assets and income, goes against the divorce etiquette mentioned earlier in this chapter. This is not taking the high road and only leads to more bitterness, anger, resentment, and even revenge. You and your ex do not have to agree on everything; in most cases, you will agree on next to nothing. Just remember, it is all about the children—that is where the agreement needs to be ironclad so the children are not the ones who ultimately suffer.

The reality is, if the children live with the ex-spouse, you want to make sure you will continue to take care of them both financially and emotionally. You don't want to see the other spouse suffer, because that is not in either spouse's best interests—especially because he or she is the parent of your kids! No one in their right mind would want to hurt their own children, even if they are living with your ex.

What I have learned from many individuals is that the children, the most important piece of the puzzle, will come to learn the truth and find out that one of you was not as honest a person as you should have been during the process. In addition, others will find out the true colors of the spouse who cries wolf all the time without any real reason for doing so.

Regrouping

Stepping back to regroup is a necessity. A lot of things are going through your mind. You need to prioritize your objectives and understand what is important to you before you begin the process. The problem is that everything goes so quickly and you may not have the time to adequately prepare. Unfortunately, you are then forced to operate in a defensive mode.

Include in your list of prioritized objectives your health, your children, your business or work environment, your friends, and your social circle. Relying on a support system will become very important. Health includes not only your physical health but also your mental health. At some point these issues may become one big blur.

Informing the Children

Divorce research has shown that children are rarely informed about their parents' pending separation. The younger the children, the less likely they are to know about it in advance. When they do find out, many times young children view the divorce as their fault. They may be indifferent at first because they don't understand what is happening. They may also refuse to believe it and in many cases will not really accept it.

Older children can usually digest more, but it may still be difficult and uncomfortable for them. The children ultimately find out, although perhaps not in a timely fashion. What may start off as shock and even denial often ends up in fear, anger, grief, and resentment. As the feeling of loss sets in, children will then begin to be concerned about how this will affect them.

Researchers have studied how children of divorced parents fare over time. Generally, the average adjustment period lasts between 18 months and three years. After five years, two-thirds of post-divorce children are coping well.

When should you tell your children about the divorce? There are pros and cons for discussing this information with the children as soon as each party decides a divorce is imminent. Some of those factors will obviously depend on the ages of the children.

Telling the children sooner rather than later keeps them apprised of everything that is happening on a timely basis so they can ask questions and try to understand. I say "try to understand" because nobody truly does understand. The children will also want answers as to which parent they will be living with. Depending on the age of the children, they may want to have a great deal of input in this decision, as well as in what their relationship will be with the parent who is moving out. What they really want is assurance that their lives will be as close to the way they were before the divorce as possible.

Likewise, there are many reasons not to tell the children immediately. First, both spouses are nervous and anxious themselves about the divorce and they are not sure exactly what to say. Second, some spouses don't want to burden the children with all of that information. Third, some parents feel that the children will not understand, so they try to protect them by not revealing anything immediately.

When talking with the children, do it together. You want the children to hear the same exact story at the same time. You do not want a slant to occur when the message gets relayed to the children, favoring one parent over another. You also want to make sure that the children realize that they are not losing a parent. The parent will still be available, love them, help them, and be all he or she can be with the child. You also want to ensure that the children don't feel that the separation or pending divorce is their fault. Perhaps a good way to start a discussion with your children is by stating something similar to the following:

> Children, as you may be aware, we have been unhappy for a long time because we fight and yell at each other so much. It has been increasing in frequency and has been taking a toll on each of us. We have tried very hard to get along better and to work things out, but we have decided it is necessary to live apart in order to preserve our friendship.
>
> We have decided to separate, and Mom (Dad) will be moving out. We have done everything possible to try and resolve our differences, including going to therapy, speaking to our clergy and to others to save the marriage, but we feel at this point there is nothing else constructive that we can do. We feel it will be in everyone's best interest if we live separately.
>
> We will try to keep things as close to normal as possible, but in no way will any of you children be at a loss monetarily, emotionally, or spiritually. We love you very much, and nothing that we do will ever change that for any of you.

After your talk, encourage the children to ask questions. Try to help them understand by giving clear, easy-to-understand answers, repeating things, branching into new areas, or just plainly reassuring them. Your children need to be reminded of your constant love and support. You must demonstrate to them that your love is real and sincere and that you will all try to make the best of a bad situation. Parents divorce each other all the time but they do not divorce their children. Tell them that they can spend as much time as they want with either parent, and that when they can't be together in person they can still communicate through phone, e-mail, texting, video, and so forth.

Again, this is an *ideal* scenario. I am aware of situations where parenting is and should be limited or supervised. Those are issues that are far beyond the scope of this book.

If your children ask you personal questions, use common sense when answering them. It is not advisable to try to make either parent look like the one who caused the breakup, for fear the children will not want to bother with that parent later on.

Negative impacts from the divorce will be minimized when the parents are in less conflict with one another and cooperate as much as possible. The parents should remain nurturing and consistent caretakers, and parent-child relationships should be encouraged by each parent. Also, while both parents should try to maintain a warm and close relationship, they must also remain consistent in their parenting role so the children do not end up taking care of the parents. Unfortunately, it often happens that the parent who did not want the divorce burdens the children with his or her financial and emotional issues, and the children feel they need to somehow resolve these problems for them. This is obviously harmful to all parties involved. Whatever the situation turns out to be, the parents need to remain the parents.

Of course, the best way to make sure things work out as well as possible for all parties involved is to reduce the conflict. If both parents can stay involved for the good of the children, or, in some cases, try to get the other parent involved, this will help make the best of an unpleasant situation.

Coming to Grips with the Reality of the Situation: Representation

Now that you are ready to proceed with the divorce process, where should you start? Should you go it alone or should you seek outside assistance? They say a fool represents himself, and I would agree. There is too much to know, be responsible for, and handle, especially if things don't go according to plan. It is worth making the investment to educate yourself.

As an educator myself, I would say that learning how the process works should automatically be something that you do from the very beginning. You need to know both the good and the bad that will arise as a result of the process, pitfalls to avoid, and things that may help the process move more smoothly and quickly. You will also want to know what the potential outcomes may be if you work it through.

Should You Go It Alone, without an Attorney?

I would strongly advise you not to handle the divorce yourself (without an attorney). Most people don't know the intricacies of the process, the motions that need to be filed, the timing deadlines, the snags that may occur, and everything else in between.

The laws surrounding the process, which vary a great deal from state to state, should automatically preclude you from doing the divorce yourself. I understand that the cost of hiring an attorney may be daunting, but better safe than sorry. You need to put yourself in the best position to succeed. Sometimes an investment up front will help you save money on the back end.

The only time representing yourself makes sense is when both parties are in agreement regarding the divorce (such as pursuing a simplified or uncontested divorce), and both want it because they simply have grown apart but still truly like each other and are genuinely concerned about the other's welfare. In this scenario the divorce is not likely to become contentious, thus avoiding all the legal maneuverings. Ideally, in this situation, each party will walk away feeling good about the division of assets, the ability to maintain a lifestyle similar to what they were accustomed to, and the ability to work together if children are involved.

I interviewed a very prominent financial planner from back East who said that after 43 years of marriage, he and his wife knew it was time to part, simply because their interests had changed. It was very amicable. He prepared a detailed listing of their assets (they had no liabilities), and she took the assets that made sense for her and which provided her with an income stream. The final division of assets was essentially equal, and now they completed the process without the skill set of an attorney. That's always the best scenario when you can achieve it.

Another example from a recent interview, also involving a financial planner, is that the two of them simply grew apart. She wanted to travel and do other things, while he was content with life as it was. They, too, were able to work things out with minimal attorney involvement. She kept the primary residence, and he kept most of his retirement accounts, paying her a lump sum of cash and some alimony to help her through the transition period. They still consider themselves to be good friends today. Again, that's making the best of a bad situation.

If you want to take a stab at it yourself, you can purchase books, kits, or other packages from stores that contain printed forms or CD-ROMs where you can fill in the blanks and print out the forms. You can also get these forms from attorneys, mediators, or others at little to no cost. There are also web sites that, for a small fee and some time investment on your part, will prepare the forms for you and provide you with instructions on how to proceed in your area of jurisdiction.

Even in the simplest kinds of divorce, it still makes sense to get another individual involved to look over what you are contemplating doing going forward. For example, when ciphering through all the issues, you may forget long-term issues that aren't present now but could be financially devastating years later. An example would be tax considerations that will come into play when you sell rental property. Depreciation recapture (especially for property held for many years) is one item that could later present not only large capital gains but also significant tax liabilities you never even thought about. An outside expert can help you look at all the issues and avoid potential pitfalls and traps.

A second long-term consideration that might be overlooked is whether one of the spouses has any retirement plan interests, especially defined benefit plans, since they do not present statements with account balances. A pension plan administrator may need to be called in to assess the value of the plan as of the date of the divorce. An outside expert, such as a financial planner, can help you factor those items into your settlement by converting the future value of the benefit amount into a number that can be used today.

A third example concerns ongoing payments made to an ex-spouse. Payments such as alimony (which has tax ramifications) and child support (which does not) can have tax consequences on both parties—the payer and the payee. Many times these tax consequences are not factored into the bottom-line number for each party when trying to arrive at an acceptable income stream.

A fourth example could involve outside parties, such as creditors. If you agree to split the house, car, or other assets which have loans associated with them, it is important to remove the name of the person who no longer owns the property after the divorce. If this is not done and, for example, the spouse who owns the car loses his job, he may no longer be able to make the car payments and could end up defaulting on the loan. If the ex is still listed on the loan, the creditors have the right to go after that party for the outstanding payments and remaining balance.

Living with someone is tough enough. Ending that arrangement can be even more devastating and difficult. If you have any concerns about doing your own divorce, listen to your gut. Two heads are always better than one. Remember, the documents themselves merely record the outcome of what you agree to do. Having some-body walk you through the process, before you get to the docu-ment stage, is much more important than the paperwork itself. Ultimately, you want the assurance during the negotiation process, because afterwards it is too late (see the discussion of negotiation in Chapter 2). You want all outstanding issues brought into the open and accounted for before you sign off on the final document. And remember, a cheap divorce can be more costly in the long run!

Hiring an Attorney

If you do not think self-representation will work best for you, then contact an attorney. Meet with several attorneys to ensure that you can work with the attorney you ultimately choose and that their per-sonality suits your needs. They say you hire a lawyer with a personal-ity similar to your own. I believe it, based on my own choice of an attorney as well as that of my ex. Sometimes the personalities gel and sometimes they do not.

Hiring an attorney will probably be one of the most important decisions you will make during this process. Besides the financial elements, future issues involving children, property division, and your ultimate security hinge on the quality of the attorney you chose to represent you.

Lawyers can be positive or negative in their approach to your case. Positive lawyers are known for being fierce advocates and paying attention to details, yet advocating for settlement and compromise at the same time. Negative lawyers are known for being aggressive and not wanting to settle the case. They have built a reputation on being difficult with opposing clients, other attorneys, and even judges. People flock to them because they think these attorneys will protect them or because, as an injured spouse, they want revenge. Sound great? Ask the spouses who have had the misfortune to deal with a negative attorney how well their family fared a few years after the divorce. Know the reputation of the lawyer you choose.

There are many theories regarding the right way to hire an attorney. I will share with you my experience, having gone through the process recently myself. Your attorney should be your mouth-piece, plain and simple. They should hear you out, identify your objectives and concerns, and then summarize them into simple and concise terms following the traditional legal format. You should feel confident that when your attorney represents you to the opposing attorney, mediator, or judge, your interests are being given full and appropriate consideration and representation. It is not about the attorney conquering in battle and winning at any cost, but rather, having them do what is in your best interests for a speedy resolution.

Believe it or not, there does not have to be a winner and loser. That is because both parties ultimately lose and the legal fees end up becoming a waste of time and money for both parties. These funds end up being channeled away from where they should go: the ultimate benefit of the children and/or keeping both parties' standard of living as close what they were used to as possible.

Your lawyer is also responsible for keeping your expectations realistic, and giving you a reality check if what you are asking for is unrealistic, impractical, or uneconomical going forward. They can do that in a constructive, meaningful way and not jeopardize your relationship with them or make you lose faith in their ability to represent you.

You, as the client, should control the attorney-client relationship, and not the other way around. I have heard of many cases where the attorney represented the client on completely meaningless issues that the client had already instructed the attorney was a complete waste of time. Sometimes it is out of your attorney's control, as the opposing party's attorney may be the one to insist on dealing with nonsensical issues for their client. However, unfortunately, I have been told that some attorneys do not heed their clients' requests, with the apparent motive of intentionally running up their clients' legal fees.

Do not hire the first attorney you interview. Interview many prospective attorneys. In each interview, see if the two of you click. Sometimes what one person considered a strong lawyer for their case may not be a strong enough lawyer for another case. Factors such as whether one spouse has their own business, or a large inheritance, may affect the ability of one lawyer versus another to handle that particular case. Since you will be sharing the most intimate details of your life with this individual, make sure you are comfortable telling the attorney you hire whatever needs to be said.

Having been through this ordeal, I think it makes sense to hire a lawyer who counteracts or can keep up with the lawyer hired by your ex. If your ex hires someone who is a yeller and screamer, who will intentionally do whatever needs to be done to secure victory for your ex, such as unfairly representing their client, lying, or back-pedaling, you will need someone who can keep pace with that type of person and situation. This does not mean that the person you hire should be a yeller or screamer also. Rather, you should concentrate on hiring someone who can counteract the opposing attorney's tactics and neutralize what they are trying to accomplish. Many of these types of attorneys like to hear themselves speak and try to dictate the final outcome by controlling all aspects of the case. It is, therefore, necessary to hire an attorney who is very detail oriented and who can calmly and reasonably handle the screaming and the potentially offensive behavior of the other attorney.

Having a lawyer who is defensive and not proactive and who just responds to issues against a type A personality lawyer will ultimately lead to great unhappiness if you believe that the other lawyer is running the show and controlling the outcome and, consequently, your destiny. In essence, your lawyer needs to keep the other lawyer honest. (Now that's the ultimate oxymoron!)

Another important consideration is that even though you can fire your attorney at any time, if you are too far into the case, it may not make sense to do so. You would have to hire someone new, get that person up to speed on the case, pay duplicate legal fees because of the additional work now created, and still be uncertain as to what the ultimate outcome will be. That is not to say that you should never fire an attorney. Just use caution when you hire them initially and make sure to use the checklist for hiring guidelines in Exhibit 1.1.

Sometimes, a lawyer is fired midstream because the client doesn't like where the case is going, or doesn't like the mediator's ruling. For example, I know of a case where a man fired his lawyer because he did not like the results of the mediation hearing, and he especially did not like the fact that his lawyer sided with the mediator. He decided to hire a negative attorney who, he felt, would fight for him, create a ruckus, and basically bully everyone into accepting what he felt he deserved or what should be rightfully his, even though his desired outcome was not practical, nor was it likely to occur.

By the same token, the new attorney should be honest in his assessment of the case and give his honest opinion to the client as to whether the previous attorney and mediator were fairly accurate in their assessment of the case. Unfortunately, most lawyers will not give an honest assessment in this regard, as they are competing for clients and will take any case with an up-front retainer.

1.	Do you feel a direct connection with the lawyer?	Yes	No
2.	Is the lawyer sensitive to your needs?	Yes	No
3.	Is the lawyer objective in his or her approach in assessing the case?	Yes	No
4.	Is the lawyer a straight shooter and will he or she communicate with you in a no-nonsense approach by telling it to you the way it is?	Yes	No
5.	Will the lawyer help minimize costs by going through other possible channels, such as mediation, direct spousal negotiation, or any other method that can be used to resolve the issues at hand without going to trial?	Yes	No
6.	Has the attorney informed you of his or her policy on returning phone calls, e-mails, fees, and billing?	Yes	No
7.	Has the lawyer provided you with the percentage of his or her cases that are settled without going to trial?	Yes	No
8.	Is the lawyer familiar with the divorce laws in your state or other states in which you have property interests?	Yes	No
9.	How frequently will the lawyer communicate with you and by what method?		
10.	Will the lawyer encourage you to ask all types of questions, even if they appear to be foolish questions, so you walk away with a strong understanding of what the immediate issues are and what is likely to transpire going forward?	Yes	No
11.	Will the lawyer explain things to you in simple language you can fully understand by repeating everything you've stated when incorporating responses to your questions?	Yes	No
12.	Will the lawyer be straightforward about billing and provide detailed support of the exact time spent on your case and deliverables that were performed during that time period?	Yes	No

Exhibit 1.1   Checklist of Top 12 Issues for Hiring the Right Lawyer

Your success with the legal process will depend on the decisions you make at each stage along the way. As you enter and complete each phase of the legal process, intense emotions may create obstacles at any turn. You can learn to understand these feelings and get past them to act constructively and rationally.

Some lawyers tend to stir the pot and create unnecessary trouble and undue hardship for all parties involved. This negative type of lawyer will create trouble by moving away from the facts and making it personal, trying to destroy the other party's credibility in a devious, underhanded fashion. For example, your ex's lawyer may constantly bad-mouth you to your lawyer, for the sole purpose of trying to make you and your lawyer nervous by stating that these charges, whether real or fictional, will be used in court proceedings, thus trying to bully you and your attorney into accepting their terms and conditions for settlement.

Some attorneys are just determined to go to court, no matter how reasonable and rational the settlement offer may appear. Many do this to satisfy their own ego trip; others do it because they have the attitude that it's either their way or the highway; and still others do it simply to give their client the opportunity to have their day in court. These types of lawyers use lies and trickery, are deceitful in their tactics, and in many cases have had grievances filed against them. Sadly, clients of these types of attorneys often end up much worse off in the long run, not only because of the excessive legal fees, but also because the final settlement worked out in court ends up being less than they would have had if they had worked more cooperatively to fine-tune the settlement agreement originally proposed.

I saw a situation where the husband offered his ex-wife a fair alimony settlement, taking into account all her reasonable future expenses. It would have provided her with about $6,000 per month for 10 years (which was over the threshold for that length of marriage). Her lawyer, however, came up with a figure of $10,000 per month for life, just because he wanted to go to court and that was where his strength was, despite the fact that it wasn't in his client's best interests. End result: The ex-wife received about 50 percent of that number as part of her final settlement. Her lawyer washed his hands of any issues and told her, "We needed to do this." For whom? For himself!

I do not mean to imply that all lawyers are like this. They are not. There are many good, ethical lawyers who want to do the right thing and work toward a fair and speedy resolution. I was fortunate enough to have one. But you need to be very careful with your selection. Again, referrals are the best way to narrow down the choice of possibilities. Interviewing many attorneys will help you to find out whether they are of the same mind-set as you, or if they are the complete opposite. The interview process will help you learn the differences among lawyers to ensure that your final selection will be the one that makes the most sense for you.

An overlooked area of importance when hiring an attorney is to make sure that the attorney is familiar with and knows the judges in the community. You would typically think that all judges provide fair rulings all the time, but this is not the case. Some judges may incorporate their own biases into their ruling, or may even refuse to accept a perfectly crafted solution that has been approved by both parties and their respective attorneys. If the attorney does not feel that you can get a fair hearing from the judge assigned to your case, your attorney will have to provide evidence that the judge assigned would not be in your best interests and seek to disqualify the judge.

Another important factor in more complicated divorces where children or business interests are involved is to find out whether the lawyer has a team of outside specialists who work with their firm. These professionals include business valuation specialists, mediators, financial planners, and CPAs. The attorney should be able to relate his experiences in working with these affiliates and attest to whether they are competent, professional, and work in a timely manner. And even though these experts may be recommended by your attorney, you may still want to take the time to interview those who may get involved in your case prior to agreeing to use them. These experts are costly and their opinions may have a significant impact on the outcome of your case. Even though I personally knew the person who performed my business valuation and felt he would be fair and reasonable, I should have taken the time to interview others before I agreed to use his firm. Once you have committed the time and money for this purpose, you are basically stuck with their conclusion, even if it is not realistic, unless you want to spend additional time and money hiring other experts to counter the opinion already rendered.

Resources to Help You Choose an Attorney

When looking for an attorney, I suggest referrals as the best source for finding a credible attorney. Many people have gone through the divorce process and have attorneys they would and would not recommend. In addition to friends, you may want to seek opinions from therapists, doctors, business associates, and co-workers. All of the state bar associations have lawyer referral services.

Choosing a family lawyer probably makes the most sense since this is a highly specialized area. General practitioners should only be used if they keep up-to-date on the many complex issues involved or if it is a simple, amicable divorce. Attorneys are becoming specialists, like other professionals, and there are many competent attorneys specializing in divorce who would be a good choice. If an attorney has received a credential as a specialist in family law, that will carry more weight. You may want to contact the American Academy of Matrimonial Lawyers (AAML), which is an elite group of attorneys who have practiced for a minimum of 10 years, 75 percent of which time has been in matrimonial law. Other groups to contact would be the International Academy of Collaborative Professionals (IACP) and the Academy for Collaborative Legal Practice (ACLP), whose mission is to achieve conflict resolution through collaborative practice.

Attorney Costs

Obviously, a major issue when hiring an attorney is cost. Most attorneys charge an up-front retainer and deduct fees from that amount. Find out what their hourly rate is, how much of a retainer will be needed, and who will be handling the case. Will it be that attorney or someone else from that office? How much time will legal assistants spend on your case (to help cut down the total charges)? And what will be your responsibilities and involvement going forward? Don't be fooled into thinking that the more you spend for legal counsel, the better representation you will receive. In most cases, you are still better off working from a referral arrangement from someone who went through the process, regardless of cost.

Another point that gets overlooked is the out-of-pocket expenses charged by attorneys. These include court filing fees, mailing fees, photocopying fees, expert witness fees, travel costs, investigation fees, and other expenses that can add up to tremendous amounts. Expert witness fees can be very costly, especially in a highly complex divorce case. Examples of expert witnesses include appraisers, accountants, psychologists, and vocational experts. If both parties can agree to have a single outside expert or firm outline many of the matters at hand, that will help in minimizing the cost of the divorce. To sum up, the level of disagreement between the spouses is the overall reason that a divorce can cost more than it needs to.

It is difficult for an attorney to pinpoint exactly what you will spend in a divorce. It will vary a great deal depending on how much gets challenged, the cooperation of the parties, what the other attorney or your attorney requests, and other factors that are case specific. Also if you are working and the other spouse is not, paying for the other person's legal costs may be a significant additional expense. Using alternative dispute resolution such as mediation or collaboration to eliminate as many contested issues as possible can save a great deal of money.

If you believe your legal fees are not accurate, you may request a detailed breakdown of the time your attorney spends on your case, if it has not already been provided to you. Under law, you are entitled to receive an itemized bill for fees that have accrued at least every 60 days, although most attorneys bill monthly. If you are concerned about being overbilled by your attorney, I would strongly suggest that you keep track of the time you are on the telephone or in meetings with your attorney and compare it to their bill when you receive it. If there are blatant discrepancies, you should address it with your attorney immediately. Keep in mind, however, that most attorneys do not bill in one-minute segments—most bill in six- or ten-minute segments, so that a one-minute phone call shows up as ten minutes of billable time. Therefore, your time records will never match exactly what they have listed, and you do not want to alienate your attorney over a few minutes here or there if you feel that he is representing you fairly and responsibly. However, if you feel that you have been overbilled and cannot resolve this issue with him, and you simply decide not to pay him, be aware that your lawyer has the right to file a special type of lien at the end of the case or at any time either you or your attorney end the attorney-client relationship. Most states have an arbitration program for disputed attorney fees, generally offered through the state bar association.

To cut down on costs, you may also consider using a family law clinic. These clinics are affiliated with various law schools that help train their law students in the divorce process under the direction of an attorney.

I operate under the premise that most attorneys will do the right thing for the client. But unfortunately, that is not always the case.

In researching this book, I spoke to many people who had major problems with their attorney or their ex-spouse's attorney. One such case involved a woman who hired a lawyer who consistently lied, telling her that everything was going great, that the settlement would be bigger than another attorney could have gotten for her, but that she could not start spending that future settlement until the case was finalized. This backed the woman into a corner and into a settlement she could not realistically live with. Another case involved a lawyer billing the client based on exactly what the client had available to spend. For whatever reason, the amount owed was equal to discretionary money remaining on a monthly basis for that individual. A third case involved a situation where a settlement was reached between the divorcing parties, but the opposing lawyer would not accept it and insisted on taking the case to trial no matter what the cost, even though it was not in the interests of either party. A fourth case involved a man who went to a large national law firm and was billed excessive amounts because the lawyer had to bring in a certain dollar amount each month. The list can go on and on. In short, be very careful when you hire an attorney and work under the premise that he or she will be around at the end of the case.

Lastly, beware of attorneys who promise you the world, a certain outcome, or a quick resolution. There are too many uncertainties in any case to predict exactly the way it will go. It is no different than relying on a stockbroker to give you specific and consistent returns from the stock market. There are too many variables that will get in the way of that happening. Some lawyers have a goal of trying to defend a high-profile case like Johnny Cochran did for O.J. Simpson, thinking it will jump-start their career in a different venue. Some lawyers will even defend people they know have no case or no realistic chance for a successful outcome. Some lawyers have a gladiator or Napoleonic complex and are looking for a victory at any cost, which, unfortunately, drives up the legal fees on the case. In addition, they tend to cause more trauma and mental anguish for the client than an attorney whose goal is to reach a fair and reasonable settlement with as little fanfare as possible.

Blocking Out the Competition

On the defensive side, if you know of potential lawyers who are tops in their field, are strong in the courtroom, and could cause your life misery, you can contact them, explain your case, and, even in the event you do not hire them, they are obligated to remove themselves from future consideration by your ex-spouse. That is because these prospective attorneys now have a conflict of interest. This strategy will remove some of the potential attorney candidates from the picture. You can do that with as many attorneys as you want. It is time consuming but could be effective in your overall strategy.

However, keep in mind that most attorneys will not give you a free consultation in a divorce case. Therefore, although this is a good strategy to remove some hard-hitting attorneys from the picture, it may be costly as well. When you call to make an appointment, you can ask what their fee is for a consultation. It may be a set fee or a cheaper rate for the initial consultation as they are trying to lock in your business from that initial visit.

Involving Others: Your Support Team

At what point, if at all, should you get others involved? By "others" I mean friends, relatives, and people who have gone through this process before. Sure, everyone wants to help right away and they all have good intentions. But that can get old rather quickly.

You definitely need someone to sound off to and with whom you can discuss your dilemmas and thoughts before you act to ensure that you are remaining rational. But over-reliance on these people can wear them down if you are not careful.

It can be especially difficult if it is a contentious situation and there are mutual friends involved, since these people may think they are compelled to take sides. Many times they do, which is unfortunate. If you find yourself in a situation where your supposed friends have sided with your soon-to-be ex and are either not speaking to you when you see them or are more interested in telling you what you should do rather than listening to what you have to say, you should not consider these people to be friends and you should not trust them going forward.

Essentially, a good combination of counsel and support from friends and relatives will help provide you with the emotional stability you need to get you through this ordeal.

Becoming Too Passive

Often the petitioner spouse in the divorce proceedings goes on the offensive and tries to run things to ensure that he or she gets his or her way. They will launch a full-blown attack to ensure that they gain sole custody of the children, keep the house, and take as much money and property as they can. They may lie, cheat, and steal. Remember, the person you married is not the same person you are divorcing. The worst thing you can do in this type of situation is to just sit back and let all this happen around you. While two wrongs don't make a right, self-defense may be a necessity to ensure that you do not mentally lose it or give in to everything just to get it resolved so the misery will be over.

The last thing you want your spouse to see is that you are too acquiescent. Many soon-to-be ex-spouses feel wronged and want revenge, so they become manipulative and do whatever they can to get what they want out of the divorce. If you are stunned by what has transpired, or if you are the one who wanted the divorce and are being made to feel guilty for it, you may be in no condition to agree to terms and conditions, much less to sign anything that is presented to you. It is important during this phase to make sure you speak with others, especially an attorney, who can provide you with guidance and help so that you do not agree to settlement terms that you would never entertain if you were thinking clearly.

Often what you need to do is counter those positions by rationally thinking out all the positions being brought up by your ex. Making a prioritized listing of what needs to be resolved will go a long way toward ensuring that you are comfortable with the outcomes from each independent area of the settlement.

What to Do Before You Leave Home for Good

If you are in the contemplating-divorce stage, make a list of all personal property belonging to both you and your spouse and keep it someplace where you will be able to access it later if you find yourself suddenly locked out of the marital home. This will provide you with a list of assets and items that you may want back which you may forget about in the flurry of the divorce proceedings. You may think that you will remember everything or that you will be able to obtain a court order to get something back, but that is not always the case.

If you are the spouse who is moving out, make sure when you go back to your old house for the last time that you take all of your personal possessions with you. This may be an uncomfortable and hostile situation but, regardless, you need to take the time necessary to gather all your personal belongings as it may be your last chance to do so. Do not leave any ammunition for your ex-spouse to look through and use against you. First take all personal and financial files and personal property; delete files off your home computer's hard drive that may be work related or may have personal meaning to you; if your computer is set up to connect remotely to your office, make sure you have that disconnected immediately; and remove all personal and sentimental items. Items like clothing and personal hygiene products can always be recouped at a later date, or purchased new if need be.

In my research, I have found many spouses who just took for granted privacy issues and were not at all concerned until it was too late. I know of a particular spouse who found out that her husband has missed over $200,000 of payroll and sales tax payments and now is concerned that the IRS will go after her. Another spouse I knew confiscated from her husband many pieces of a valuable antique collection which had been left to him by his grandfather. She sold the collection and pocketed the money. In another situation, a spouse left without realizing that his home computer was still hooked into his office computer, and his soon-to-be ex spent a great deal of time reading his e-mails and gathering information that she hoped to later use against him in court.

The point is to make sure anything of value is removed from the house at the same time you decide to leave.

Rattiner's Planning Tips

1. Be comfortable with your decision to pursue the divorce (regardless of who initiated it).
2. The divorce process is a business decision. Keep emotions in check and pursue it as you would any other business deal.
3. Do not act until you are 100 percent certain that divorce is the best option for you.

4. Get a handle on your finances. Start with a budget so you can determine the assets, debt, and income issues that need to be addressed. Try to have the entire picture outlined in advance.

5. Trial, permanent, and legal separations are geared towards the same thing, but demonstrate different ways of getting there. This goes back to answering the question, is divorce right for you?

6. There are many different ways to approach divorce. Select the method that gives you the least amount of discomfort. A method that helps maintain your health is primary. If it is also easier and cheaper for both spouses, that is a major plus. In addition, it offers you the best chance of a complete overall recovery in the shortest amount of time.

7. The person you divorce is not the same person you married.

8. Don't sweat the small stuff. Pick and choose your battles carefully. Look at the big picture. Not everything is a major battle or a huge catastrophe.

9. Don't be a part of the blame game. Take it from a CPA: Two wrongs don't make a right.

10. Take the high road always. It all comes out in the wash.

11. Always work with an attorney. Don't go through the motions without any counsel walking you through the process. Even if your ex asks you not to work with one, you owe it to yourself and your ex to become as educated as possible.

12. Work with an attorney who understands you, is similar in personality to you, and can counter your ex's attorney's moves. Rely on referrals.

13. Interview many attorneys and other outside experts. Receive price quotes from each of them. Verify how they will communicate with you going forward.

14. Rely on a close family member or friend to bounce ideas around.

15. Don't be too hasty. Step back from the situation, try to look in from the outside, and act rationally.

16. Remember, it's ultimately all about the children! Don't make waves with your children by trying to get revenge on your ex.

17. Look at various scenarios including a best-case and worst-case picture. This will provide you with some boundaries as to what to expect.

18. A passive approach towards divorce will leave you very frustrated because you will think that all is not being done to further your cause. You will need to be proactive to counter your ex's negative lawyer's future moves.

19. Protect yourself before leaving home. Don't give your ex too much ammunition to come after you.

20. No matter how bad it seems now, just remember my mother's favorite saying: "This, too, shall pass."

C H A P T E R

2

Minimizing the Damage

Nothing is to be gained by going through the divorce process. As stated repeatedly throughout this book, it is a lose-lose proposition. However, once the process starts, you need to take steps to minimize the damage to you, both financially and emotionally.

With that in mind, your objective should be to lose as little as you can. It's inevitable that you will be on the losing side—unless, of course, you are standing on the other side of the platform as one of the providers of paid services. These are the people who are hired throughout the process and earn money at your expense. Therefore, the overall goal is to minimize the damage that will be created.

Negotiating Your Way out of a Trial

When going through the divorce process, your ultimate objective should be to negotiate a settlement on all issues so you don't end up in trial. Custody, property, alimony, child support, or other key issues should be the main focus. It's always cheaper not to go the trial route, and mentally it's less draining. In fact, over 90 percent of court cases settle before the trial begins, so why even discuss this alternative?

For starters, staying out of court is the best way to minimize the damage. Second, it moves the process right along and keeps each spouse focused on those things that are of greatest importance. I learned long ago that you need to pick your battles. You can't battle everything, otherwise you begin to lose focus. Stay focused on the key topics at hand and negotiate those first. That will help lead to a settlement each spouse can live with. It will never be perfect, nor will either spouse receive all that they want. But it will keep costs down, provide you with more assets to divide, and keep your sanity.

Negotiation isn't a simple process. It involves making an unlimited number of offers and counteroffers. Sometimes you can luck out with two cooperative spouses and settle quickly. Other times it will become a dragged-out fight to the bitter end. After everything is said and done, people often find out that many of the issues that were negotiated during the process were really not that important in the end.

Your settlement will reflect the personality of your ex. If he or she has been demanding, unreasonable, or has lost sight of the big picture, you can expect the settlement to go that way, too. But be careful. This one is for the long haul, so you need to approach it right.

Early-on Negotiations

Step One: Always Be Prepared

As I tell my students, always be prepared! Do your homework. Be alert. Study your assets. Know your debt. Calculate your income. Resolve alimony and child support issues. Then figure out what-if scenarios. That means once you see the entire picture of what you are dealing with in total, set up a spreadsheet that can be helpful for reaching a fair and equitable settlement.

Here's how you do your homework. List all of the major categories (assets, debt, income, expenses, (including alimony, child support) on the left side of a spreadsheet. Then make a column for you and one for your ex, and assign each separately titled asset and debt to its appropriate column. For example, your own pension plan should be listed in your column. After that, divide the joint assets and debt equally among both columns. See Exhibit 2.1.

Step Two: Design a Spreadsheet to Decipher Your Options

To the right of the two spouses' columns, create several more columns, showing different percentages and various possibilities for splitting any or all of these assets between the two of you. Remember, this is not a proposal. You are sorting through all of your options as to what could make sense for you, before you ask.

Negotiation Sample Spreadsheet

Mr. and Mrs. Itz O'vernow   What If Scenarios

	Step 1			Step 2		
	Total	Husband	Wife	Possibility #1	Possibility #2	Possibility #3
Assets						
Primary residence (J)	600,000	300,000	300,000			
Husband's 401(k) (H)	300,000	300,000				
Wife's IRA (W)	500,000		500,000			
Rental Property (J)	400,000	200,000	200,000			
Car (H)	10,000	10,000				
Car (W)	16,000		16,000			
Total	1,826,000	810,000	1,016,000			
Debt						
Mortgage on Primary (J)	400,000	200,000	200,000			
Rental Property (J)	250,000	125,000				
Car Loan (H)	8,000	8,000				
Car Loan (W)	12,000		12,000			
Total	670,000	333,000	337,000			
Net Worth	**1,156,000**	**477,000**	**679,000**			
Income						
Wages (H)	100,000	100,000				
Wages (W)	150,000		150,000			
Interest Income (J)	2,000	1,000	1,000			
Dividend Income (W)	3,000		3,000			
Rental Income (H)	5,000	5,000				
Total	260,000	106,000	154,000			

Exhibit 2.1   Negotiation Sample Spreadsheet

	Step 1			Step 2		
	Total	Husband	Wife	Possibility #1	Possibility #2	Possibility #3
Expenses						
Alimony Payment to.... (H) or (W)	?					
Child Support Payment to... (H) or (W)	?					
Other Expenses	80,000	40,000	40,000			
Total	*80,000*	*40,000*	*40,000*			
Surplus/ Deficit	**180,000**	**66,000**	**114,000**			

J-Joint
H-Husband
W-Wife
Step 2: The "Possibilities" column represents probable settlements that make sense for each spouse.
Step 3: Revisit the statement (Step 1) and determine which items you wish to keep.
Step 4: Try to work out a fair compromise (from Step 1 items you have identified) using the items you listed as your starting point and hopefully your ending point.

Exhibit 2.1   (Continued)

Step Three: Revisit the Issue of What You Want to Keep

After you have entered all that information, take a good hard look at the assets you wish to keep and those you don't. This step differs from the previous one in that here you are revisiting those assets that make sense for you to hold on to, whereas in step two you were dividing up assets based on many scenarios and exploring different final possibilities.

These decisions can also trickle down to the amount of alimony and child support paid or received. Keep the main assets separate from the little ones. Your issues will probably be with keeping those big assets that are important to you. When dividing the little stuff, write all the items down and then take turns going back and forth. Most of these items probably represent more sentimental feelings than actual hard dollars.

The objective is for each party to end up with roughly half the value of the overall asset picture, which is easier said than done. But what if those numbers don't work for you? What about possible contingencies (i.e., income drying up, change in overall level of assets) or anything else that can affect the agreed-upon split just a little while after the divorce becomes final? Therefore, know what you are comfortable with ahead of time. Know your limits as to what you are willing to give and get. Put yourself in your ex's position and see if it makes sense from his or her viewpoint. Before you start negotiating, know your bottom line.

Step Four: The Negotiation

Once you have done your homework, looked at possible division scenarios, and figured out which assets and debt make the most sense for you to keep, then you are ready to negotiate. On your spreadsheet, you should have a model sampling of how you would like to see the property and debt divided, with each spouse's preferred interest represented. That means one spouse may want the retirement plans over the rental properties because he or she does not have time to deal with those issues. Or a spouse may want income-producing investment assets that generate a rough dollar amount every month.

Some things will be more easily divided than others. For those issues that cannot be worked out, ask your ex if he or she would be fine with having a mediator, arbitrator, or judge on call to help with the final division of assets and debt.

As negotiations begin heating up, tempers may flare, spouses could become hostile towards one another, or other issues can develop. At that point, it is best to call time-out, walk away to cool off, and then start again. You may have to experience many cooling-off phases during the process.

Can You Negotiate What You Want?

You can attempt to negotiate what you want, but you won't walk away feeling like a winner across the board. Negotiation is about give and take. Therefore, prepare yourself for a position of compromise. You need to walk away in a win-win scenario. However, since you're engaged in a lose-lose proposition, this is an extremely daunting task.

Now that you have all the assets listed, you need to assign a priority scale next to each objective you lay out for yourself. You need to go into negotiations expecting to win on several fronts (but not all of them). Furthermore, if you try to bully your way through, you stand a chance of not getting your settlement approved by the judge. The judge doesn't want to see a one-sided settlement.

When presenting a spreadsheet for your ex and the attorney to evaluate, divide your page into four components. List all your assets down the first column. Put the dollar amounts down the second column. Make an attempt to assign each of these amounts into either the third column (yours) or the fourth (your ex's). Base each assignment on the likelihood that you or your ex would want to control that asset after the divorce. Remember, you're not saying this will definitely happen. Instead, you are saying that this is a bona fide, good-faith, first attempt to ease the splitting of property, and one of you has to take the initiative to begin the process. The bottom line is that the dollar totals should be somewhat equal for you and your ex.

Negotiating through Your Lawyer

A good lawyer will continually write settlement proposals throughout the process in an effort to end the case. He knows that it is in each spouse's best interests to accelerate the process. The lawyer's work in settlement negotiation should consist of constantly rewriting the proposal after the other side counters or addresses their chief concerns, to help bridge the gap. A disinterested lawyer keeps tossing counterproposals in the trash and threatening trial.

Be careful. Many times lawyers won't initiate this negotiation process for fear of getting wrong what you ultimately end up with.

Last-Minute Negotiations: The Settlement Conference

Sometimes early-on negotiations won't work and the next round of negotiations will occur through a settlement conference. This is usually required shortly before trial begins. The court will assign you a settlement conference judge to try to help you settle.

The settlement conference judge gets an executive summary of where things stand now, what differences exist, and what offers and counteroffers have been proposed, and will then try to bridge the gap. Sometimes it works and sometimes it doesn't. And even if no settlement was reached, the lawyers can continue the negotiation process during the eleventh hour.

Remember, going to court is such a crapshoot, once you enter the courtroom you really will have no feel as to how it will all work out when you leave. You're better off not placing yourself in a situation where you have no way to control your success and will have to live with the consequences, if unfavorable. Therefore, get down to it and negotiate your settlement.

There are many things you can do to minimize the damage that will result from the divorce process. Following is a list of 11 things that can lessen the harm and help you manage the damage control that could potentially be inadvertently done to you.

Rattiner Damage Control Tips—The Top 11

1. Take care of yourself since it's all about me now!
2. Take care of your family.
3. Protect your mail.
4. Protect your computer.
5. Close joint accounts.
6. Establish your own credit.
7. Protect your separate property.
8. Filing a tax return.
9. Relief from joint liability.
10. Temporary support agreements.
11. Reentering the workforce.

Let's talk about how you prepare yourself in each one of these planning pointers.

Take Care of Yourself—It's All About Me

Once you have started your divorce, the work of rebuilding has begun. You need to keep busy, finding a consistent routine for yourself and your children that fits your newly separated life.

Allow time each day just for you. Be aware of your own stress level and pause when you are feeling overwhelmed or exhausted.

There is no question that divorce is one of, if not *the* most stressful periods in your life other than perhaps the death of a family member or a close friend. You probably have never been through it before, and hopefully, you never will again. Because of the possibility of a breakdown, state of confusion, anxiety attack, or prolonged depression, your main focus needs to be how to minimize emotional damage and take care of yourself.

Think of it from this perspective: You will not do anybody any good if you are not focused first on yourself. That is because other people are depending on you. Think of the message that flight attendants communicate to the passengers on an airplane: "Place the safety mask on yourself before you help those around you." That is because you will not be able to function properly or do anybody else any good if you are unable to breathe.

Your children will need you now more than ever. You will also need to gather all sorts of documents, adhere to all kinds of legal proceedings, and be running in multiple directions, probably even more than you normally do. Your healthy survival is essential to the proper handling and well-being of all those important things in life.

Even if you are the plaintiff who is initiating the divorce, you will still feel the effects of the stressful emotions. Essentially, there is no getting around it no matter what side of the fence you are on. Often, a good place to start to get a handle on yourself, your emotions, and your psyche is to visit with a therapist or a counselor.

Free to low-cost counseling can be found through your insurance program, a member of the clergy, schools that train social workers and psychologists, and community health care centers. Support groups may also be a good fit. Directed by therapists or active volunteers, support groups can provide the opportunity for you to meet people who are in the same situation you are in. One-on-one counseling may be the best starting point for many people as it is often hard to discuss personal details in front of an entire group, especially when emotions are still raw.

The demands on your time during this process can be quite overwhelming, especially if you are employed and juggling various outside commitments with children, church, and other previous engagements. But the upside is that now, as a suddenly single person, you can change your house and your life to just the way *you* want. That thought should lift your spirits and turn a difficult time into a healthier and happier outlook.

The bottom line is you just cannot sit at home waiting for the world to change. You need to be proactive in your assessment of the divorce situation and your ability to take control of your situation. The sooner you do that, the better you will feel. See Exhibit 2.2 for a list of questions to ask therapists to help you choose one who can help you.

Take Care of Your Family

Of course, if you do not take care of yourself first, you are not good at caring for your family. However, that does not mean you should ignore your family and their needs during the divorce process. There may be factors entirely out of your control here, because in order to best take care of the family, both parties need to be on the same page. Unfortunately, that is often not the case, as the spouse who did not want the divorce may delight in turning the children against the other parent. This is extremely unfortunate, and often backfires, as children are healthiest mentally and emotionally when they have two stable, loving parents involved in their lives.

1. How do you establish measurable goals at the beginning of the sessions?
2. Do you have extensive experience in the field of divorce? Let me explain my personal situation to you.
3. Cost: What are your fees? Do you accept insurance? And are rates negotiable?
4. In what states are you licensed to practice?
5. What is your educational background and training?
6. Are you a clinical member of the American Association for Marriage and Family Therapy (AAMFT) or a member of any other professional association?
7. How often do you meet with patients and what is the average session time?
8. How do you know when treatment of someone like myself has been completed?
9. Do you use psychological testing?
10. Do you think that you can help me based on what I've told you?

Exhibit 2.2 Rattiner's Questionnaire for Finding a Qualified Therapist

Research has shown that at some point all children want to have a relationship with both of their parents, unless there were extreme conditions that make it an unhealthy situation. Often those who lived with the parent who vilified and tried to prevent contact with the other parent, even for a period of several years, sought that parent out when they were older and developed loving and warm relationships with them, even to the point where many of those children ended up living with or close to the vilified parent.

A parent's desire for revenge, however, often overshadows the well-being of the children, and things are said and done that cause severe damage to a parent-child relationship. If parents can put their differences aside, especially during the initial divorce process when emotions are raw, and work together for the best interests of the children, all parties will be much happier and more stable overall. Many children are involved in sports, music, religious activities, and other events which both parents should be kept apprised of and attend as often as possible. Although you do not have to sit together and be chummy, it will be good for your children to see you being civilized and cordial to each other.

This, unfortunately, is the ideal scenario, which seldom occurs. Too often children are brought into the middle of the process. Some are even brought into court to testify as to which parent they want to live with and why, and are made to justify their position. Other children are told every detail of the divorce and made to feel that the other parent abandoned them or does not care about them anymore, while still others are simply ignored and left to fend for themselves. All of these situations can be extremely damaging to an otherwise healthy and stable young child.

Most children can benefit from some sort of counseling or therapy. Sometimes that counseling can be most beneficial if it is one-on-one with the child; other times, one or both parents should be involved. As with attorneys, there are many different types of counselors. Some of them specialize in helping families or children cope with divorce, while others are general practitioners. They can range from psychiatrists, who can prescribe medication if necessary, to psychologists, who usually have more training in counseling, or general therapists. Your child's school may also have some form of counseling available. You should research carefully and get recommendations from trusted sources prior to committing to such a course of action. Be aware that once your child starts with a particular counselor, they may become attached or may be agitated if they are hearing things that are outside their comfort zone.

Refer to Exhibit 2.2 for questions to help you choose a therapist.

Protect Your Mail

This is an often overlooked issue because your private mail is still going to your previous primary residence or may be accessible by your soon-to-be ex-spouse. You may not be living in the family residence but, for whatever reason, you may not have your mail forwarded right away; or, as often happens, the post office may not have forwarded all of your mail. In this situation, your soon-to-be ex has access to all your mail and may feel entitled to open it, even without your permission.

If you need to have confidential communication with anyone, including your bank, lawyer, financial adviser, or friends, it is better to be safe than sorry. Individuals or companies that send items such as confidential legal documents, investment statements, paychecks, bank statements and canceled checks, personal and confidential correspondence, and any other personal items should all be alerted that any and all such personal items should be sent to a new address. The unauthorized opening of your mail is a federal offense. As soon as papers are served, or before if you are doing advance planning, have your mail forwarded to a post office box, your office, a friend's house, or a temporary residence to ensure privacy. However, as stated previously, the post office is not 100 percent reliable in this area and you should, therefore, contact all individuals or companies, either by telephone or online, to make sure that they have a new address to which they should sent any and all future correspondence.

You should also be aware that many financial institutions, investment companies and credit card companies, in an effort to "protect your identity," will send a letter to you at your previous address to verify that you have requested the change. If you do not want your soon-to-be ex to know where you are having these items sent, you need to address this matter with each of these companies directly.

However, it has been my experience that there really is no privacy in these areas and most companies are notoriously bad about keeping personal information confidential.

Protect Your Computer

If you have a family computer or a personal computer in your previous residence with confidential work or personal information on it, you should delete all such information entirely off the computer, including out of the recycle bin, before you leave the house for the last time. Be aware that suspicious or nosy spouses may look through your computer before you leave, to find additional ammunition which they will then try to use against you during the divorce process. Keep in mind, however, that even deleting items from the computer and then the recycle bin may not entirely delete the item from your hard drive. The best option would be to take the entire computer, or at least the hard drive, with you when you leave.

Stop using e-mail accounts that can be easily accessed, and make sure you change your password. Further, if you had computers which you used to log into your office server, make sure your company's information technology (IT) department is aware of the situation so they can make whatever changes are necessary to block all future access from those computers. Even if you think your computers are safe, you should still speak with your IT department as they may have other ideas and suggestions for computers you used for work-related items which you are leaving behind. Too many times, the ex will find information on the computer that they really should not have had access to at all, especially sensitive employment/work-related information. Computer-literate spouses have been known to restore e-mails that had previously been deleted from an unsuspecting spouse's computer. Once papers are served, especially in a contentious divorce situation, all future e-mail should be sent exclusively to you and should remain off limits to your soon-to-be ex-spouse.

If you are not sure how to permanently delete computer files, you should hire a computer professional to assist you. They can help you determine the best way to delete information from your computer while not losing the information you need to keep for yourself. This may include saving information onto a portable hard drive, zip disk, or other media, so you can take the information with you. Be careful, however, of leaving any of this information around in a hard copy.

Close Joint Accounts

Bank Accounts

Hopefully, you and your soon-to-be ex can sit down and amicably decide who will pay for what expenses or how the family bills will be paid until things are finalized with the divorce. Unfortunately, in many instances spouses cannot agree on this and will try to punish the other spouse by either withholding money, if they are the major wage earner, or by draining all money out of the joint accounts, leaving no money to pay bills as they become due. Remember, the term *joint* means that either spouse can take out all of the money in that account. Essentially, the first one to the bank wins! This obviously creates hardship, and credit issues, for both spouses as well as the children. Often these situations result in court hearings wherein temporary support orders are issued to deal with these financial matters.

Once it has been decided how the family bills will be handled, either amicably together or through a court order, it is best to close all joint accounts and to open accounts in your name alone. There are situations where continuing to maintain a joint account for a period of time may be a good idea. For example, if you will be receiving a tax refund which will be in both names or if there are other assets or accounts that need to be liquidated in which a check or transfer may be payable jointly, it is easier to have an account established where those funds can be deposited, again keeping in mind that either spouse can take money out of that joint account. If trust and communication have totally broken down between you and your soon-to-be ex, and everything is being channeled through your attorneys, it is best to close all joint accounts and immediately sever those financial ties.

Even if you do maintain a joint account for a period of time, it is important for you to establish your own bank account so that you can more easily track what expenses you are paying individually. If your soon-to-be ex is being unreasonable and withholding money, it may be necessary or warranted to have some of the expenses you are paying brought back into the equation when you are doing a final division of assets.

Credit Accounts

If you are in the phase of seriously thinking about divorce, you will want to start establishing credit in your own name as soon as possible (discussed later in this chapter). This is especially true if you have been the non-wage-earning spouse for several years and most of the credit during the marriage has been established in your spouse's name. Apply for a credit card or two in your own name. It is up to you whether you want to tell your spouse about them. However, keep in mind that if you run up a large credit card bill on an account in your own name, of which your spouse had no knowledge, you will most likely end up being solely responsible for this bill upon the final division of bills and assets.

If you are unable to get a credit card in your own name, you will have to contemplate carefully the advantages and disadvantages of keeping any joint credit accounts opened. The advantage may be that you will have something to fall back on if you are not getting the money you need to pay for your and/or your children's needs. The disadvantage, of course, is that with any joint credit, your soon-to-be ex can max out your credit cards or lines of credit even above and beyond your limits. Neither spouse needs permission, a signature, or even notice from the other in order to do this if the account is in both names. Only you can know what is best for you in this situation.

During the divorce process you and your soon-to-be ex will continue to be responsible for these joint credit debts. If you decide not to close joint credit accounts, and your spouse decides to use those credit accounts to incur additional debt, you will need to be extremely careful in order to avoid being responsible for these debts. If your ex does run up the debt and does not pay it back, the creditors will come after you regardless of the date of separation, since you are the other owner on the account. Community property states may work a little differently. (See discussion on community property in Chapter 8.)

Once you and your soon-to-be ex have agreed, by either working it out together or through a court order, how the credit accounts will be divided and paid, you should then immediately close all joint credit accounts. Credit card companies are usually reluctant to simply transfer the responsibility for the account from one spouse to the other, and will require you to open a new account in your name alone. This is usually a better option anyway, as your soon-to-be ex will have information on the old account and may be able to use it in the future to get detailed information such as purchases made, payments, and so on. If there are still balances on accounts that you are closing, the credit card company can either transfer the balance to a new credit account or they can simply close the account so that no future charges can be made, and you will continue to make payments until the balance is paid in full.

Another important point about closing credit accounts is to make sure you write to each credit card company and request to have the account permanently closed. This means neither of you can reopen the account at a later date, and it will show up as a closed account on your credit report. An 800 number and mailing address are usually provided on the monthly statement or can be found on the Internet. If you do have current charges on the account, then ask the company to close the card for all new charges going forward.

Prior to signing a final settlement agreement, you should obtain a copy of your credit report so that you can verify all credit accounts in your name alone and jointly with your spouse. You do not want to be surprised after the fact with a large credit balance that you knew nothing about. You will also be able to tell by looking at your credit report whether the credit companies have honored your request to close the accounts.

Beware of attorneys who tell you to run up credit account balances. Many will tell you to put your attorney fees on a joint credit card. This is a common practice because credit accounts are considered to be marital debt and your ex will have to pay for half of the balance. This is generally not a smart thing to do for a couple of reasons. First, it's morally wrong. Second, when each spouse maxes out the credit card debt (especially before filing for divorce), then each spouse may have difficulty paying off his or her share or getting any other type of credit. If you run into trouble paying off this credit card debt, your overall credit rating can be in jeopardy. An explanation of credit card ratings is given in a later section of this chapter.

Utilities

If you are going to continue owning the house, change the name on the utility bills to reflect your name only. Remove the ex if he or she is still on the bills so there is no issue about changing them later and receiving approval after the divorce becomes finalized. If you are not going to continue owning the house, then remove your name from the utility bills for the house.

I learned through hard experience that although we have gone to great lengths in this country to protect each individual's privacy, no such protection exists in a divorce situation. Your soon-to-be ex will be able to access bank account information, credit card information, frequent travel account information, and so on, with only a phone call. Even though I went to great lengths to protect this information, I was amazed over and over again how easily accessible it is if a person has an account number, your social security number, and can answer some basic questions. A utility company even sent my ex a check for a credit balance on a utility account *in my name alone* because she had called them and reinstated her name on the account. Fortunately, she was not able to cash the check because it was issued in both names and required my signature. Remember, the person you married is not the same person you are divorcing, and you must take all precautions necessary to protect yourself, especially in a contentious situation.

Establish Your Own Credit

Getting your own credit card will be dependent on factors such as your employment, your credit rating, and any past credit-related issues. Your rating will carry over to other things you do, such as renting an apartment, applying for a mortgage or car loan, and so forth. It is imperative that you manage your credit with a fine-tooth comb during the divorce process, because any negative impact on your credit rating can hurt you in the long term and may make things you try to do more costly. For example, interest rates that mortgage companies charge are determined by how high your credit rating is—the better your rating, the lower the interest rate you will be able to obtain.

You are entitled to receive one free credit report each year under federal law. When ordering the report, you must provide the credit reporting service with the following personal information: name, address, social security number, and date of birth. You may also have to provide information that only you would know, such as the amount of a mortgage or car loan payment. To order your free credit report, call Annual Credit Report Service at (877) 322-8228, visit their web site at www.annualcreditreport.com, or write to them at P.O. Box 105281, Atlanta, GA 30348-5281.

You can also order your report from any of the three major credit bureaus, Trans Union, Experian, and Equifax, each of whom must provide you with a complementary credit report. Their contact information is as follows:

TransUnion: P.O. Box 2000, Chester, PA 19022-2000; (800) 888-4213.

Experian: P.O. Box 2002, Allen, TX 75013; (888) 397-3742.

Equifax: P.O. Box 740241, Atlanta, GA 30374; (800) 685-1111.

If you are having problems paying your debts due to the divorce, or if you believe that may become a problem, you should call your creditors immediately to discuss your options. Many creditors will try to work with you if you are diligent about making your payments on a timely basis. They may be willing to make adjustments based on your current situation and your ability to repay debt. There are also companies that claim to be experts at helping you solve your credit problems. I would caution you to beware of these companies. Many of them charge high fees, and I know of instances where they have collected payments on behalf of the creditors but never forwarded the payment to the creditor to pay off the debt and have then gone out of business themselves. You are then out all the money you paid to them and you still have the credit balance to contend with.

If you are leaving the marital residence and have poor credit, no work history, or no money, you may have to ask family, friends, or your religious or other organizations to help you through the initial transition. This may include having someone cosign for an apartment, utilities, and so on. If that is the case, sign a short-term lease, if possible, and make timely payments so that you can start establishing your own credit history. If you rent from a private individual, make sure they provide you with receipts so that you have evidence of your timely payments.

Divorce is a very expensive ordeal. There are no two ways about it, you are going to need money for a divorce. You may have to support yourself and your children with minimal to no help from your soon-to-be ex. This will be especially hard if you have been dependent on your spouse and your spouse decides to cut off support. You will also need money to hire an attorney. If you have to borrow money from friends or relatives, be sure to sign a promissory note so the court will look at this as a loan and not as a gift that does not have to be paid back.

Do not panic if your credit has been adversely affected in your marriage or through the divorce. Although it may take some time, if you are diligent in working with the credit companies and strive to make timely payments, your credit can be restored to a workable level within a year or two.

If there is ever a time to guard against contingencies, the divorce process is certainly the time! Some advance preparation may be in order to protect yourself. However, there is a fine line between *protecting yourself* and trying to *punish* the other party. It is reasonable to assume that both parties should have sufficient money to live on and that one, or both, of the parties may need to take some money out of a joint account in order to establish personal accounts of their own. Ideally, you and your spouse should be able to discuss this and come to an agreement. Often, however, this is not the case and one spouse ends up acting rashly and taking all of the money out of the accounts. This only causes more headaches for both parties, especially if it is done without notice and you have automatic payments set up to come out of the account or have written numerous checks with the understanding that money was in the account. Keep in mind that such actions can adversely affect your credit as well as your spouse's. Plus you can quickly incur large bank charges for overdraft fees, which is a waste of money.

Protect Your Separate Property

It is probably a wise decision to move all valuable separate property from the house before your soon-to-be ex can damage or misplace those items. If large property is involved, it makes sense to rent a storage unit to temporarily store those items until you have a new place to live. Smaller items, like jewelry, life insurance policies, account records, or important papers can be stored in a safe deposit box or held by trusted family or friends.

A much overlooked scenario is to document or videotape all personal property in your marital residence prior to the initiation of the divorce process. As mentioned before, you will not remember everything you had in the property, especially if you have lived there for a number of years and have stored important items that you do not use very often in an out-of-the-way area of the house. If you did not prepare a list or a videotape ahead of time, speak to friends and family members to see if they may remember items, especially family heirlooms, that you may have forgotten about. Make sure you perform these tasks before any divorce papers are finalized.

Filing a Tax Return

Should you file a joint return with your spouse during the divorce process? It depends on how the divorce is going and the trust factor present. Even married people are not always keen on filing a joint return. An example comes from one of my Certified Financial Planner (CFP) education courses. A woman mentioned to me that she had been married for 23 years and had filed her tax return as "married filing separately" for the past 22 years. When I asked her why, she stated that she had no clue what her husband did for a living!

When you file jointly with your ex, you are both considered jointly and individually liable and responsible for any tax, interest, and penalty issues that arise from the filing of that return before the divorce. This means that one spouse may be held liable for 100 percent of the entire joint tax liability, even though the other spouse may have earned all of the income. Furthermore, this liability applies even if the divorce decree states that the former spouse will be responsible for any amounts due on previously filed joint returns.

Generally, married filing jointly provides for greater tax relief and the least amount of tax liability, especially in situations where one spouse is the predominant breadwinner. However, filing jointly can incur a marriage penalty. This occurs where both spouses earn roughly equal amounts. That is because this can now push you up into a higher overall income tax bracket.

As with being 100 percent liable for any taxes due from the filing, if you file jointly and are getting a refund, then you must also split the refund, unless you can agree otherwise. This leads to another disadvantage in that any overpayment shown on a joint tax return may be used to pay the past-due amount of the ex's debts. However, a spouse can get their share of the refund if they qualify as an injured spouse.

If you are concerned about the liability from your ex-spouse, then married filing separately would be a better alternative. Filing separately means that you are only responsible for the tax liability reported on your own tax return. Filing separately also makes sense if one of the spouses had certain high itemized deductions, such as medical expenses, casualty losses, or miscellaneous expenses (all subject to deductibility limitations).

Filing separately presents a problem in that if you itemize, then your ex must also itemize. The ex is precluded from using the standard deduction in that case. Also, married filing separately imposes higher income tax rates and each spouse will end up paying more in income tax liability. Furthermore, income tax rates are higher at the lower levels of income when filing separately than they are when you file jointly; the exemption amounts for calculating alternative minimum tax will be half those used when filing jointly; you can only write off $1,500 of capital losses (rather than $3,000); and the spouse may not be able to take the child and dependent care credit, the adoption credit, higher education expenses pertaining to the Hope and Lifetime Learning Credits, or the write-off for student loan interest available from cashing in qualified U.S. Savings Bonds to pay for college.

Also, after the due date of a return, usually April 15, the spouses cannot file a separate return if they previously filed a joint return. An exception exists whereby within one year from the tax return due date, including extensions, the personal representative for a decedent can change from a joint return elected by the surviving spouse to a separate return for the decedent spouse.

Your filing status will also depend on when the divorce process started and when it is likely to be completed. You can file jointly in any year the divorce has not become final, but once it is final, then you must file separately. If you have dependents, such as children, then you are better off filing as head of household.

Relief from Joint Liability

There are a few ways you may be able to minimize the tax liability if you decide to file jointly. These include being subject to the innocent spouse rule for tax filing and the injured spouse relief for tax filing rules.

Innocent Spouse Rule for Tax Filing

This may apply to joint filers. In this situation, the IRS recognizes that some spouses sign their name to a joint return without ever reading it or understanding what is included as part of the return. In these cases, a spouse may try to hide behind the *Innocent Spouse Rule*, which states that a spouse who unknowingly signs a fraudulent tax return can be excused from liability for penalties based on that return. From a practical standpoint, it is difficult to prove you were the victim under the Innocent Spouse Rule, but it may be worth pursuing. You can find out more about this by downloading IRS Publication 971 at www.irs.gov.

Injured Spouse Relief for Tax Filing

You can be an injured spouse if you file a joint return and all or part of your overpayment is expected to be or was actually applied against the ex's past-due federal tax, state income tax, child or spousal support, or federal nontax debt, such as a student loan.

As an injured spouse, you can get a refund for your share of the overpayment that would otherwise be used to pay the past-due amount. In order to qualify as an injured spouse, you must file a joint return and not be required to pay the past-due amount. In addition, you must either have reported income, or have made and reported federal withholding or estimated tax payments or claimed the Earned Income Credit. Community property state residents only have to comply with the first two items. Lastly, refunds received in a community property state are dictated by local law.

Temporary Support Agreements

When you are creating temporary support agreements, make the goal about support—both spousal and child. That should be the focus. Other things that coincidentally happen and miraculously show up should be discounted and not factored into the agreement unless it involves some type of support.

The goal here is to ensure that the basic expenses are covered until things become finalized. If you are the primary breadwinner, it makes the most sense to continue business as usual. Continue paying the bills so the family is minimally disrupted. Also, if your ex drives you to court over this issue, you may end up being liable for both sets of attorney fees.

If you separate from your spouse and you do not have a job or other reliable source of income, you may soon find yourself financially needy and dependent on others. If you cannot come to an agreement with your spouse and/or he or she will not pay you voluntarily, then you need to get the court involved. A court can and will issue a temporary support order which is called *pendente lite* or temporary support in this type of situation. Keep in mind, however, that if your spouse is cooperating and you are getting money to pay bills and live on but you think you can do better by taking him or her to court, you may be surprised. In some instances, a spouse may end up getting less than was being provided to them voluntarily. States have strict guidelines that they follow to come up with support amounts. This is usually based on the income of both parties and a specific percentage of the difference in income. Factors such as special needs or the number of children may also play a role in this equation.

If you cannot afford an attorney, many states, through their family court or support division, will help you prepare and file the necessary paperwork to obtain support. If you are not able to get the court papers filed immediately yourself because of other things going on or because of the upcoming battle you anticipate, then have your attorney get this done on your behalf. Even though having money to pay your attorney may be an issue, the court process will accelerate the cash flow to you, so obtaining an advance from a credit card or a loan from a family member may be a worthwhile debt to incur.

From a practical standpoint, any support you ultimately get, both temporary and permanent, will need to be documented in order for each party to be protected and so that each party can understand the tax consequences involved. Simply put, if payments are considered child support, there are no taxable consequences. Money is not deductible by the payer nor taxable to the payee. Payments should be specified as child support for the cleanest results on taxability. Spousal support, however, is a taxable event. It is deductible by the payer and taxable to the payee.

Reentering the Workforce

If you are a stay-at-home spouse and young enough to reenter the workforce, then that may be where you are headed. It could be grueling, especially if you left the workforce many years ago to care for the children. A vocational expert will be needed to assess how much money such an individual is capable of earning.

So unless you are independently wealthy, you will need to come to grips with your career plans. What you will need to do immediately is brush up on your skill set. If you have a professional license or certification, you may need to take continuing education courses, attend a professional conference, and register with headhunters or other employment agencies. You will need to work up your resume, perhaps update your wardrobe, and research job prospects.

If you have been thinking about changing careers, make these moves before you discuss a divorce with your spouse. A court is less likely to upset your plans if you have already started down that path. If you have been out of the marketplace for an extended period of time, your ex should provide you with the funds to become retrained so you can ease back into your previous career.

Start looking for a job as soon as possible. In most situations, if a spouse is able to work, they will be required to do so, or at a minimum the income they could have earned will be taken into consideration in a final settlement either as a deduction from alimony/child support or in the form of a reduced financial settlement. A judge may not look favorably on the fact that you had several months to find a job, especially if you are well qualified and have chosen not to do so. There will not be any additional time to ride it out like some people do during the temporary orders and the divorce process.

Further, going back to work should help stabilize your situation, both financially and emotionally. You will have control of your own income and, hopefully, health and retirement benefits that come with your new employment. Also, you will have the opportunity to meet new people, become involved in new projects, get a whole new spin on life and the world, and think about things other than the divorce. When divorcing spouses do not work, they often spend too much time dwelling on the divorce process, trying to figure out ways to get revenge or hurt their ex, or, in some cases, become very depressed, believing they have nothing to live for anymore. These spouses can get so caught up in trying to destroy the other person or remain depressed for such extended periods of time that they cannot move on with their life, and they become bitter and angry at the world. This is obviously not constructive for them and can be especially destructive if there are children in that environment.

As stated throughout this chapter, your objective is to come out of the divorce process as minimally scathed as possible. Both your financial and emotional health are going to be severely at risk during this process, especially if it is a contentious situation. There is a strong possibility that you will be blindsided by your ex, so you need to be prepared, both emotionally and financially. The planning tips found in this chapter are designed to lower that risk and provide you with the knowledge you need to minimize the risk when going through the divorce process.

Rattiner's Planning Tips

1. Negotiation is the best way to minimize damage. Trials are costly, personally damaging, and a waste of time in the grand scheme of things.
2. Be prepared and do your financial homework first before you even attempt to negotiate. You need to know what you have and what you want before the process can begin.
3. Don't try to win on every negotiating point. Go in thinking compromise. Just prioritize those assets you want to end up with. That way, you'll consider the process a victory.
4. Offer a settlement that is fair to your ex. Otherwise, it won't happen. Remember, it has to be signed off by a judge.
5. Going to court is a crapshoot. It doesn't make sense to take chances with a judge who may be having a bad day.
6. Taking care of yourself is your first priority. If your needs aren't being met, you won't be able to take care of others.
7. Taking care of your family means not alienating the children from the other parent. All children need two loving parents.
8. If you know you are leaving the family residence, take all precautions to protect your mail. Angry exes will open your private mail if it's there.
9. Delete or remove your hard drive from your personal home computer. There can be significant and harmful files that you thought you removed from your computer but actually didn't.

10. Close all joint accounts. That includes your bank accounts, credit cards, utility bills, and other accounts on which both names are listed.
11. Establish your own credit, especially if you were the at-home spouse and may not be able to gain credit after a divorce becomes final.
12. Rent a storage unit or have your personal separate property stored at a friend's house to ensure that you will receive all of it when the divorce is final.
13. Don't file a joint tax return if you are concerned about tax liability issues going forward. Both signers are equally responsible for any monies owed the IRS.
14. The Innocent Spouse Rule may help free you from joint tax liability. But if you have a grand lifestyle in the eyes of the IRS, don't bet on it.
15. Temporary support agreements will help control your ex's spending habits during the divorce process.
16. The at-home spouse should want to get back into the workforce right away to earn a living and also to occupy him- or herself to alleviate some of the anguish created by the divorce process.
17. A therapist for you, your ex, or your children can help you talk through those critical issues that are bottled up inside.

CHAPTER 3

Paying for Divorce

Why is divorce so expensive? Because it's worth it! Or so the saying goes. Divorce is very expensive both during and after the process. Determining how to pay for divorce represents a huge financial challenge since monies that typically fund one household now must fund two or more. It is again worth repeating: There are no winners that result from this process, only losers.

Costs Involved

There are many costs involved in the divorce process. Some are recurring everyday costs that you have paid blindly for years and others are newly added costs that only appear in the divorce process.

Costs incurred in everyday life include fixed expenses such as mortgage, rent, utilities, insurance, and taxes, as well as discretionary expenses such as food, clothing, transportation, car expenses, credit card payments, travel and entertainment, vacations, contributions, personal care, dues, and so forth. Additionally, there are the divorce costs. These can include lawyer and specialty fees such as business valuations, mediators, arbitrators, vocational experts, and therapists. As stated throughout this book, the divorce costs are wasted monies that hopefully can be minimized so that each spouse makes the best of a bad situation.

Your goal is to pay these expenses as they are incurred, even with many of them being new. This is easier said than done for most people. You may have had a hard enough time paying your normal expenses before the divorce; now, with these additional divorce-related expenses, the situation is magnified. And to make matters worse, it is not just your expenses that are affected but all your ex's expenses as well. Two for the price of one! Therefore, you need a strong game plan to distinguish what you should be paying for, how to pay for it, and for how long.

What Should You Pay for in the Divorce?

Ideally, you would like to know up front who is responsible for what expenses. The problem is, depending on your situation, you may be called upon to pay for both your expenses and your ex's expenses. It boils down to who is in the best position to pay for these expenses.

Generally, the courts and the attorneys determine that the primary wage earner should be responsible for the expenses of the divorce. Sometimes they may issue an executive order to enforce this issue. Or, if one of the spouses is behaving badly, such as spending excessive amounts of money, running up joint credit card debt, and so on, then the temporary order may be used to limit the amount of money that can be spent by that spouse. Or the temporary order will establish a set amount of support which may limit what each spouse is able to spend.

Temporary orders are supposed to be just what the term implies—temporary. However, beware: Just as in the rest of life, there are no free rides in divorce, either. The temporary order may set the stage for what is to come, especially if the divorce gets delayed and takes longer than it should. This is especially true in matters of child custody and visitation. Ideally, temporary orders should be created between you and your spouse, but in most cases, especially in a contentious situation, the attorneys and often the judge or mediators get involved. Just remember, if you do come to terms with your spouse regarding matters addressed in temporary orders, which would include financial and visitation issues, formalize these matters in writing to make sure each party is clear on what they are supposed to do and that they uphold their end of the agreement.

How Long Will You Have to Pay These Expenses?

Good question. It is anybody's guess. Theoretically, the divorce expenses will continue for the entire period during which both spouses are slugging it out and perhaps even afterward. "It ain't over till it's over," as the great New York Yankee philosopher Yogi Berra said. That is why it is imperative to keep the divorce process as short as possible. Divorces can take from one month to several years. Obviously, the shorter the time frame, the cheaper it should be for everyone.

To keep the process alive for infinity and beyond does not accomplish the goals of either spouse. It is no different than a business proposition. Figure out what you want to do, figure out a way to accomplish that goal, and then, as the Nike slogan states, "Just do it!" But it sounds a lot easier than it really is.

Looking at it from outside the box, you can see all the nonsense that accompanies a divorce and you just want to say, "Let's cut to the chase and be done with it—it's time to move on." That is when it pays to have friends and relatives involved. They are far enough away from the situation that they may be able to provide you with good, independent, objective advice. When you are in the midst of the divorce process, you are just too emotionally caught up to be able to think things through rationally.

A good attorney will try to expedite the process. He will try to get right to the issues and use alternative forms of dispute resolution to minimize the process. This will help save costs and emotional wear and tear. As I stated before, my attorney attempted to do this. Unfortunately, you need someone on the other side who is also willing to make that logic work. That often does not happen. There are some attorneys who will wait until the money well dries up before they will consider trying to resolve the issues and settle the case. Unfortunately, in my research for this book, that is mostly the type of attorney I heard about. Perhaps attorneys stir such anger and are the brunt of many jokes for a reason!

How long the divorce goes on will also depend on what each person wants to get from the process. In theory, it should be simple: The spouses can no longer coexist under the same roof so it is time to move on. But as most people come to know and realize, logic plays a very minimal role in the entire process. It is truly run by emotions and nothing more.

Some soon-to-be ex-spouses refuse to settle because they want to punish the other spouse for leaving, lying, cheating, spending lavishly, abuse, or other issues that have come up. Others simply do not want to get divorced, so they try to latch on to anything they can as a ray of hope that the ex will come back, and they drag the process on indefinitely. This is always a recipe for disaster. Other soon-to-be ex-spouses are just plain nasty and inconsiderate, and may have nothing better to do with their time. This seems to be especially true in situations when one spouse is not working and the children are either grown or at least fairly independent, allowing the parents too much time to dwell on the divorce process to the point where it is all that keeps them going. In any event, the longer the parties delay the inevitable, the worse it is for everyone and the more expensive it becomes.

Creating a Budget

The first step necessary to determine what each spouse will pay for during the divorce process is to develop a budget. There is only so much income and it has to go a long way toward paying current and possibly future expenses. Therefore, take it one step at a time. Remember, not every financial decision needs to be made at this juncture. Some things will begin to fall into place during the process.

A budget is a necessity because it tracks what you make and the amount you spend. Also, it will be required during the process to determine the needs of each party. Be careful, because one or both sides will attempt to exaggerate their numbers. You should be proactive in looking at the document your soon-to-be ex provides, as no one will know how accurate those numbers are better than you. Make sure that expenses are claimed by only one spouse as there is obviously no need for both spouses to pay the same mortgage, credit card bill, and so on.

Once you have reviewed the financial information submitted by your soon-to-be ex, make notes and comments for your attorney so that they have a firm understanding of what the real income and expenses are, which will likely be very different from the inflated numbers your spouse provided. Each spouse initially assumes, then comes to find out over the course of the months or years of the divorce process, that if they artificially increase their needs, the party responsible for making a decision, whether it be a judge, mediator, or another party to the final settlement, will award them these inflated, unrealistic larger amounts, thus providing that spouse with a greater share of income. As it is often said, do not assume anything, because you are likely to be wrong!

For example, I knew of a budget where a person put down such an unrealistic amount of income that it was greater than the family (during the marriage) ever earned. It was completely unrealistic and any judge would ultimately see through that, especially if expenses are validated. Another example would be where one party puts new expenses (never before paid by the family) on the budget, since that person has always wanted to do these things and is now hoping to be able to do so because of the divorce. Using that approach, the spouse who puts down the unrealistic numbers will find out that they will not receive anything near what they anticipated and will actually reduce what they ultimately receive.

Ideally, it is easier to work together with the spouse when undergoing the development of a budget, but that may not be possible. An honest approach tends to benefit both parties, but emotions may not allow that to happen for the reasons already stated. If working together is impossible, then calculate your expenses accurately and estimate what your spouse's living expenses should be.

To begin the budgeting process, list all the major categories that you spend money on. Fixed expenses, which are present in roughly the same amount every month, should be your starting point. Examples include mortgage, rent, insurance, and taxes. Other expenses over which you tend to have more control are listed afterwards. You can find out what these expenses are by examining your checkbook and credit card statements, or simply keeping a cash log on a memo pad whenever you go out and writing down each amount as you spend it. To complete this exercise, use the form in Exhibit 3.1 to complete your budget.

Litigation Budget

Ask your attorney to develop a litigation budget. Many attorneys are uncomfortable with this as they fear that you may take it too literally and expect the expenses to directly correlate to the amounts they provided to you. Even worse, the spouses may try to hold the attorneys to those amounts. It is very difficult, even for attorneys, to predict the course of action the litigation will take. Unexpected problems often come up and require a great deal of effort, attorneys' time, and your money (would it be anyone else's?) to solve.

Monthly Expenditures	Amount
Auto loan payment	$
Auto maintenance	$
Child care	$
Clothing	$
Contributions	$
Credit card payments	$
Dues	$
Entertainment	$
Food	$
Household maintenance	$
Income and Social Security taxes	$
Insurance	$
Personal care	$
Property taxes	$
Rent or mortgage payment	$
Retirement plan investments	$
Savings/investments	$
Transportation (gas, fares)	$
Utilities	$
Vacations (monthly allotment)	$
Other	$
Total Monthly Expenditures	**$** _____

Monthly Receipts	Husband	Wife
Wages or salary	$	$
Capital gain (long-term)	$	$
Capital gain (short-term)	$	$
Dividends (mutual funds, stocks, etc.)	$	$
Interest (CDs, savings account, etc.)	$	$
Pension	$	$
Rental and/or royalty	$	$
Social Security	$	$
Other taxable	$	$
Other nontaxable	$	$
Total Monthly Receipts	**$** _____	
Net Cash Flow = Total Monthly Receipts – Expenditures	$	

Exhibit 3.1   Your Monthly Budget

In any event, it is reasonable for you to assume that you can have the attorney's help and insist on some type of budget.

With the litigation budget you are better off starting with a range of expenses as opposed to trying to predict the exact dollar amount. This budget should also have a couple of broad categories rather than many detailed categories. These categories would include items for discovery, negotiations, alternative dispute resolution, trial preparation, and trial. Litigation costs can easily be upwards of $25,000, even in a fairly amicable divorce if there are unresolved or complex issues. This is why it is always advisable to avoid litigation at pretty much all costs.

Analyzing Your Income

Many people do not truly know what their current income is. Sure, they know what their W-2 form states, and other sources of income perhaps, but most people equate income with what they can buy—in other words, with the expenses they actually incur. This process provides a rude wake-up call for what spouses truly earn and can afford. Now, all of a sudden, they need to make their income stretch for all these unforeseen expenses they are about to incur.

To start off, you will need to list all income for both you and your spouse. (See Exhibit 3.2.) This will provide you with a starting point for what you have to spend on the divorce process. Ouch, the ultimate wake-up call!

Once you complete the income portion of your budget, you will then need to see how much money you can really spend—after taxes. Too many spouses simply ignore this calculation because it is too difficult for them, they cannot be bothered, or they simply do not know how to complete this step. But, as they say in business, it is not what you make, it is what you keep. The same rules apply here. You need to figure out what you are walking away with.

Keep Your Income Separate

If you do not have a separate bank account, immediately open one, as discussed in Chapter 2. Start depositing your paycheck into it. Even if you are the sole wage earner in your family and you and your spouse have agreed to keep a joint account for paying family

	Total Income (Community/ Separate)	Allocated to You	Allocated to Your Ex
1. Wages (each employer)			
2. Interest income (each payer)			
3. Dividends (each payer)			
4. State income tax refund			
5. Capital gains and losses			
6. Pension income			
7. Rents, royalties, partnerships, estates, trusts			
8. Taxes withheld			
9. Other items such as Social Security benefits, business and farm income or loss, unemployment compensation, mortgage interest deduction, etc.			

Notes: _____

_____

_____

_____

Exhibit 3.2   Income Allocation for You and Your Ex

expenses, make sure the money you earn goes first into your own account before being transferred to the joint account. As soon as you have permanently separated, your income becomes your own, separate property. Having your own account clearly states that you are now separated and your income is now your own.

Going Solo

Now that you have begun the process of dividing assets, your next move is to get an accounting of your separate assets and begin to keep your assets solo. These are assets that are listed in your name only.

Solo Assets

You have the right to withdraw or borrow up to 50 percent of your retirement account, but that may not be a good idea, for several reasons. First, you are only allowed to borrow money from certain plans and there are specific limits as to how much you can withdraw. For example, with a 401(k) plan it is 50 percent of the account balance up to a maximum of $50,000. However, this money must be paid back within five years to avoid having to take the money as a withdrawal. Second, depending on your age and the type of retirement plan (e.g., 401[k], IRA, Roth IRA, etc.), there may be penalties for early withdrawal. Third, there are normally tax consequences associated with any retirement plan withdrawal. Finally, judges will see that you were intentionally trying to reduce your assets, especially with retirement dollars, in an effort to keep that money out of the final financial settlement.

Sometimes it is necessary to dip into retirement/investment money to pay ongoing expenses during the divorce process. The real issue may then be whether your retirement account is sole property or joint property. If it is considered a joint asset, you can make the argument that taking half of the account is within your rights, especially if you are using this money to pay attorney's fees and other divorce expenses. Of course, the negative attorney can say you are intentionally reducing your assets so there is less money to split down the road, or that you are taking those funds in order to hide them, give them away, or for some other nefarious purpose.

Separate Property

Do not confuse solo assets with separate property. Separate property is what you bring into the marriage, and as long as you keep it apart from your spouse's property, it will remain your separate property. This includes assets or debts that either of you had before your marriage, or that you acquired after the permanent separation. Generally, each of you will keep your separate property and be responsible for your separate debts, but in some states separate property can be divided at divorce.

Separate property is titled in your name and is allowed to be kept separate because you have not commingled it with your spouse's property. Separate property also includes gifts and inheritances brought into the marriage or received during the marriage as long as it is, again, not commingled with your spouse's property. In some states, any increase in separate property will be considered marital property.

Joint Assets

And the father said to the son, after looking down at his kingdom from his castle, "Son, someday, all of this will belong to . . . your ex-spouse's attorney!" Translation: What was an impressive array of joint assets that would suit either spouse's needs for years to come, or possibly until death, will ultimately be gone, unless you and your ex get a wake-up call and begin to become logical and reasonable during the process.

How you handle joint assets depends on whether divorce papers have been filed. Before either of you file, you can use joint assets any way you see fit. Once divorce papers have been filed, you are legally prohibited from doing anything that would harm your jointly owned interests, nor can you do anything that would harm your spouse's separate property. Jointly owned property must be managed for the benefit of both parties.

Exhibit 3.3 demonstrates how to construct a balance sheet. If you already have this information assembled in a format of your own design, you can skip this exercise. When you have filled out the form, attach copies of brokerage, financial adviser, and mutual fund investment statements, and any other necessary documentation, and your balance sheet will be complete.

Determining Your Net Worth—Analyzing Your Assets and Liabilities

Personal Assets

Name of Asset	Current Value
Primary residence	$
Secondary residence	$
Automobile(s)	$
RVs (boats, campers, etc.)	$
Household belongings, etc.	$
Other personal assets	$

Cash Reserves

Bank Name	Name of Asset	Current Value	Rate of Return (%)	Maturity Date	Annual Additions	Purpose
	Checking accounts	$				
	Savings accounts	$				
	Credit union accounts	$				

Company retirement plan:						Retirement
Company retirement plan:						Retirement
Company retirement plan:						Retirement
Company retirement plan:						Retirement
IRA:						Retirement
IRA:						Retirement
IRA:						
Other:						
Other:						
Other:						

Exhibit 3.3   Your Balance Sheet

Non-Retirement and Business Investments

Name of Asset	Current Value	Rate of Return (%)	Maturity Date	Annual Additions	Purpose
Real estate:					
Real estate:					
Real estate:					
Real estate:					
Personally owned business:					
Other business interests:					
Note receivable:					
Note receivable:					
Note receivable:					
Life insurance cash value:					
Life insurance cash value:					
Life insurance cash value:					
Other:					
Other:					
Other:					
Other:					

Exhibit 3.3   (Continued)

Liabilities

Name of Liability	Initial Balance	Current Balance	Monthly Payment	Interest Rate	Payoff Date
Home mortgage:					
Home equity loan 1:					
Home equity loan 2:					
Second home mortgage:					
Auto loan 1:					
Auto loan 2:					
Credit card:					
Credit card:					
Credit card:					
Credit card:					
Real estate loan:					
Real estate loan:					
Real estate loan:					
Business loan:					
Business loan:					
Business loan:					
Retirement plan loan:					
Retirement plan loan:					
Other loan:					
Other loan:					
Other loan:					
Other loan:					
Other loan:					

Exhibit 3.3:   (Continued)

Taking care of joint assets is viewed as a fiduciary responsibility, similar to what financial advisers have to adhere to when managing their clients' money. In a nutshell, each spouse owes the highest degree of care and responsibility to the other as if they were managing the other's money. Each spouse owes the other an undivided amount of fiduciary responsibility. But what if you are concerned that your ex will not adhere to this aboveboard legal obligation? What if he or she clears out the joint bank accounts or other joint property?

Before Divorce Papers Have Been Filed

Before either spouse files for divorce, there is not much you can do about protecting the joint assets. This is a difficult situation, since the nature of how you work in this area is directly determined by how much you trust your spouse. Keep in mind once again that the person you married is not the same person you are divorcing! As stated in Chapter 2, when it comes to joint accounts, remember, the first one who gets to the bank wins! Both you and your ex have a legal responsibility not to do anything that would harm the other with regard to joint interests. The property must be managed for the benefit of both parties. Unfortunately, it does not always work that way.

If one spouse takes half of the account, as long as harm is not intentionally caused to the other spouse, that may just be the lay of the land. To be safe, however, that spouse should keep the money in a separate account under his or her name and show what the money was used for, as this money will have to be brought back into the final accounting of assets to be divided. If the spouse takes all of the money in the account, that may be construed as hiding assets, which the courts will not look favorably upon. Further, if this causes undue hardship to the other party, a judge or mediator may insist that part or all of this money be returned to the account, given to the other spouse, or, at a minimum, brought back into the final accounting of assets to be divided.

Technically, at least half of the joint assets are yours. Therefore, if you pull out any of the money found in a joint account, does that put you in some type of jeopardy? The answer can be yes if it is viewed as being done in anticipation of the divorce. The attorney for the other spouse may have fun trying to prove that. Also, if your divorce was amicable up to this point, it will certainly not be afterwards.

After Divorce Papers Have Been Filed

After divorce papers have been filed, the court automatically issues an order that restricts both of you from taking or transferring any of your jointly owned property. You and your spouse are required to leave your joint savings, checking, and investment accounts and everything else as they are unless you and your spouse agree to use them. It is wise to agree in advance on how any joint monies should be used and to get it in writing so that there is no dissension down the road as to whether it was mutually agreed upon or not.

If one spouse takes more than his or her fair share, that money may need to be repaid later or worked back into the settlement, as previously stated. Unfortunately, this happens quite often. You can protect yourself in these events. You can notify the bank, brokerage house, or insurance company that you are in the process of a divorce and that they should not allow for withdrawals or transfers of any monies from any of these accounts without the written consent of both parties. Further, send the financial institution a letter stating that it must adhere and honor the court orders that are an automatic part of the divorce.

You can also do the same thing regarding retirement accounts by contacting your ex's plan administrator, and for home equity lines of credit by contacting the bank or financial institution. Also, if your spouse trades securities or performs other financial transactions over the Internet, send an e-mail to the trading firm advising them that a divorce action has been filed and that no further transactions should be made on the account without both spouses' authorization.

Again, if you and your soon-to-be ex can agree that one or both of you can use the joint assets, make sure you get it in writing! You may agree to use joint assets to pay for the legal fees and other divorce or support expenses. Keeping records of bank statements showing withdrawals and payments, as well as copies of the bills that were paid, will ensure that the money is going for its intended purpose.

What Is Truly Important

The most important thing is for each party to have sufficient assets to feed and shelter each person until the divorce is final, which hopefully will only be several months as opposed to several years.

With the passage of time, what works out financially and what does not will become more apparent.

Again, using joint assets to pay for a divorce is a waste of money because a lot of these assets will be used, unfortunately, not for your betterment. As many ex-spouses find out too late, usually after the fact, there are many cheaper alternatives to employ when going through the divorce process. (See Chapter 4.) But you may not have an option, as we will discuss in a moment. Further, attorneys who know how much you have in joint assets can keep the case going until all of the assets are depleted. As I stated before, not all attorneys do that, but I have seen and heard about many who do. As we explore in the next chapter, there are better ways of going about the divorce process so that it can be more of a win-win scenario.

How to Pay for It: Avoid Paying for Your Ex's Legal Fees

If you are the major wage earner in the family, one of the biggest problems you are going to face in the divorce process is that not only will you be obligated to pay your own legal fees but you may very well end up having to pay your ex's legal fees, too, as well as all of the other divorce-related expenses. This will especially hold true if you are the breadwinner and your ex is the at-home spouse.

The goal here is to use monies that belong to both of you so that you are not stuck footing the entire divorce bill out of your share of the marital assets. Some of the inequities that arise from this process are that the breadwinner uses his or her money to pay for divorce, such as from a business or other account. This lowers the breadwinner's assets, and then the remainder is split, so a gross injustice is served to the breadwinner.

You may be wondering what happens if the ex has his or her own money. That takes us back to the discussion of whether the ex's money is separate property. If it is considered separate property, such as an inheritance or gift received during the marriage or prior to the marriage and those funds are kept separate, then those monies are exempt from having to be used to pay for any joint expenses. So in essence your ex can have more separate money than there is joint money, and yet you can be held responsible to pay for the joint bills! What a system!

Then you have to try to figure out what the best way is to begin paying the legal fees. Most people are not millionaires, nor do they have an unlimited amount of money they can tap into and throw into the black hole of the divorce process. Again, from the attorneys' standpoint, they look at the bottom-line asset number and view you as having all of those assets to use in the divorce process. After the divorce, if you account for the percentage of assets you have remaining versus the total amount you had prior to the divorce, you will most likely see a huge percentage decrease in your net worth. The question then becomes, how can you leverage the situation so that you are not solely responsible for paying these fees on top of the split of assets and income that will follow later on?

A good place to start is to begin liquidating joint assets under the premise that your joint assets will bring in money that can temporarily be placed in a liquid account (such as a money market or savings account) to pay the fees associated with the divorce. Of course, if the assets are jointly held, then you will have to have your ex sign off on it. Your rationale is that you have to provide the funds to make those payments and ultimately both of you can be held responsible to pay those debts either during the divorce process or afterwards.

A second option, if you are not the primary wage earner, is to put your attorney fees on a joint credit card, although, as stated in Chapter 2, this is not a great idea as it may cause great hardship down the road if you do not receive enough money to pay these bills in full. However, because it is a joint debt your ex will also still be liable for this debt. This is part of the reason we give in Chapter 2 for closing joint credit accounts as soon as is practical. The rationale for placing these expenses on the joint credit account is that the primary wage earner will be responsible for most of these bills as the lower wage earner has no money to pay the bills.

Still another approach is to take out a joint loan to pay those bills. Perhaps a home equity line of credit makes sense. A home equity line of credit is a preapproval from the bank, stating that you have sufficient equity in your home and strong enough credit scores to borrow against the house for whatever reason. Further, since it is secured against the house, you can also deduct the loan's interest on your tax return.

Using the same rationale, taking out a mortgage or home equity loan in advance for what each attorney may quote the legal fees at would also make sense. Add up the two legal fees, and take out a mortgage for about 125 percent of that amount. There are always cost overruns—ask anybody! This way the money is there to pay the lawyers. If you do not pay the attorneys, they could secure a lien on the house. Again, the interest on the mortgage or home equity loan is tax deductible.

Tax deductibility of expenses helps minimize the sting. As a precaution, it is generally not a good idea to go into debt, especially to pay for divorce-related expenses. However, if it is a joint obligation, then perhaps the debt can be shared by both spouses once the final settlement is reached. The debt and assets typically are split and hopefully each party will take a share of both the debt and the assets. Keep in mind, however, that unless the property securing the mortgage or home equity line of credit is sold, or money is used from another source to pay off those loans, there will still be liens against the house for whichever party obtains that asset in the final settlement.

You can always make the case to use retirement assets to pay for divorce expenses. Even though, as stated before, there are restrictions and repercussions, and you may need to seek permission to do that, these assets then become part of the pool of monies to be divided between the spouses. If you are able to borrow against qualified retirement dollars (see Chapter 7), you should. However, if you take monies out of an IRA or other personal retirement account, then borrowing is not allowed. You have to withdraw that money, and that could incur a 10 percent early withdrawal penalty on top of the ordinary income tax you would have to pay for accessing the retirement accounts today.

You can also sell rental real estate or other assets. Selling rental real estate may be a good solution because the tax implications of selling the property later may not adequately be taken into consideration if the property is simply transferred to a spouse a part of the marital settlement. (See Chapter 6.) Capital gains and recaptured depreciation with rental real estate will effectively lower your tax basis and thus increase your tax liability. Having that accounted for during the process will make you both liable for the tax consequences and you will not get stuck footing the tax bill alone if you decide to sell the property after the divorce. For example, if you owned a piece of real estate jointly since 1990 and now roughly 20 years have gone by, you may have used up much of the depreciation on the property, so your adjusted basis is next to nothing. Therefore, when you sell the property, you are realizing all profit, especially in a down market. With an up market, the numbers are a lot worse. Take a look at the following example.

Example

John and Jane purchased a rental house back in 1990 for $200,000. During the divorce process, they sell the rental house for $700,000. Their tax liability would be $111,250 based on the following:

Purchase price	$200,000
Depreciation	$145,000
Adjusted basis	$55,000
Sales price	$700,000
Capital gain	$500,000
Tax Liability	
$145,000 × 25%	$36,250
$500,000 × 15%	$75,000
Total tax liability	$111,250

Therefore, if you keep the rental house, be prepared to pay tax on it when you sell it, unless you opt for an IRC Section 1031 election (see Chapter 6 on tax issues).

A sidebar bit of advice is to have your attorney keep track of the expenses being paid that represent tax-deductible expenses. For example, if much of the advice you are seeking stems from tax or investment issues surrounding the assets, those expenses may be deductible on your tax return. The benefit to that is it helps lower your overall legal expenses since you may be able to write off a portion of those expenses. Check with your CPA on that issue.

The resulting bottom line is that the more that goes to the attorneys, to the other specialty parties involved in the process, or is just wasted on other nonsense, the less money will be available for you and your spouse as well as for your children, either while you and your ex are alive or upon your deaths. This can obviously have a negative impact on you as well as on your children, especially if they are used to being abundantly provided for and now are not getting what they are used to getting. This may cause resentment and hostility between the parents and the children. As I have reiterated many times throughout this book, it is in everyone's best interest to resolve these matters with the least amount of legal maneuvering and expense. Again, the divorce process is a lose-lose situation.

Rattiner's Planning Tips

1. Many costs show up for the first time during the divorce process. Take an accounting of what each one represents before you act on it.
2. Try to shorten the divorce process, where possible. The longer it goes, the more expensive it becomes.
3. When figuring out how much each spouse needs during the divorce process, the first thing you should do is to create a budget.
4. Lawyers will provide you with a litigation budget if you request one.
5. Once the divorce process is under way, keep your income separate from that of your ex.
6. As long as separate property has not been commingled, it should remain separate property after the divorce.
7. Joint assets should be taken care of in a fiduciary capacity by each spouse during the divorce process.
8. Your responsibility for using and caring for joint assets differs before and after divorce papers have been filed.
9. Taking out a mortgage or home equity line of credit, liquidating assets in a joint account, credit cards, and retirement accounts are all sources for paying legal fees during the divorce.
10. Don't forget the tax angles of your expenses, since this will determine what you truly have to spend during the divorce.

CHAPTER 4

Plan of Attack:
Let the Games Begin!

There are many ways to play the divorce game. Unfortunately, both spouses have to agree to play it the same way; otherwise the automatic default option is attorneys. Need I say more?

Taking Your Ex Out

When I used to coach my three kids in basketball, soccer, and baseball, I was a staunch advocate of taking the early lead and having the other team follow your game plan, and not the other way around. They played on your terms which were dictated by you at the very start. Call it the intimidation factor, but it usually worked, as our winning records indicated.

Following the same logic, should you go after your ex that same way? As much as you're tempted to get the early lead, and place the intimidation factor front and center, and you have every good reason to want to do that, it is generally not advisable.

Many spouses do not follow that logic. They go for the killas early and often as they can. What I've learned is that after all is said and done, 90 percent of those people I interviewed said they wish they hadn't done that, for a variety of reasons. These include the long-term damage it does to the children, who may not be able to forgive you; the resources it wastes; the general hostility and anger displayed toward you by others; the fact that the two of you don't cooperate on kids' issues when you should; and, probably even more important and overlooked, your health—both mental and physical. Sometimes the damage is so severe, you never get over it and thus never recover. Too little too late, is how I view it.

If you are still considering taking your ex-spouse out, remember this saying, "When tempted to fight fire with fire, remember that the Fire Department usually uses water."

Remember

Remember, this author is not licensed to dispense any legal advice. The following information is presented to alert you to some of the things you may experience. For a complete, unbiased, and more informed picture of the entire legal process, you should contact an attorney to discuss any planning issues and your options as it relates to your divorce.

Litigation

Generally, litigation should be avoided at all costs. That's because it is very expensive, time consuming, open to the public, and can cause considerable long-term harm. Most attorneys do not end up in litigation and do not want to go to court in the first place. As stated in Chapter 1, if your attorney ends up in court more than 5 percent of the time, he is above traditional averages and you may want to reconsider using that attorney.

If both spouses know the trial is fast approaching, they tend to get more reasonable. Even though you don't want to go in this direction, you'll need to prepare for war but pray for peace! Last-minute glitches in settlement agreements seem to be almost the norm. In fact, many cases are settled at the eleventh hour, literally right up to the trial date.

I would say "Never say never" with respect to going to court. The main reason why cases end up before the court has to do with custody issues. There may be other instances where it makes sense, but those are few and far between. First, the court costs, lawyer fees and prep time, additional time off from work, and other hidden expenses can drive the cost up to $20,000 or more. Second, as I found out from those unfortunate few who did go to court, between your attorney discrediting the other party and vice versa, you will be mentally drained from the experience. Fortunately, I did not have to go to court.

In the weeks and months preceding the trial date, your attorney will probably suggest or discuss settlement options with you.

The judge may urge the settlement upon both you and your spouse in a pretrial hearing. However, if both of you refuse to budge, then you will see each other in court.

Your spouse may want to take you to court to prove that you are a louse! They may want to air their grievances about you to everybody and would be looking forward to this day at all costs. An angry spouse would probably not care about the stress involved, but rather would like to place your alleged offenses against you on public record.

If this describes your ex, then you can expect a nasty day in the courtroom. Anticipate the ex calling friends, neighbors, business associates, or even people who have nothing to do with the case, who know you just as a mere acquaintance perhaps, to become involved in the drama for the sole purpose of humiliating you.

Judges don't want you to come before them. They don't like the responsibility, generally. Also remember that both parties may not be happy upon leaving the courtroom once the judge renders a decision.

No matter how unproductive and uncouth your spouse is acting, you always need to maintain your cool in the courtroom. You need to clearly focus on your mission in the courtroom, which is to protect your interests. These include custody of your children, future inheritances, protecting your children against an abusive spouse, and so forth.

Your lawyer should prepare you for the trial process in advance. You will have to accompany your lawyer to court. Knowing what to expect will help set the expectations going forward. The attorney needs to inform you that all hell will break loose and you just have to grin and bear it. Knowing in advance what to anticipate will hopefully make it more tolerable. Probably the most important thing for you to remember is, don't tick off the judge! Remember, ugly divorces can continue beyond the trial.

If you do go to trial, the process and formality in the courtroom are pretty standard. First, attorneys give opening statements. The petitioner will call witnesses, introduce evidence, and present the case. The respondent will follow. The petitioner may then present a rebuttal. The respondent can then provide a surrebuttal. Lastly, the parties present their closing arguments.

The judge then may request memoranda or briefs to be filed on legal issues before or after the trial. It could take the judge ample time to determine the ultimate outcome and decision of the trial. In a worst-case scenario, that means property divisions, custody, support, and responsibilities of the spouses may not be determined for a long while, possibly as long as two years. Hopefully, it will be much sooner.

Your testimony can be given to the court in the form of a signed statement called a *declaration of affidavit.* In that case, you won't have to speak. But everything you do will make some type of impression on the judge. The judge is the only one deciding your case. The judge might preside over your trial, so your demeanor in the courtroom matters. Dress well, be respectful, be on time, and be prepared. Always present yourself as reasonable and mature.

Many times, however, you will have to approach the witness stand, so you should try to get an inkling of what to expect. You'll probably prepare in advance with your attorney. Make sure your attorney knows exactly what to expect before the trial. This is not the time for your attorney to come across surprises. Remember, your attorney needs to be fully prepared going into the courtroom as to what the outcome should be. Many people have told me that an attorney never asks a question without knowing the answer in advance. From that perspective, people sometimes view it as a game—an unfair one at that!

If you don't like the outcome, you can chance an appeal. That means you take the case to the next highest court, which would be the state court of appeals, or the state supreme court. It is the job of the appellate court to review the decision of the lower court and determine whether the decision was based on legal error, whether the decision was supported by adequate evidence, or whether the judge went outside the boundaries of his discretion. Different standards may be applied to different cases.

Many times appeals are brought by the spouse who thought the initial settlement wasn't fair and is seeking to change the terms of the settlement. But beware. Appeals are expensive and time consuming. If the appeal is frivolous, sanctions can be imposed against the party bringing the appeal. Make sure the dollars and the terms are worth fighting about.

Again, hopefully you won't end up in court, but if you do, there are things you can do to give yourself a leg up. That means, first of all, engaging in behavior patterns that are more respectful. For example, if you are seeking to obtain custody of your children, decrease the number of hours you work and your out-of-town travel. On the flip side, if you are looking for more money from your ex, cut down on the frivolous purchases and show the court you are using money provided to you to benefit your children.

Second, maintain boundaries set by your attorney both before and during the trial. Don't scream at, hit, or threaten your spouse; don't withhold money earmarked for the children or put the spouse's property on the front lawn. You must maintain good conduct.

Third, it is unwise to become friends with your lawyer during the process. That's because the lawyer could lose objectivity since he may feel a personal attachment to you and may fight to represent your interests to the bitter end, as opposed to settling the case, which may make more sense for everyone involved.

Fourth, don't succumb to outside advice. Friends, family members, business co-workers, and others will give you advice on how to "win" the divorce trial. While their intentions are good, it may not be in your best interests to follow their specific words of advice. In many cases people have told me it caused them to lose their case!

But probably most important of all, you don't know how the trial is going to end up. It is based on factors that may be outside your control or based on irrefutable evidence about your marital estate, your finances, your past behavior, and so forth. It is a complete crapshoot which, for a few hours of uncertainty, can determine your deal for the rest of your life. There are lots of reasons why. The judge may have had a bad day, or you might get a judge who could be biased in his approach or rulings. Going to court is too risky and definitely not worthwhile. Good attorneys try to avoid going to court at all costs.

Just remember, if this is the path you each choose, minimize the damage by accelerating the timeline and lessening the cost.

Anything Other Than Litigation

If given the choice, you're probably always better pursuing your divorce with means other than litigation. Basically, that can be accomplished by using some type of alternative dispute resolution (ADR). This term refers to procedures for settling disputes by means other than litigation and includes mediation, collaborative divorce, and arbitration. We discuss each in the following sections.

Mediation

Mediation is defined as hiring a third party to help you resolve various forms of disputes with your ex. Mediation is designed to help you and your ex resolve these issues without having to involve a court in your decision-making process. The rationale is that it can save you time, money, and hurt feelings. As a side note, it can be a wonderful way to improve your relationship with your ex. The benefit to that is to have the two ex-spouses work together to solve a mutual problem, such as child issues. It also teaches cooperative skills that will be valuable for both of you, should a problem arise down the road.

If you want to do your divorce without hiring a lawyer, you may want to consider mediation. But you can also hire both a lawyer and a mediator. Many lawyers are used to working with mediators. That means they will cooperate with your mediator and keep the court process to a minimum while helping you work through your divorce.

In order for mediation to really work, you both have to agree that you have the children's interests first and foremost. And regardless of mediation, that is always the first priority, as stated throughout this book. That means you both have to act as rational adults. Easier said than done! You have to see past your own nose and see past the conflict with your spouse.

Mediation can work best for you if any of the following situations exist:

- Both spouses are pro-kid (kids come first).
- Abuse towards the ex is stalling negotiations.
- Each spouse is locked into an unreasonable position.
- Neither spouse wants to accept alternatives beyond their respective positions.
- Poor communication exists between the spouses.
- Most issues have been settled but a few more remain outstanding.
- Attorneys are contributing to the mess by trying to win at all costs, by not listening to each other or to their clients, and by pushing their client's position on the mediator and the other attorney.

Sparring spouses are generally not set up for mediation, because there is too much anger through the divorce process. Those conflicts have little chance for being righted. The following is a list of situations where mediation will probably not work:

- Spouses have money issues.
- Retaliation is the ex's normal personality.
- The ex is looking to punish you.

- The spouse poses a danger threat.
- Either spouse is lying on a variety of issues, and honesty is not present.
- You are not good at articulating your position.
- The lawyers are not present to intercept things headed in the wrong direction.

However, I will point out that if the mediator's skills are top-notch and she knows how to communicate to these types of personalities during this process, the mediation can work and should be attempted.

For the sake of cost reduction and peace of mind, mediation is becoming a more popular choice for resolving disputes concerning custody, asset division, and child support. In addition, it allows families to model their own court orders by tailoring it to their unique circumstances. That's because immediate court pressures to resolve the case are not much of an issue. Mediation sessions can be scheduled to work around your schedule and for your convenience. You can also involve others, such as your CPA, CFP, psychologist, or other adviser, in your mediation session.

Research indicates that mediation is faster, cheaper, and creates a less adversarial way to approach the end of a marriage or a custody negotiation compared to court intervention. It also tends to result in fewer returns to court for modification after divorce. In fact, many states require mediation before you go to court.

Spouses who opt for mediation tend to select joint legal custody more often than spouses who utilize the court system, partly because of how well the partners got along to begin with. You can have professionals assist you in the mediation process. Most parties report high satisfaction with the process, and despite myths to the contrary, there is no advantage given to either the man or the woman.

The Mediator

A trained mediator acts as an impartial third party and assists in reaching resolution on relevant issues in the divorce. That's important. You do not want the mediator to act as an adversary. You want them to be impartial and recommend a fair settlement which everyone can live with and which is an acceptable ultimate framework for a document that the lawyer drafts upon completion of the mediation process.

In essence, the mediator serves as a master communicator, referee, and problem solver, working to balance both spouses' interests and to assist them in reaching fair decisions. Mediators can charge anywhere from $100 to $400 per hour. A mediator typically contracts with you for a set number of sessions at a set hourly rate or fixed price. It can range anywhere from two through ten hours.

Here's some real practical advice that cost me thousands of dollars to learn, but I include it for you with the inexpensive purchase of this book. I hired two mediators. The first one was a therapist, the second one was a judge. The first one was a complete waste of time and money; the second was phenomenal. This is all from a business context. And I don't say that because the second mediator took my side. Quite the opposite!

Overall, I thought the second mediator worked out a better deal for my ex. The reason I thought the second mediator was great was because when I met him for the first time at 8:00 A.M., he came into the meeting room that I was occupying, looked me square in the eye, and said that we were not going home until we came to a total agreement. He was right. I had scheduled a flight to New York that night for a class the next day and had to postpone my flight to the following day. To me, his greeting started the day right and set the tone for what was yet to come. It also established him as a no-nonsense guy who would not stand for any nonsense going forward. And that was definitely true. While his decisions weren't all correct for either side, he did his best to make sure it came out fairly in the end. And I believe it did.

This second mediator was a retired judge who had opened up a mediation practice with other judges. He knew the laws, he'd seen it all before, and he was receptive to each of our opinions. He let each of us speak, formulated the facts, and rendered his decision. It was quick, abrupt, and he kept us focused and on track.

The first mediator was not a judge. Honestly, I am not sure what her background was. But my ex and I were in separate rooms, as with the second mediation. She ran back and forth like a schoolgirl and basically used the approach "he said, she said." No constructive conclusions. I didn't feel like I got my money's worth simply because nothing constructive was decided at the end of the day.

In my view, a mediator is supposed to bring the parties together towards a final resolution. She didn't take the facts and try to use them to tie us closer together in our wants and needs, nor did she bridge the gap. She reported to my attorney and me in a way my kids could have done. Personally, she was fine and pleasant, but as far as business was concerned, she was not very effective. A complete waste of money in my book! I knew, after the session was over, we were no better off, and mentioned to my attorney that the next time in mediation we should get a judge to hammer out the tough issues.

A mediator does not have to resolve or become involved in every issue. You can hire a mediator on select issues, such as child custody, asset division, alimony, or child support. The whole goal of mediation is to resolve the issues ahead of time, before you would have to get the courts involved. Even if you are just a little successful with mediation, you still get to keep more of your money in your own hands and reduce the overall cost.

Hopefully, the mediator will be able to resolve important issues for both you and your ex. But even if that happens, you should still consult a lawyer throughout this process to make sure you understand what issues the mediator is providing suggestions on and how these recommendations will affect the divorce going forward.

Once you finalize the agreement, then have your lawyer officially review it and formalize it for the court to review and approve. See Exhibit 4.1 for questions you should ask when selecting a mediator.

The Mediation Process

Usually, there are four processes to mediation: (1) establishing the ground rules, (2) coming to grips with the key issues, (3) clearly communicating problem-solving options, and (4) refining and recommending solutions.

Establishing the ground rules involves educating both you and your spouse about what the process will involve, emphasizing the importance of setting aside feelings in favor of what's best for the children, being flexible, and being respectful of the other person. Coming to grips with key issues on the table has each spouse spelling out what is acceptable to him or her in terms of the final settlement. Since the mediator is there to find the common ground between the two of you, she has to remove the obstacles that get in the way, such as the anger, hostility, and resentment of each spouse towards the other, and to state your positions clearly.

The mediator needs to clearly communicate problem-solving ideas to each party as to where things stand in negotiation, the deadlock

1. What is your style of mediation?
2. Do you have a specialty?
3. Do you see couples separately and/or together?
4. How do you charge and what are your fees?
5. How many mediations have you performed? Is this your full-time job?
6. What kind of background or training do you have? Are you a judge?
7. How do you work with spouses who each have their own attorney? Are attorneys part of the process or do you refer legal issues to them directly?
8. What do you do if you see the mediation process breaking down?
9. Do you work with and refer spouses to other professionals, such as CPAs, CFPs, attorneys, therapists, and so on?
10. How is confidentiality handled?
11. Are you willing to testify in court, if need be?

Exhibit 4.1   Checklist for Hiring a Mediator

that has occurred, and suggesting alternatives neither party has considered for breaking the deadlock. The mediator must also recommend solutions to the parties so that each spouse agrees in principle. First, the mediator restates and refines each solution, making sure each spouse accepts it in more specific articulation. The mediator then creates a written document that can be used by the lawyers to forge ahead with a legally binding settlement. While the results of mediation aren't legally binding, the solutions it forges can help lawyers resolve even the most difficult divorce situations.

Collaborative Divorce

Collaborative divorce is a newer type of divorce method that uses collaborative law in solving disputes without going to court. It focuses on an interdisciplinary team approach where the groups of professionals work with a divorcing couple to help them reach a fair resolution of all issues without litigation. These professionals include people who deal with financial, legal, spiritual, physical, and emotional issues.

The process stresses honesty, cooperation, and compromise with an orientation towards the future. It helps set the tone by maintaining respect for each party, prioritizing the needs of the children, working in an ethical manner, working cooperatively with the ex, and maintaining the control of the divorce process without having to go to court. If the negotiations do fall apart in a collaborative divorce, both parties will be required to get new lawyers to represent them in court.

Collaborative divorce provides for a free flow and exchange of information. It can make the divorce go smoother and more quickly than a contested divorce and, best of all, you don't end up in court. It's somewhere between mediation and litigation. The main points spouses wish to get across with the collaborative effort include settling.

Part of the issue here is whether both attorneys are capable of making this happen. When I chose my attorney, she was an expert and leader in this field. It was supposed to be an easier, smoother, and cheaper ride all the way around. Unfortunately, my ex's attorney was the complete flip side, more of a litigator than anything else. The collaborative process won't work if both attorneys are not on the same page with their lawyering style.

Arbitration

Arbitration occurs when each party agrees to hire an independent person, usually a judge, also called an arbitrator, and agrees to let that person rule on the case. Each side prepares arguments and evidence and submits their case to the arbitrator. The arbitrator makes a ruling after hearing the facts from both sides. Arbitration can also occur through a panel. Arbitrators are typically paid by the hour. Court records are made public, just like with a trial.

If the arbitration is nonbinding, then the arbitrator's ruling is not final and either spouse can appeal. If it is binding, the case ends when the arbitrator makes his ruling, and it cannot be overturned. Both parties agree to this type of ruling in advance. Arbitration is used in the financial services field where securities lawsuits are brought by disgruntled customers.

Arbitration does have its advantages due to the speed with which the case is heard; it's cheaper and more impersonal.

The Preliminaries: Gathering the Evidence

The next stage revolves around accumulating sufficient evidence that can be used for trial. It also involves supporting documentation to help you present your case. There are formal procedures that need to be followed in gathering the evidence. A summary of the process is explained below.

Discovery

Discovery is a legal method used to obtain information about your case from your ex or other sources. It allows each spouse to ask the other questions and request documents about any subject that may be relevant to the case. This includes full disclosure of all assets, documents, and information essential to a fair resolution. That is the premise for all types of divorce cases.

Discovery may follow formal guidelines according to the court's rules so the judge can intervene if the parties are not cooperating, or informal guidelines if they are. Any spouse who refuses to follow the rules may be forced into a pretrial hearing. The spouse who is found at fault may have to pay the other side's attorney fees and costs for making the judge enforce this action.

Discovery mechanisms generally fall into four categories: releases, interrogatories, depositions, and subpoenas.

Releases. If you or your ex-spouse do not possess various documents that have been requested by the other party's attorney, you may have to sign a release to allow the other side the ability to access and copy those documents. The IRS has a special standard release form (IRS Form 4506) for requesting old copies of your tax returns. You'll need to send a minimal check as well. Examples of the types of documents your ex's attorney will request include past tax returns, bank statements, pay stubs, retirement account statements, and so on.

Interrogatories. These are questions to which you must provide answers under oath in paper format (paper discovery). They are usually supplemented by a request for documents, which is a list of requests for copies of documents to be provided along with the interrogatory responses.

Discovery may also include a request for inspection. This is a request to appraise or examine items that are in the possession of the other person and cannot be easily duplicated or provided. Examples would include a home, boat, closely held business, or real estate.

Questions are fairly broad and generally tie to information that would be considered admissible at trial. Since the questions are an attempt to gather sufficient evidence from your entire marital relationship, they tend to be open-ended and anything asked is probably fair game. If you're not comfortable with any questions, run them by your attorney.

Depositions.   These are sworn testimonies, given under oath in an informal setting such as a lawyer's office or in front of a court stenographer. The stenographer records word for word everything you say. It represents a great way to gather information to be used at trial and also alerts your attorney to what your ex will say about you at trial.

Depositions enable you to find out what arguments are going to be used, witnesses that your ex's attorney plans to call, and what your ex plans to say about you on the stand. Even though this is serious business, it's easier to provide a deposition in an informal setting as opposed to providing it on the witness stand.

Unfortunately, depositions are expensive and time consuming, and if you don't go to trial they can be considered a waste of money. That's because your attorney will be with you at the deposition, and the hiring of the court reporter is also quite expensive. But they are needed in the event you do go to trial. Depositions settle more cases than any other vehicle available to you.

Subpoenas.   Subpoenas are legal documents requesting that certain witnesses be available at the trial date. Subpoenas are usually served by the sheriff's office and must be done in advance of the trial date. The most common purposes are to obtain wage, retirement plan, and bank records.

Working Discovery's Usefulness.   Proceed with discovery in a logical order and work for cooperation first. Start early enough by asking to do the discovery step-by-step. Start by asking for a voluntary exchange of documents and releases. If your spouse is uncooperative, then use subpoenas or interrogatories. See if you can uncover suspicious items that make sense to investigate further. If that is the case, look for hidden assets and/or income.

Discovery can be quite expensive but it is necessary. Most people have their money in relatively few places. If the bank records don't provide full disclosure to your satisfaction, you can issue a subpoena to the bank or brokerage house. "Do it once and do it right" is what I normally tell my students. I am telling you the same thing.

Extensive discovery is a full-blown attack, probably not necessary due to the cost. For example, issuing 30 subpoenas that can cost you thousands of dollars to locate a few thousand dollars is not a good use of your time or money.

Going after Hidden Income and Assets

Hidden income or assets will surface even though you don't report any of it on your financial statements that you submit to the court. If hidden income or assets exist, the case can later be reopened for fraud, or wind up in the prosecutor's office if the judge doesn't like what he sees.

Hiding income or assets is never an option. It clearly is not worth it. Think of it this way. You are going to receive 50 percent of the income anyway while your ex gets the other 50 percent. After taxes, the income will be less. Further, the amount of money that the ex is going to spend to try to uncover that amount of money will take you back to square one. You'll spend that excess defending yourself and ultimately you'll lose. You probably will end up with less than you started with, let alone the aggravation you will put yourself through. Remember what I said earlier: Mental and physical stress on your health take a real toll during divorce, especially over the long run. As I stated before, it's easier and more pleasant just to take the high road.

Income is reported on a W-2 and appears on the tax return. It can be further verified by contacting the employer about what was on the W-2. If people work off the books or under the table, it presents a challenge just because of the secretive nature of receiving the income. This type of payment is obviously illegal. Unless you believe that there is substantial money floating around, it's probably not worth pursuing.

An easier way to take notice is examining the ex's lifestyle. If he or she claims to be making $40,000 per year and seems to be living well above those means, that could be an indicator. Another way is to look through the check register and credit card receipts. If your ex's income is $40,000 and $75,000 was written as checks during the year, that kind of new math doesn't add up! Also try looking in the safe deposit box for clues that may surface. Whatever you do, take good notes.

Finding hidden assets is relatively easy, for two reasons. One, there are paper trails that usually tie assets and income together. Even looking at the tax return, you'll be able to see income on your Schedule B (Interest and Dividends) that will have to have originated from some source. You can research back into what the asset value is if need be.

Second, with the advent of the Internet, we're just one small world now and it is relatively easy to find information if you have the time and the money to go searching. You can even hire a private investigator to take the lead for you. Many of them have databases to search offshore banks and stock holdings. If you do this yourself, you can save significant money by not obtaining the services of a professional and still wind up with most if not all of the information.

Finding Hidden Income

Look at these sources if your spouse has a closely held business:

- Company car.
- Meals and entertainment.
- Business trips to exotic locales.

Contact disgruntled current and former employees who worked at the closely held business. Also check for prepayment of debts, charge accounts, expensive supplies, or assets for the closely held business.

To find retirement plan assets, contact the plan administrator. Most retirement plans are held at the employer or brokerage firm. If you don't know the name of the firm, you can use the interrogatories or a deposition to find out.

You can contact a Social Security office to find out about your ex's benefits. You will need your ex to sign a release or you can issue a subpoena.

Credit reports are a strong source of information since most people tend to want a good credit score and therefore don't withhold positive information. On the credit report, you can find wage information, employment, and other possible income sources. Again, you will need either a signed authorization by your ex or a subpoena. You'll need documented proof as to why you need it if you take it before the court. A good reason is if the ex is refinancing, has a bad credit report, and you are trying to find out why that is happening.

Loan and credit card applications are another strong source for finding hidden assets. On these forms, people are trying to look as good as possible, so they should reflect a maximum amount of income, assets, and so forth. If the two of you recently refinanced a home or tried to, you may have such an application floating around. This information can also be used to establish your ex's income at trial if your ex is not being forthright about his or her earnings. Furthermore, it can challenge your ex's credibility if what the ex is telling you is different than what has been reported on the application.

Personal Fault Issues

If you are concerned about the ex hiding assets or income, you also may become suspicious about other behavior. That includes spousal affairs, illegal activities, and other venues your ex may be involved in. Pursuing these issues may determine whether your suspicions are correct and help you decide whether you wish to obtain a divorce. Even more important is determining whether you want to find out what the real scoop is.

If you're concerned about your ex having an affair, you can look at his or her cell, office, and home phone bills and see if you recognize all of the phone numbers listed on the bill. You can have your ex followed by a private detective or a friend, or even do it yourself. But just be careful if the ex has a violent personality—it could end up being counterproductive.

So what have we learned from all this? For starters, it is better to cooperate, settle differences, and minimize the damage. The damage can be quite extensive in the form of money, emotional upset, and health issues. It's not worth getting sick over because then you'll carry it around for the rest of your life.

Grudges may develop and be drawn out for many years, perhaps forever. The real suffering that occurs throughout the entire process is that of the children. Because of this, you should alter your plan of attack and instead consider taking the high road. Remember, as I stated before, it's always about the children. Brush your egos aside, and make sure that the potential damage to the children as a result of a long-drawn-out and abusive process is reduced.

As I've learned throughout this process, the worst thing that can occur (other than the children issues) is the loss of money, both income and assets. But you can always make more money or buy new assets. In fact, you will likely want to buy new assets to escape the memories left behind, rather than cling to the things you salvaged from the divorce. Until you realize and accept that, you'll have a hard time with the divorce process because you will be too emotional, bitter, or just plain angry to let go. It's not worth it.

Just remember, you cannot undo the damage caused to children or others. You may be set back financially a few years or longer from your ultimate financial goals, but you can still achieve them down the road. You'll still get there! It took me a long time to understand that. Many people over the years tried to convince me of that, but I was either too stubborn or too dumb to realize it. Now I have seen the light.

Rattiner's Planning Tips

1. It never pays to take your ex out. Be smart about the entire divorce process. Look at the big picture.
2. Avoid litigation at all costs. It is too expensive, too demanding, and will not enable you to get the result you are trying to achieve. You can't control the ultimate outcome.
3. Mediation is a better bet if you and your ex can agree to it. Having an independent person be the referee allows for a more equitable settlement. Remember, you'll never be happy with the final outcome, but it will help minimize the damage and hopefully provide you with a settlement you both can live with.
4. Hire a former judge as the mediator. That person has the experience necessary to understand the issues, close the gap, and wrap up the case. You always want to employ a no-nonsense approach to be implemented by a no-nonsense judge.

5. Make sure you understand the mediation process before moving forward. It puts both spouses on the same playing field looking for similarities between the parties rather than differences.

6. Collaborative divorce is another good option because the whole goal is to avoid going to trial. You need both sides to be open, honest, and cooperative with each other. And you need both attorneys to feel the same way.

7. Arbitration is usually a winner-take-all scenario. If binding, you lose your right to challenge the decision. If nonbinding, you're probably not going to get from it what you should.

8. Discovery is a necessary step because it helps gather all the information you need to make the right decisions about the final outcome of the case. If you have your doubts about things, it forces the other spouse to act.

9. To go after hidden assets, make sure it is a worthwhile investment. It can be expensive if you get other people involved and not worth the cost.

10. Trying to prove personal fault issues is not really necessary in the grand scheme of things. It doesn't get you closer to your ultimate goal of settling the case and moving on with life.

CHAPTER 5

Alimony and Child Support Issues

Alimony: Maintenance and/or Spousal Support

Alimony, maintenance, or spousal support (used interchangeably throughout this chapter) represents a payment made to an ex-spouse, which is not paid as part of an Internal Revenue Code (IRC) Section 1041 property settlement, under a divorce or separation instrument. It does not include voluntary payments that are not made under a divorce or separation instrument. It may be made in one lump sum or in installments. It can also be temporary or permanent. Alimony rules can be found under IRC Section 71(b).

The rationale from moving away from the term *alimony* to *spousal support* is that alimony used to imply a permanent awarding of monetary payments to the payee spouse for long periods of time or even for life. Today, since most spouses work outside the home or are capable of doing so, the support is designed to help the lesser-earning spouse or the at-home spouse gain the necessary training and provide sufficient time to reenter the workforce and earn as much as that spouse is capable of.

These awards are designed to be temporary and to better match the individual circumstances of the spouses involved. Also, since the roles have changed in many families where the men have sacrificed their careers to stay at home with the children, a greater proportion of spousal awards have been going to men.

Alimony payments are concerned with the future needs of each spouse. The amount may be negotiated as part of the final settlement. It helps to think of alimony as separate and apart from your property settlement. It may continue indefinitely or until the death or remarriage of the ex-spouse receiving the support. As stated in Chapter 1, each spouse should take the high road and figure out exactly what each one needs to make it all work. Make an honest assessment of the situation. This doesn't mean gouging the other or even giving up your right to receive it. It means trying to be as fair as possible. Try to make it as much of a win-win situation for both of you as you can.

Many factors are involved in the awarding of alimony. These include the length of the marriage; each spouse's age; vocational skills of each spouse; time necessary for the spouse to get up to speed in his or her occupation; standard of living during the marriage; the health, occupation, and needs of each spouse; conduct of the parties during the marriage; who will maintain a household for the children; liabilities of each spouse; the previous sacrifice of one spouse's future earning capacity because he or she was an at-home spouse raising the children and put their career on hold; and the economic circumstances of each spouse.

When negotiating your alimony agreement, make sure that you don't tie the termination of the alimony payments to any issues related to your children. In other words, don't tie it to the time they graduate college or leave home. If you do, the IRS might consider the payments to be child support rather than alimony. And you'll soon find out that child support payments are not deductible.

Courts do not award alimony for marriages of short duration, defined as five years or less. Instead, courts prefer to return each spouse to the position they were in prior to the marriage. Long marriages of 20 years or more where one spouse stayed at home to raise the children can basically bank on incorporating alimony as part of the settlement. Marriages in between can encounter many different offshoots of this.

It is important to be aware of your state's laws regarding how alimony works.

Calculation of Alimony (Maintenance)

When courts calculate the amount of alimony to be paid by a spouse, each spouse's ability to earn an income is usually taken into account. Past actual earnings as well as projected future earnings come into play. Also taken into account is the spouse's ability to earn more if they choose to do so or whether that is a realistic possibility. Some states apply the amount of alimony based only on past earnings without regard to future earning capacity.

The court will look at the spouse's ability to earn outside the home given their marketable skills. If the ex-spouse refuses to work outside the home but is capable of doing so, that factor will be taken into account by the courts when awarding alimony.

In many states, no alimony is awarded if both spouses are able to support themselves individually. Other states provide a cap on the amount of alimony payable and require payment of alimony during a transition period only until the other spouse is in a position to support him- or herself. In fact, there are several states that do not award alimony. You must establish residency first to be considered falling under the rules of that state.

Receiving alimony payments will not put you in a situation exactly like you previously enjoyed. You may have been fortunate that you were able to do whatever you wanted, but now the game has radically changed. The lifestyle you enjoyed before is now a thing of the past, realistically speaking. That's because two independent households now exist. Therefore, the standard of living will ultimately go down.

The age factor may come into play, especially if one spouse has been out of the workforce for a long time. Health issues also come into play, especially if it is not feasible for the other spouse to work. Similarly, a spouse closing in on retirement or with poor health may not be in a position to pay alimony. Courts will factor these things in when arriving at the actual number.

See Exhibit 5.1 for deductibility of certain payments as alimony.

How Long Is Alimony Paid?

Alimony can be awarded for any length of time depending on the circumstances. Generally, alimony is paid for a period of years or ends at death or when the other spouse gets remarried. In fact, in some states, if the supported spouse begins living with a partner in a marriage-type setting but has not remarried, payments can stop as well.

Alimony can also be awarded on a temporary basis pending the outcome of a divorce. If one spouse is making voluntary payments to the other, that amount could be used as a precursor or

IF you must pay all of the . . .	AND your home is . . .	THEN you can deduct and your spouse must include as alimony . . .	AND you can claim as an itemized deduction . . .
Mortgage payment (principal and interest)	Jointly owned	Half of the total payments	Half of the interest as interest expense (if the home is a qualified home)
Real estate taxes and home insurance	Held as tenants in common	Half of the total payments	Half of the real estate taxes and none of the home insurance
Real estate taxes and home insurance	Held as tenants by the entirety or in joint tenancy	None of the payments	All of the real estate taxes and none of the home insurance

Exhibit 5.1   Alimony and Itemized Deductions
Source: Adapted from IRS Publication 504 Divorced or Separated Individuals (2007), p.12.

to establish a pattern or routine for the payment of alimony in that amount. Therefore, that amount becomes finalized based on what has been happening throughout the divorce process. The court may reason that since the spouse has been getting along on that amount during the divorce process, then the amount of payment should remain the same and continue as before.

Can the Payee Spouse Receive an Extension for Alimony Payments? The short answer is yes, as long as you make the request prior to the alimony period expiring. You would have to show the court a change in the circumstances supporting your request for extension.

Remarriage. When the payee spouse remarries, alimony payments stop. That's because the court views the payee spouse as now receiving more money within the new marriage than as a single person. If the payer spouse remarries, however, the payee spouse will probably not be able to increase the amount of alimony currently being received unless the payee spouse can show need.

Initial Payment of Alimony

Alimony is generally paid monthly, but it can be paid on a weekly basis or as a lump sum paid in advance. By paying it as a lump sum, you are locking yourself in and won't be able to alter that decision later on. But it also can be a blessing in disguise.

The amount of a lump-sum alimony payment is based on the length of time the alimony payments would be required to be paid based on past state case law, and then discounting those payments back to a dollar value as of today at an assumed discount (interest) rate. In other words, it is the present value of the future cash flow payments.

The recipient spouse gets all the money up front, which can be a good thing for him or her because if that spouse wants to get remarried soon, that spouse would have collected all of the alimony payments already. Remember, alimony generally stops upon remarriage. A lump-sum payment also assures the recipient spouse that he or she will get all the alimony payments and will not have to worry about the other spouse skipping town, paying late, not paying, or other factors that may come up. You also need to take into account the tax elements of the alimony payments since it is deductible by the payer spouse and taxable to the payee spouse. (See the later subsection on deductability.)

For the payer spouse, it's a crapshoot. By paying all the money up front, you are choosing door number one. Essentially, you know what you are responsible for, and the payee knows exactly what's being received. However, this arrangement does not allow for a change in factors and circumstances, which means that if the payer spouse earns more money in the future, or less money, the alimony amount cannot be altered to fit the new situation. Therefore, if the payer spouse stumbles upon hard times, that's too bad for the payer spouse. Likewise, if the payer spouse earns triple the salary or wins the lottery, that's too bad for the payee spouse.

Modification of Alimony Payment

Other than payout of alimony as a lump sum, alimony can be modified. It can be changed by the spouses by modifying the alimony terms of the final decree. It can also be made without court approval, although that is never a smart way to go. It can also be made by one of the spouses filing a request for modification with the court. The party requesting the change will have to show proof for why the change is necessary. The rationale behind this rule is it helps stabilize the prior arrangements and prevents the court from becoming too overburdened with change requests.

Alimony can also be increased or decreased based on changing circumstances. Examples of changing circumstances include:

- Cost of living adjustments (COLA).
- Escalator clause in the agreement ties to the payer spouse's increase in income.
- Payer spouse loses job.
- Payer spouse experiences a severe downturn in business (similar to the current state of the economy) and is not making as much money as previously.
- Payee spouse's needs change.
- Payee spouse's income increases.
- Payee spouse becomes disabled or sick.

Hiring a Vocational Expert

If you were married to an at-home spouse who had a prior career, you may want to employ the services of a vocational expert to forecast the future earning potential of that spouse. That will go a long way in reducing the amount of alimony you will be required to pay since that potential income will be compared to your actual income and the difference will be used in the alimony calculations.

Vocational experts can help spouses who are facing a change in circumstances to identify what type of work they wish to pursue, what additional education or training they will need, their chief capabilities and limitations, how long training will take, realistic expectations as to starting salaries, and whether outside assistance, such as mental health counseling, will be necessary before the spouse will be fully capable of self-support.

Deductibility

Alimony is deductible by the payer and must be included in the spouse's or ex-spouse's reported income. Each spouse should consider the tax ramifications of receiving and deducting alimony payments.

To be considered alimony, a payment must meet the following requirements:

- The payment must be mandated under a divorce or separation instrument.
- The payment must be made in cash.
- No provision in the divorce or separation instrument designates the payment as not being alimony.
- If separated under a decree of divorce or separate maintenance, the spouses cannot live in the same household.
- It must be mandated that payments must end at the death of the payee spouse.
- Payments cannot be considered child support.
- The two spouses cannot file a joint tax return with each other.

The Payment Must Be Made under a Divorce or Separation Instrument. The term *divorce or separation instrument* means a divorce decree or a separate maintenance written instrument incident to that decree. It can also refer to a written separation agreement or a decree or any type of court order requiring a spouse to make payments for the support or maintenance of the other spouse. An interesting tidbit is that a premarital agreement that provides for support can be considered to mandate alimony payments if incorporated into the decree or separation agreement.

The Payment Must Be Made in Cash.   Cash payments that qualify as alimony include checks and money orders. However, transfers of services or property, execution of a debt instrument, or the use of property do not qualify as alimony.

A planning tip here: Cash payments to third parties can qualify as alimony if made under the terms of the divorce or separation instrument, or pursuant to the ex-spouse's written request. These payments qualify if they are made in lieu of payments of alimony directly to the spouse; the written request states that both spouses intend the payments to be treated as alimony; and a written request is received from the spouse before the taxpayer files the return.

For example, Stan Roberts pays the mortgage on behalf of his ex, Lisa Roberts, who owns the home as part of the divorce settlement. Stan pays the mortgage directly at $3,000 per month, or

$36,000 for the year. The $36,000 payment can be considered alimony and deductible by Stan and taxable to Lisa.

If the home is owned jointly and the taxpayer spouse is required to make all the payments, then one-half of the payments may qualify as alimony. Lastly, utility payments can be considered as alimony.

No Provision in the Divorce or Separation Instrument Designates the Payment as Not Being Alimony.   Both spouses can designate qualifying payments not to be considered as alimony. This is done by having a provision in the divorce or separation instrument stating the payments are not deductible as alimony from the payer spouse and are excludable from the payee spouse's income. Any written statement signed by both spouses is treated as a written separation agreement. For temporary orders, the designation must be made in the original or a later temporary support order. Lastly, each spouse must attach a copy of the written instrument to their tax return filing in each year the designation applies.

If Separated under a Decree of Divorce or Separate Maintenance, the Spouses Cannot Live in the Same Household.   Quite frankly, I never did understand this point. Why in the world would you want to live with your ex anyway? Well, what do I know?

Payments to your ex while you and your ex are members of the same household are not alimony if you and your ex are separated under a decree of divorce or separate maintenance.

However, when the parties are not legally separated under a decree of divorce or separate maintenance, a payment under a written separation agreement, support decree, or other court order may qualify as alimony even if the parties are members of the same household.

It Must Be Mandated That Payments Must End at the Death of the Payee Spouse.   As I discuss with my financial planning class, what kind of hazard does this create? A moral hazard!

Payments made to a spouse must end at death if it is considered to be alimony. If the spouse makes payments for any period after the ex-spouse's death, *none* of the payments made before or after death are considered to be alimony. Unless state law automatically requires payments to end at death, the divorce or separation instrument should state that there's no liability for continued payments after death.

Here's an example: Per the divorce decree, Jack is required to pay Diane $2,000 per month for a period of 10 years. The divorce decree further states that in the event of her death, the balance of the payments are to be made to Diane's estate. If Jack makes 12 payments in year one, how much of the total payment can be deducted as alimony on Jack's tax return? Answer: None, because in order for the payments to be considered alimony, they must end at death. Therefore he has no write-off on the alimony and Diane does not have to include the $24,000 ($2,000 times 12 months) as part of her income.

Payments Cannot Be Considered Child Support.   The decree or separation instruments must clearly state a fixed amount for child support, or the entire payment will be deemed alimony. Where confusion exists as to whether past child support or alimony has been paid, the presumption is that child support has been paid.

You and Your Ex Cannot File a Joint Tax Return with Each Other.   Payments are not considered alimony if the spouses file a joint return. Therefore, couples who were married on the last day of the tax year must file as married filing separate or head of household for any payments to be considered alimony.

Alimony Recapture: Too Much Alimony Paid Too Soon

Many payer spouses demand that their ex-spouse take larger payments in the form of alimony on an ongoing basis (typically within the first three years) as opposed to receiving those monies up front. The payer spouse may come up with an excuse stating that the payee spouse can't handle money, he or she will blow it, or that it's easier to pay the payee spouse on a pay-as-you-go-plan.

There's only one reason why payer spouses would do this: The payer spouse wants to deduct those excessive monies when paid out as alimony as opposed to being included as part of a property settlement under IRC Section 1041. This only applies to the first three years of alimony payments. The reason the rule is capped at three years is that the IRS says most of these cases occur during the first three years after the divorce becomes finalized and they want these disguised payments to be part of the original property settlement negotiated at the time of the divorce.

Little does the payer spouse know that any payments considered excessive will have to be recaptured. This means that it is not deductible to the payer spouse and not taxable to the payee spouse.

If the payer spouse is subject to this rule, then the payer spouse must include as income in the third year the part of the alimony payments that were previously deducted in the prior two years. That means the ex-spouse payee can deduct in the third year the part of the alimony payments such spouse previously included in income.

The three-year period starts with the first calendar year a payment qualifying as alimony under a divorce decree, separate maintenance, or a written separation agreement was made. Payments made under temporary support orders are not included here. The three-year period includes the second and third year regardless of whether payments are made during those years.

How It Works

The recapture rule is triggered in the third year if the alimony paid in the third year decreases by more than $15,000 from the second year, or the alimony paid in the second and third years decreases significantly from the alimony paid in the first year.

Payments not included in the recapture calculation include payments made under a temporary support order; payments required over a period of at least three calendar years which represent a fixed part of business, property, or self-employment income; and payments that decrease because of the death of either spouse or the remarriage of the payee spouse.

It should be noted that alimony recapture rules only apply when the payments are decreasing in amount each year. Therefore if payments in year two are more than payments in year one, no recapture scenario exists.

Let's run through an example (see the opposite page). This is a tough calculation. My students have a hard time with this one, too. The format can be found in IRS Publication 504. Use the form in Exhibit 5.2 to calculate your own alimony recapture.

Child Support

Child support is the amount of money that the noncustodial parent pays to the custodial parent to help pay for the everyday needs of the child(ren), such as housing, food, clothing, and education. Child support rules can be found under IRC Section 71(c).

Example

Nick pays his ex-spouse, Carla, $60,000 alimony during the first year, $35,000 during the second year, and $12,000 during the third year. Calculate the amount of alimony recapture. Note: Do not enter less than zero on any line.

1. Alimony paid in second year	1. $ 35,000
2. Alimony paid in third year	2. $ 12,000
3. Floor	3. $ 15,000
4. Add lines 2 and 3	4. $ 27,000
5. Subtract line 4 from line 1	5. $ 8,000
6. Alimony paid in first year	6. $ 60,000
7. Adjusted alimony paid in second year (line 1 less line 5)	7. $ 27,000
8. Alimony paid in third year	8. $ 12,000
9. Add lines 7 and 8	9. $ 39,000
10. Divide line 9 by 2	10. $ 19,500
11. Floor	11. $ 15,000
12. Add lines 10 and 11	12. $ 34,500
13. Subtract line 12 from line 6	13. $ 25,500
14. Recaptured alimony: Add lines 5 and 13	*14. $ 33,500

*If you deducted alimony paid, report this amount as income on Form 1040, line 11. If you reported alimony received, deduct this amount on Form 1040, line 31a.

All states have specific guidelines that must be followed in the determination of how much child support is to be paid and allocated for each of the children of the marriage. Parents cannot opt out of child support laws. That's because all children have the right to be supported by their parents. As a result, parents cannot agree in advance to waive or alter significantly the amount of child support paid.

The flip side is also true. One spouse can agree to pay more than the guidelines established by the state. That's because it is always in the child's best interests to receive more child support.

Child support must be paid in cash to the custodial parent or to a third party, such as the child's private school, in accordance with the parents' binding agreement or the court order. Many people don't know that the noncustodial parent must pay the full amount of the child support owed even though that parent showers the child with clothes, presents, and more during each visit.

Note: *Do not enter less than -0- on any line.*

1. Alimony paid in second year   1. _____
2. Alimony paid in third year   2. _____
3. Floor   3. _____
4. Add lines 2 and 3   4. _____
5. Subtract line 4 from line 1   5. _____
6. Alimony paid in first year   6. _____
7. Adjusted alimony paid in
   second year (line 1 less line 5)   7. _____
8. Alimony paid in third year   8. _____
9. Add lines 7 and 8   9. _____
10. Divide line 9 by 2   10. _____
11. Floor   11. _____
12. Add lines 10 and 11   12. _____
13. Subtract line 12 from line 6   13. _____
14. Recaptured alimony: Add lines 5 and 13   *14. _____

_____

*If you deducted alimony paid, report this amount as income on Form 1040, line 11. If you reported alimony received, deduct this amount on Form 1040, line 31a.

Exhibit 5.2   Recapture of Alimony Worksheet

This is because child support is designed to help offset the custodial parent's costs of providing the child with a proper home, proper transportation, and other things. The rationale here is that if the noncustodial parent only showered the child with gifts, the custodial parent would not have enough funds to support the child.

The use of child support payments is left solely to the discretion of the custodial parent. Children's extracurricular activities can be paid by additional child support dollars or arrangements can be made to augment a divorce agreement with additional child support payments.

To determine how much child support you can count on, see Exhibit 5.3 and contact your appropriate state web site.

Taxation of Child Support

Per the IRC, all worldwide income earned by any U.S. citizen is considered income from whatever source derived. The only exception to that rule is if in the Code it specifically states that something is

State	Support Information/Calculators
Alabama	No official calculator
Alaska	http://webapp.state.ak.us/cssd/guidelinecalc.jsp
Arizona	www.supreme.state.az.us/childsup
Arkansas	No official calculator
California	https://www.cse.ca.gov/ChildSupport/cse/guidelinecalculator
Colorado	www.coloradodivorceinfo.com/child-custody/childsupportcalculator.htm
Connecticut	www.jud.state.ct.us/Publications/ChildSupport/2005CSguidelines.pdf
Delaware	http://courts.state.de.us/family (click link for child support calculation)
District of Columbia	http://csge.oag.dc.gov/application/main/intro.aspx
Florida	www.myflorida.com/dor/childsupport or http://flcourts.org/gen_public/family/forms_rules/902e.pdf
Georgia	https://services.georgia.gov/dhr/cspp/do/public/SupportCalc
Hawaii	www.hawaii.gov/jud/childpp.htm
Idaho	No official calculator
Illinois	www.ilchildsupport.com/calculating.html
Indiana	www.in.gov/judiciary/childsupport
Iowa	https://childsupport.dhs.state.ia.us/guidelines.asp
Kansas	www.kscourts.org/rules-procedures-forms/child-support-guidelines/default.asp Microsoft Word worksheet and schedules are included in guidelines, which are complex.
Kentucky	http://chfs.ky.gov/dis/cse.htm
Louisiana	Guidelines: www.dss.state.la.us/index.cfm?md=pagebuilder&tmp=home&pid=146 PDF worksheet: www.dss.state.la.us/docs/searchable/OFS/overview/SES/Ses_OBL_A_330.PDF

Exhibit 5.3 State Child Support Calculators

State	Support Information/Calculators
Maine	www.courts.state.me.us/maine_courts/specialized/family/child_support.html
Maryland	www.dhr.state.md.us/csea/worksheet.htm
Massachusetts	www.cse.state.ma.us/parents/Calc2.htm
Michigan	www.courts.michigan.gov/scao/services/focb/mcsf.htm
Minnesota	http://childsupportcalculator.dhs.state.mn.us
Mississippi	www.mdhs.state.ms.us/csemdhs.html (very basic child support table)
Missouri	www.courts.mo.gov (click on "Know Your Courts," then the Supreme Court link, and follow the "rules" links to find the support guidelines)
Montana	http://www.dphhs.mt.gov/csed/packet/guidelines.shtml
Nebraska	http://supremecourt.ne.gov/rules/amendments/worksheet5amd.pdf
Nevada	No official calculator
New Hampshire	www.dhhs.state.nh.us/DHHS/DCSS/child+support+calculator/default.htm or www.egov.nh.gov/DHHS_calculator/calc_form.asp
New Jersey	www.judiciary.state.nj.us/csguide/index.htm
New Mexico	https://elink.hsd.state.nm.us/csed/guidelines.html
New York	https://newyorkchildsupport.com/child_support_standards.html
North Carolina	http://info.dhhs.state.nc.us/olm/manuals/dss/cse/man/CSEcj-02.htm#P175_16711
North Dakota	www.nd.gov/dhs/services/childsupport/progserv/guidelines/guidelines.html
Ohio	No official calculator
Oklahoma	www.okdhs.org/onlineservices (under "citizens," locate link for calculator)
Oregon	www.dcs.state.or.us/calculator

Exhibit 5.3 *(Continued)*

State	Support Information/Calculators
Pennsylvania	www.humanservices.state.pa.us/CSWS (links to statutory guidelines, but not calculator)
Rhode Island	www.cse.ri.gov/services/establishment_childsup .php (no calculator, just general guidelines)
South Carolina	www.state.sc.us/dss/csed/calculator.htm
South Dakota	www.dss.sd.gov/childsupport/services/ obligationsdetermined.asp
Tennessee	www.state.tn.us/humanserv/is/incomeshares.html
Texas	No official calculator
Utah	http://orscsc.dhs.utah.gov
Vermont	www.ocs.state.vt.us (downloadable free software)
Virginia	www.dss.state.va.us/family/dcse_calc.cgi
Washington	www.courts.wa.gov/forms/documents/CSWorksheet.pdf
West Virginia	www.wvdhhr.org/bcse/chapter48a2.cfm
Wisconsin	www.dcf.wisconsin.gov/publications/ dwsc_824_p.htm
Wyoming	No official calculator

Exhibit 5.3 *(Continued)*

not reportable as income. Most of the exclusions consist of social exclusions which are for the betterment of society and really are not designed to have true income consequences. They are considered more like reimbursements. Child support is one of those exclusions. Child support is neither taxable to the recipient spouse nor deductible to the payer spouse.

Modification of Child Support

Like custody orders, child support orders are not set in stone for the remainder of the child's youth. Courts will modify support if circumstances have changed substantially since the time of the original order.

What this means is that if the income goes up substantially or goes down even more, the courts can adjust the child support either up or down to reflect the changing circumstances of the noncusto-dial payer parent. Therefore, a custodial parent trying his or her luck in bringing the noncustodial parent back to court can have a rude awakening if the money the custodial parent now receives is reduced.

Courts will also consider increasing child support in cases where significant inflation exists, or the costs associated with rais-ing the child have increased. Likewise, if child support is being paid on multiple children, and one reaches an age where child support is not required any longer (typically anywhere from age 18 to 21, depending on the state), support will be reduced. However, because the cost of raising children is not proportionate, it will not be an even division just because one child is no longer being supported. For example, if there are three children receiving support, and one child turns age of majority, then the custodial parent of the remain-ing two children will probably continue to receive more than two-thirds of the payment since there is not a one-third reduction in the cost of raising the remaining two children. Therefore, the guideline figures reduce proportionately as the number of children declines.

If a court determines that a reduction in child support is appro-priate, the court will generally apply that reduction only to future child support payments. The rule is that the courts do not apply changes to payments retroactively.

Stepparents and Child Support

Stepparents do not have an obligation or a responsibility to pay for child support. The only exceptions to this rule are the following:

- The stepparent has sought visitation rights.
- The stepparent has interfered with the stepchild's ability to obtain support from the natural parent.
- The stepparent has agreed to pay child support in a divorce agreement.

Temporary Child Support

Temporary child support is typically awarded by the court at the out-set of the case to ensure that the children do not have a reduction in their standard of living pending the outcome of the divorce dispute.

Another important planning tip is to make sure that the custodial parent seeks an appropriate level of temporary child support because if they do not, they run the risk that the amount of support initially awarded could become the final amount of child support.

Child Support Ends

Child support ends when the child reaches age 18 to 21, depending on state law, and/or if the child becomes emancipated. Becoming emancipated means that the child gets married, becomes self-supporting, abandons the parental home, goes into the military, reaches the age of majority, or it is appointed by court order.

Failure to Pay Child Support

Penalties for failure to pay child support are quite substantial. Every state imposes criminal penalties on parents who fail to pay child support, and the states can proactively monitor whether the payments are made going forward. States can garnish wages, cancel driver's licenses, gain access to federal and state tax refunds, or even

When negotiating child support, consider the following issues:

1. Special issues related to the child, such as physical, emotional, or health.
2. Physical custody arrangements.
3. Support of parent to other former households, including alimony and child support.
4. Other financial obligations of the parent which are not tied in to child support.
5. The income capabilities of each parent.
6. Child's future college costs.
7. Child's summer vacations, camps, or costly recreational activities.
8. A parent's extraordinary needs, such as high medical expenses.
9. Travel expenses associated with one parent assuming full or partial responsibility.
10. Child's actual expenses, including health care.

Alimony and Child Support Summary Chart

	Deductible by Payer	Taxable to Payee
Alimony	Yes	Yes
Child support	No	No

arrest the payer parent for failing to pay child support. In addition, states can block the transfer of property, enter liens against property, or revoke professional licenses.

Using a qualified domestic relations order (QDRO) to collect child support from a retirement account has tax implications. While child support is not a taxable event, withdrawals from a retirement plan are. Thus, payments made from a retirement plan to fund child support will result in taxable income to the ex-spouse receiving the child support.

Rattiner's Planning Tips

1. Alimony is tax deductible for the payer spouse and taxable to the payee spouse.
2. Child support is neither taxable nor deductible by either spouse.
3. Alimony is generally not awarded for short-term marriages which have durations of less than five years.
4. Make sure you call in a vocational expert to help assess the at-home spouse's ability to earn income after the divorce.
5. If spouses agree to a lump-sum award of an alimony payment, it cannot be altered in the future.
6. Regular monthly payments of alimony can be modified by the courts in the future.
7. Alimony payments always end at the death of the spouse and usually at remarriage.
8. If you front-load alimony to the tune of greater than $15,000 between years one and two or between years two and three, some of the alimony may need to be recaptured.

9. Child support payments can always be modified.
10. Awarding temporary alimony may not always be a good idea because it can be used as a precedent for awarding permanent alimony.
11. Don't use a QDRO to collect child support. If you do, it will be considered taxable income.
12. Keep alimony and child support separate from property division issues.

CHAPTER 6

Divorce Can Be Taxing!

One of the things you need to stay on top of are the tax ramifications surrounding divorce. Family law attorneys are probably not going to be your best source of information here. Sure, they'll know about dividing property, but a lot more goes into it than just the splitting of family assets. And many won't even know where to begin concerning the tax aspects of those property splits. For example, if you have rental property, or have engaged in like-kind exchanges, then consideration must be given to depreciation recapture and capital gain issues. Further, if a spouse wants to sell the family home awarded to her, she needs to know about capital gain issues, especially if the spouse has lived in the house for many years.

When negotiating is all said and done, the crucial thing to ensure is that the amount of money you bargain for is the amount you will end up with and that your share will not shrink because of tax consequences either now or in the future.

Property Settlements

Under IRC section 1041, no gain or loss is recognized on a transfer of property from one spouse to the other if the transfer is incident to divorce. Nonrecognition treatment applies even if the transfer was in exchange for cash, the release of marital rights, the assumption of debt, or other consideration. There are no income or deduction issues that arise from the general division of property. The income tax issues may arise when property is given beyond the initial settlement through alimony or child support.

A transfer is *incident to divorce* if it is made within one year after the marriage terminates, or it is related to the marital termination. A property transfer is presumed related to the marital termination when required by a divorce or separation instrument (either original or modified), and the transfer is not more than six years after the marital termination. If a taxpayer transfers property to a third party on behalf of the former spouse, the property is treated as if it had been transferred to the spouse or former spouse, and the spouse or former spouse immediately transferred it to a third party, provided the transfer is required by a divorce or separation instrument or the transfer follows a written request of the recipient spouse.

Transfers of an interest in a health savings account (HSA) or medical savings account (MSA) are not considered taxable transfers. After the transfer, the interest is treated as the spouse's HSA or MSA. See Exhibit 6.1 for an IRS summary of property transfers pursuant to a divorce.

Code section 1041 does not apply in the following situations:

- Taxpayer's spouse or former spouse is a nonresident alien.
- Certain transfers in trust.
- Certain stock redemptions, which are taxable to a spouse under the tax law, a divorce or separation instrument, or a valid written agreement, as discussed in Reg. 1.1041-2.

Purchases Between Spouses

Under IRC § 1041, the selling spouse is not taxed on the transfer, but the buying spouse cannot increase the basis of the property, even by amounts they may have paid to the other spouse for the property under Temporary Regulation § 1.1041-1T. Thus, a spouse who buys property from another spouse is disadvantaged as compared to a third-party purchaser.

The nonrecognition rules of IRC § 1041 do not apply to nonresident alien spouses. The rationale is that since nonresident aliens would not have to pay U.S. tax on the sale of property outside the country, there would be no reason for them to receive property tax-free incident to a divorce.

Transfers in Trust

Section 1041(a) does not apply to the transfer of property in trust when the transferred property is encumbered by an obligation in

IF you transfer . . .	THEN you . . .	AND your spouse or former spouse . . .	For more information, see . . .
Income-producing property (such as an interest in a business, rental property, stocks, or bonds)	Include on your tax return any profit or loss, rental income or loss, dividends, or interest generated or derived from the property during the year until the property is transferred	Reports any income or loss generated or derived after the property is transferred	Publication 550, Investment Income and Expenses (See Ownership Transferred under U.S. Savings Bonds in Chapter 1.)
Interest in a passive activity with unused passive activity losses	Cannot deduct your accumulated unused passive activity losses allocable to the interest	Increases the adjusted basis of the transferred interest by the amount of the unused losses	Publication 925, Passive Activity and At-Risk Rules
Investment credit property with recapture potential	Do not have to recapture any part of the credit	May have to recapture part of the credit if he or she disposes of the property or changes its use before the end of the recapture period	Form 4255, Recapture of Invest-ment Credit
Interests in nonstatutory stock options and nonqualified deferred compensation	Do not include any amount in gross income upon the transfer	Includes an amount in gross income when he or she exercises the stock options or when the deferred compensation is paid or made available to him or her	

Exhibit 6.1   Property Transferred Pursuant to a Divorce
Source: Adapted from IRS Publication 504, Divorced or Separated Individuals (2007), p. 19.

excess of the property's adjusted basis and such obligations are assumed or taken subject-to by the transferee.

A taxpayer spouse who makes a transfer in trust must recognize gain to the extent that the liabilities assumed by the trust, plus the liabilities to which the property is subject, exceed the total of the adjusted basis in the property transferred. Also, gain or loss is generally recognized on a transfer in trust of an installment obligation.

Passive Activity Loss Property

When a spouse gives passive activity property to the current spouse or ex-spouse, the basis in the gift is increased immediately before the transfer by the amount of any passive activity losses allocable to the property as per rules IRC § 469(j)(6) and § 1041(b). These losses cannot be deducted for any year pursuant to IRS Publication 504. In a community property state (see Chapter 8), half the property would get a basis adjustment under this rule.

Deferred Tax Liability

The courts rarely consider the deferred tax liability impact of property divisions unless the taxable event is likely to occur in the near future or a sale is ordered by the court. The rationale is that taxes are considered highly speculative and subject to change or offset. If the tax impact is uncertain, the later taxes may be ignored. If this is a critical issue for you, the only way to have them considered is in negotiation or mediation settlement.

Record-keeping Requirements

Under Temporary Regulation Section 1.1041-1T, the transferor spouse must at the time of the transfer supply the transferee spouse with records sufficient to determine the adjusted basis and holding period (the length of time the property has been held) of the property.

Where potential credit recapture exists (such as with rental real estate), the transferor spouse must also supply the transferee spouse with records sufficient to determine the amount of the potential tax liability. However, no sanctions are specified for failure of the transferor to comply with these rules. Therefore, consideration should be given to incorporating these rules into the divorce decree.

Here's another practical tip. This is an area where you do not want to rely on your attorney. Bringing in your own CPA, Certified

Financial Planner (CFP), or financial adviser to help you calculate these amounts will be worth your weight in gold. For example, if you hold on to a property for longer than the depreciation period, all of the original cost basis will need to be recaptured and will result in a huge gain and tax liability.

Gift Tax Issues

The transfer of property to a spouse or former spouse is not subject to gift tax if it:

- Is made in settlement of marital support rights.
- Qualifies for the marital deduction.
- Is made under a divorce decree.
- Is made under a written agreement, and you are divorced within a specified period.
- Qualifies for the annual exclusion.

Property Basis

When one spouse transfers property to the other spouse, the receiving spouse picks up the basis from the transferor spouse. There is no step-up in basis if the fair market value is higher at the time of the transfer than what it was at the time of acquisition. Step-up in basis only occurs at death. Sounds tempting?

The transferee spouse receives the marital basis even if the asset is subject to liabilities exceeding that basis. It can result in a deferred tax liability. A Section 1041 transfer is treated as a gift for income tax purposes. The transferee spouse receives no added basis on purchase.

Filing Status

Your income tax filing status is determined as of the last day of the tax year. The filing status also depends on your marital status at year end. This is important because applying the appropriate filing status will save you megabucks when filing your tax return.

Therefore, if the spouses get legally divorced on December 31, then each person can file either singly or as head of household (if that person qualifies). If two people get married on December 31, they can choose either married filing jointly or married filing separately. Then how come the spouses can file jointly if married only one day of the entire year? Oftentimes it feels like an entire year! Seriously, marital status is determined on the last day of the calendar year.

If spouses are considered unmarried, their filing status is single, head of household if certain requirements are met, or a qualifying widower. A spouse is considered married for the entire year if they are separated and have not yet obtained a final divorce decree by December 31. An exception to this rule is that if the spouse lives apart from the soon-to-be ex-spouse, then that spouse may be considered unmarried and be able to file head of household. What's the advantage of that? Head of household has more favorable tax rates than married filing separately.

Two interesting exceptions are worth noting. If you and your spouse obtain a divorce at the end of the year for the sole purpose of filing as single taxpayers during the current year, and at the time of divorce you both have the intention of remarrying after the first of the year, then you and your spouse must file as married taxpayers.

Another exception exists when you are granted an annulment (as opposed to a divorce), which means that you were never recognized as being married in the first place. The IRS takes the same position. In that case, you must go back and amend up to your last three years of tax returns to either single or head of household filing status. If you were married less than three years, then only amend the years in which you filed as a married couple. An amended tax return is called a 1040X. The reason you need to do this is because in the eyes of the IRS you were never recognized as filing married filing jointly or married filing separately. The reason you have to go back only a maximum of three years is due to the statute of limitations. The statute says that in most cases you can only go back and amend up to three years of tax returns. No amendments are required prior to the three years.

Before you even decide on which filing status to use, get an estimate of what your tax liability will be at year end. You don't want any surprises. There are many tax programs that can help you sort through the numbers. Otherwise, ask your CPA to work out the numbers for you.

There are five tax filing statuses. They are single (S), married filing jointly (M/J), married filing separately (M/S), head of household (H/H) and qualifying widow (Q/W). Notice that all the filing statuses have two letters, other than single. It used to—originally it was called single and happy (just kidding).

Let's take a look at comparing the different filing statuses.

Single

This filing status will subject you to the highest tax rates. You would use this filing status when you are unmarried and have no dependents (children or parents) that you can claim as a deduction. That means given the same taxable income as a married couple filing jointly, more overall tax is paid by the single person.

If both spouses have significant income, then it may be better to delay the divorce until the following year so you get the lower tax rates of married filing jointly in the current year. If you stay married until the beginning of the following year, it will save you money in the current year. However, don't do things solely for tax purposes!

Married Filing Jointly

You will be required to select one of the two marital filing statuses if you are not legally divorced yet, with few exceptions. Even though I stated previously that it may be cheaper to use married filing jointly, there are liability issues to be aware of. When you file jointly with your ex, you are both considered jointly and individually liable and responsible for any tax, interest, and penalty issue that arises from the filing of that return before the divorce. This means that one spouse may be liable for 100 percent of the entire tax liability even though the ex may have earned all of the income. Furthermore, this liability applies even if the divorce decree states that the former spouse would be responsible for any amounts due on previously filed joint returns.

Generally, married filing jointly provides for greater tax relief and the least amount of tax liability mainly in situations where one spouse is the predominant breadwinner. Filing jointly could institute a marriage penalty. This occurs where both spouses earn roughly equal amounts. That's because combining your incomes can push you up into a higher overall income tax bracket.

If you do file jointly, you are 100 percent liable for any taxes due from the filing. Likewise, if you file jointly and are getting a refund, then you must decide how to split the refund. This leads to another disadvantage in that any overpayment shown on a joint tax return may be used to pay the past-due amount of the ex's debts. But a spouse can get their share of the refund if they qualify as an injured spouse.

Both spouses must sign a joint return. If one spouse refuses to sign and files a separate return, then you must as well. The only way for you to file jointly without cooperation from your ex is if all the following requirements are met: He or she has always filed jointly in the past, has not filed a separate return, refuses to file a joint return, and had no income in the current year.

What happens if there is an IRS bill that you are unaware of? You can try hiding under the Innocent Spouse Rule (see Chapter 2) but chances are that if you are living the high life, the IRS won't buy that. You can have an indemnity clause included as a hold-harmless agreement as part of the divorce agreement. However, the IRS won't accept that and it is not binding on you. That means the IRS can come after you for nonpayment of taxes by your ex. I interviewed someone who is in that exact situation, where the husband did not pay payroll and sales taxes for the better part of five years and now the IRS is attaching a lien on that wife's family home. Furthermore, if you remarry, the IRS could come after your new spouse for tax liability due.

Lastly, if you and your ex are likely to receive a tax refund, that amount of money is considered a marital asset and subject to property division.

Married Filing Separately

If you are concerned about liability for your ex-spouse's taxes, then choosing married filing separately would be a better alternative. When in doubt, file separately. Filing separately makes you responsible only for your tax liability reported on your tax return. If one of the spouses had certain high itemized deductions, such as medical expenses, casualty losses, or miscellaneous expenses (all subject to deductibility limitations), then it may be cheaper to file separately.

Filing separately presents a problem in that if you itemize, then your ex must also itemize. The ex is precluded from using the standard deduction in that case. Also, married filing separately poses higher income tax rates and each spouse will end up paying more in income tax liability. Additionally, income tax rates will increase at lower levels than by filing jointly; the exemption amounts for calculating alternative minimum tax will be half of filing jointly; you can only write off $1,500 of capital losses (rather than $3,000); and the spouse may not be able to take the child and dependent care credit, the adoption credit, higher education expenses pertaining to the Hope and Lifetime Learning Credits, or the write-off for student loan interest available from cashing in qualified U.S. Savings Bonds to pay for college.

Also, after the due date of a return, the spouses cannot file separate returns if they previously filed a joint return. An exception exists whereby within one year from the tax return due date including extensions, the personal representative for a decedent can change from a joint return elected by the surviving spouse to a separate return for the decedent spouse.

Except in community property states, if you file a separate return, you generally report only your income, exemptions, credits, and deductions. If your spouse had no income, you can claim an exemption for your spouse. If your spouse refuses to provide the information necessary to file a joint return, you should file a separate return.

Lastly, your filing status will also depend on when the divorce process started and when it's likely to be completed. You can file jointly in any year the divorce has not become final, but once it is final, then you must file separately. If you have dependents, such as children, then you'll probably use the head of household filing status.

Head of Household

This filing status is a better alternative than single if you qualify. Generally, you must be unmarried or considered unmarried as of December 31. You must also have paid more than half the cost of keeping up a home that was the main home for more than half the year of your unmarried children, or provide more than 50 percent of the support of your parents if they are considered dependents. Children away at school are not affected by that provision.

Children include an unmarried child, grandchild, adopted child, and foster child. Foster children have to live with you the entire year. If your children are married, you can still file head of household status if you claim these children as exemptions on your tax return.

Qualifying Widow

This is a filing status used by the surviving spouse for the two years following the death of a spouse. In the year of the spouse's death, the couple still files either married filing jointly or separately. The benefit of this filing status is that it uses the same cheaper tax tables as married filing jointly as opposed to single (how you would file if you had no dependents) or head of household (how you would file if you maintained the home for a dependent during the calendar year), where the tax rates would be higher on the same amount of income. The rationale here is that it works as a two-year transition period for the surviving spouse from a tax standpoint. This filing status is not likely to be applied in divorce situations.

Seven Ways to Pass the Qualifying Relationship Test

1. Your child, stepchild, legally adopted child, eligible foster child, or descendant of any of them.
2. Your brother, sister, half brother, half sister, stepbrother, or stepsister.
3. Your father, mother, grandparent, or direct ancestor, but not foster parent.
4. Your stepfather or stepmother.
5. A son or daughter of your brother or sister.
6. A brother or sister of your father or mother.
7. Your son-in-law, daughter-in-law, father-in-law, mother-in-law, brother-in-law, or sister-in-law.

Here's a thought: Any of these relationships that were established by marriage are not ended by death or divorce. How does that translate? Once an in-law, always an in-law! Ouch!

Parents and Qualifying Relatives

Parents can be claimed as dependents even if they don't live with you. In fact, they could be living in another state or even in a nursing home. Qualifying relatives can be any relatives for whom you claim an exemption. There is no age requirement. The key here is that you have to provide greater than 50 percent of their support.

Lastly, a tax planning tip you may be able to use is that if you have two children, and each of you can claim one child as a personal exemption, then each of you may be entitled to filing as head of household as opposed to one spouse filing single.

Four Ways to Meet the Qualifying Relative Requirements

The qualifying relative must:

1. Not be the taxpayer's child (for example, your 20-year-old son is not a qualifying relative, since he is your qualifying child);
2. Be a member of the household or pass the relationship test (the qualifying relative must either live with you all year as a member of your household, or be related to you as described earlier).
3. Pass the gross income test (the qualifying relative must earn less than the personal exemption amount for that year).
4. Pass the taxpayer support test (taxpayer pays more than 50 percent of the qualifying relative's support during the calendar year). To calculate, compare the taxpayer's provided support to the entire amount of support received from all sources.

Remember, the taxpayer support test does not apply to qualified children.

Exemptions

Exemptions come in two types: personal and dependents. A personal exemption is one you claim for yourself. An annual dollar amount, adjusted for inflation, is provided for each year that you claim yourself on your tax return. Dependent exemptions are ones previously discussed, including your children, grandchildren, parents, and, if you get married again, your spouse.

In the case of divorce, which parent gets to claim the child as an exemption? Generally, the rules are complex, especially if joint custody is awarded. If parents are awarded joint custody of a child, they should have the divorce decree clearly state who is entitled to the exemption. When the parents do not have an agreement, the parent having actual custody for a great portion of the year gets the dependency deduction under IRC § 152(e).

Form 8332

The custodial parent can sign Form 8332, Release of Claim to Exemption for Child of Divorced or Separated Parents, or a similar statement, agreeing not to claim the child's exemption. The exemption may be released for either a single year, a number of specified years (for example, alternate years), or all future years.

Example

Is there any way for the dependency exemption to be awarded to the noncustodial parent? The answer is yes if all of the following apply:

- The parents either (1) are divorced or legally separated under a decree of divorce or separate maintenance; (2) are separated under a written separation agreement; or (3) lived apart at all times during the last six months of the year.
- The child is in the custody of one or both parents for more than half of the year.
- The divorce decree or separation agreement provides the noncustodial parent can claim the child as a dependent or the custodial parent signs a written declaration (Form 8332) that he or she will not claim the child.

The noncustodial parent must attach the release to their tax return. If the exemption is released for more than one year, the noncustodial parent must attach the original release to their return the first year and a copy of the release each of the following years.

Multiple Support Agreement

If two or more people pay over half a dependent's support, but no one alone pays over half, one of those people can claim an exemption if all of the following apply:

- The person paid over 10 percent of the dependent's support.
- If not for the support test, the person could claim the dependent's exemption.
- The person attaches a signed Form 2120 from every other person who meets the previous two requirements.

The multiple support rules do not apply to qualified children since the support test does not apply to them.

Medical and Dental Expenses

For medical and dental expenses, a child of divorced or separated parents can be treated as a dependent of both parents if all of the following apply:

- The child is in the custody of one or both parents for more than half the year.
- The child receives over half of his or her support during the year from the parents.
- The child's parents either:
  - Are divorced or legally separated under a decree of divorce or separate maintenance.
  - Are separated under a written separation agreement.
  - Lived apart at all times during the last six months of the year.

Sale of the Principal Residence

When the principal residence is sold, the general rule is that single taxpayers can exclude up to $250,000 of capital gain; married filing separately taxpayers can each exclude $250,000; and married taxpayers filing jointly can exclude up to $500,000 of capital gain as long as they have lived in the house for two of the past five years (it's two of the past ten years for people in the military). In addition, during the two-year period ending on the date of the sale, neither spouse may have excluded gain from the sale of another home.

For this to happen, certain criteria must be met by each spouse, depending on filing status (see box).

Single or Married Filing Separately

1. The individual meets the ownership test.
2. The individual passes the use test.
3. Only one capital gain exclusion from the sale of a primary residence can occur every two years from that spouse.

Married Filing Jointly

1. Spouses file their return as married filing jointly for the year.
2. Either spouse meets the ownership test.
3. Both spouses meet the use test.
4. Only one capital gain exclusion from the sale of a primary residence can occur every two years from either spouse.

Ownership Test

An ownership test must be met regardless of filing status. During the five-year period ending on the date of the home sale, the spouse must have owned the home for at least two years and lived in the home for at least two years. The rules are somewhat modified in cases of divorce. Generally during the divorce process, one of the spouses is likely to leave and thus not continue to be an occupant of the primary residence. When that happens as a result of the divorce decree, and the first spouse grants the ex-spouse a right to temporary possession of the home but retains title to the home, and the home is later sold, then the nonoccupying spouse will be considered to have owned the home for the period of time that the occupying spouse owned the home as that spouse's principal residence.

Co-Owning the House.   Anytime you extend your obligation with the ex-spouse, it's probably a bad move because then you have to agree on spending money to fix it up, living there, or selling it. For a spouse who continues to own the house but doesn't live in it, there's a risk that the $250,000 exclusion might not apply when the house is sold. To avoid losing the exclusion, it's important to have written documentation of the agreement that called for one spouse to stay in the house and the other to leave but remain a co-owner. If it is clear that the arrangement was pursuant to a divorce settlement or court order, then the nonresident spouse can still take the exclusion on the basis of the resident spouse's occupancy of the house during the required period of time.

Use Test

In the event either spouse transfers a residence to the ex-spouse pursuant to a divorce decree, the transferor spouse shall be able to include the transferee spouse's use period in computing his or her own use period.

Remarriage

What happens if one spouse ends up getting remarried prior to the sale of the home jointly owned with the former spouse? If that situation occurs, then the remarried spouse can use the new spouse's time in the home to meet residency requirements in order to use the married filing jointly exclusion amount.

Planning Tips

If one spouse buys out the other, the selling spouse doesn't have to worry about capital gains tax because the sale was part of the divorce.

However, a planning tip that you shouldn't overlook is that if the spouse who ends up receiving the primary residence intends to sell it after the divorce, waiting until after the divorce becomes final may not be the best move from a tax standpoint for the spouse who keeps the home. That's because the $500,000 exclusion for couples filing jointly is not available any longer and the $250,000 exclusion is. If the gain is greater than $250,000, then the spouse who ends up with the house may have to pay capital gains tax on the sale. Often this is not factored into the final division of assets. If two spouses own a home jointly and file separate returns, each of the individuals can exclude up to $250,000 of capital gains from the sale of their respective interests during the year they are still married.

For example, if a house was purchased in 1990 for $200,000 and today it is worth $600,000, waiting till after the divorce becomes final changes the tax filing status of the new single homeowner from married filing jointly to single. Excluding other costs, here's what would happen if the spouse who ended up with the home then sold it:

Single Spouse Selling the House after the Divorce

Sale price	$600,000
Cost	$200,000
Gain on sale	$400,000
Exclusion	$250,000
Taxable amount	$150,000
Tax liability @ 20 percent (Fed/State)	$ 30,000

If you are not officially divorced, you are still considered married and can thus continue to file married filing jointly. In that case, the couple can still take the $500,000 exclusion.

In the next example, look what happens if the spouses sell the house while still legally married and filing jointly.

Married Filing Jointly Taxpayers Selling the House During the Divorce Process

Sale price	$600,000
Cost	$200,000
Gain on sale	$400,000
Exclusion	$400,000 (can go as high as $500,000)
Taxable amount	$0
Tax liability	$0

This is a far cry from the first scenario whereby the spouse who kept the house would face a tax liability to the tune of $30,000, assuming a 20 percent tax rate. Therefore, make sure that the tax element of the house is factored into the final split of marital property.

Exception to the Two-Year Rule.   An exception exists to the two-year rule if the house is sold due to unforeseen circumstances. In these cases you can prorate the gain on the house. Unforeseen circumstances include moving for any of the following reasons:

- Job change
- Health issues
- Divorce

Since divorce is listed among the criteria, the gain can be prorated such that some of the gain can be deferred but not up to the full $250,000/$500,000 exclusion. See the box on the opposite page for an example of how that works.

For more information on the tax implications from the sale of a primary residence, you can also review IRS Publication 523 or visit www.irs.gov for more information.

Tax Deductibility of Divorce Costs

Under Internal Revenue Code Section 1041, property transferred to either spouse is not deductible because it is part of the initial property settlement. Under Section 1012, legal fees paid specifically for a property settlement can be added to the basis of the property received.

Example

John and Jane Smith purchased a house for $300,000. Six months later they were legally divorced. Jane, who is now single and is the sole owner of the house, decides to sell the house for $400,000 after the sixth month. How much of the gain would be taxable to Jane?

Step 1

Sale price	$400,000
Cost	$300,000
Profit	$100,000

Step 2

$250,000 single exclusion $\times$ 6/24 = $62,500 can be excluded from the sale of the house.

Step 3

Profit	$100,000
Excluded gain	$62,500
Taxable gain	$37,500

Note: The 6/24 represents living in the house for 6 months out of 24 months (two-year requirement). Also, if Jane sold the house at the end of two years (instead of six months), then the entire gain (up to $250,000) would have been excluded from capital gains tax.

Also, legal fees and court costs for getting a divorce are not deductible under Regulation 1.262-1(b)(7).

However, fees are deductible in the following cases:

- In connection with the collection or refund of any tax.
- For the production or collection of income (i.e., alimony).

Another point worth mentioning is that a debate exists as to whether you can write off the investment and tax fees in connection with the divorce. Many CPAs state that if you receive an itemized bill from your attorney specifying what part of the legal fees dealt with investment or tax advice, you have grounds to write off only that portion of the bill as a miscellaneous itemized deduction subject to the 2 percent limitation.

What constitutes investment advice? Having the lawyer assist you in determining which property you should keep and the investment ramifications of, say, rental houses or stock and bond portfolios, or determining income requirements to live on, would constitute investment advice. The tax implications of all of that information can be counted as tax advice. Other examples include depreciation recapture calculations, capital gain issues, and so forth.

Tax Implications of Living Together

Couples living together cannot file jointly. To file joint returns, they would have to be legally married. A few states have provisions for common law marriages but such cases are rare. Working couples with similar incomes will often find a tax advantage in not marrying. However, couples with only one income source or with widely different incomes will come out better taxwise if they do tie the knot.

Like-Kind Exchanges under IRC Section 1031

The IRS encourages citizens to reinvest in the infrastructure of our society in many different ways. One way is to allow the purchaser of business investment property to write off the cost of that property over several years. That's called *depreciation*. There are many types of depreciation write-offs, all dependent on the type of property being purchased. Depreciation represents a noncash charge against income because it enables you to take a write-off on your tax return for the expense even though it isn't out-of-pocket to you. It furthers your loss or reduces your gain for tax purposes on an annual basis.

Like-kind exchanges represent the next level of IRS involvement in having investors invest in the infrastructure of our society. That's because the IRS prefers that investors not cash out their investments, but instead roll them into more expensive property. In return, the IRS will allow investors to defer the tax on their gains from selling the first property and rolling it into a second, more expensive property.

The key for working with a like-kind exchange is that the properties have to be qualifying properties and the investor must work within the stringent set of rules mandated by the IRS. The three essential elements of a like-kind exchange are:

1. The properties must be exchanged.
2. Both the property exchanged and the property received must be held by the same taxpayer for productive business use in the taxpayer's trade or business or for investment.
3. The properties must be of like kind.

Like-kind does not mean identical. It means similar. It can occur in many situations, but real estate tends to be the most popular. Examples within real estate that work include selling an apartment building for an office building; selling an office building for a farm; selling a farm for a ranch; and selling a ranch for an apartment building. All qualify as like-kind, which means the gain from these properties would be deferred until the properties are sold outside a like-kind exchange. If dissimilar property accompanies the sale (such as cash, securities received, or debt relieved), those items are called *boot.* In those cases you must pay taxes solely on the boot received and can defer the taxes on the similar or like-kind property exchanged.

The only requirement necessary outside of the foregoing rules is that whatever asset you sell, you have to purchase an asset more expensive in order to defer the gain. If you purchase an asset that costs less, then you will have to recognize the difference as income right away. The joke in my CFP financial planning classes is one of trading spouses. If you trade your 40-year-old spouse for two 21-year-olds (42 years total), the numbers work!

How it can work in divorce is in the following manner. If one spouse takes over the rental real estate, that spouse can trade it for another property without incurring taxes on both the capital gains and the recaptured real estate. Sometimes the spouse who ends up with the property may decide that keeping that property poses too many bad memories and may be looking to start over and replace the property with another one representing a new beginning.

The gains on the property can be quite enormous. For example, if you have held rental real estate for more than ten years and have depreciated it each year (which is a requirement), then your recapture tax alone could be astronomical, let alone the fact that if you sell the property for more than you paid for it, you'll have significant capital gains tax as well. It all adds up. Worse yet, you may not have the funds to pay the taxes currently. Therefore, if you want to keep that type of property for your own enjoyment (i.e., a rental at the beach, in the mountains, and so forth), you can have your cake and eat it, too. In addition, it does not have to be a one-for-one exchange. For example, you can have three properties with a total sale price of $1 million and perform a like-kind exchange for one property costing $1.2 million. As long as you spend more than you are taking in, it qualifies. So your exchange can be five properties for one, or more.

In order to do the like-kind exchange, you have to use a qualified intermediary. That person or entity can be a title company, real estate broker, attorney, or someone in a similar capacity. The intermediary has to physically hold the money and release it to the seller of the property you end up purchasing.

In addition, there are time constraints on the process. After you sell your property, you must identify as many as three properties you plan to purchase. You don't have to purchase them all, but you do have to purchase one of them. You have 45 days from the date of escrow to identify the property you plan to purchase, and 180 days from the date of escrow to close on any one of them. If the like-kind exchange doesn't work this way, you run the risk of the entire gain becoming taxable immediately.

Installment Obligations

IRC Section 453B provides for the recognition of gain on the disposition of an installment obligation. A transfer between spouses or former spouses incident to divorce does not result in the recognition of gain or loss under IRC Section 453B(a) except for transfers made in trust. The transferee spouse is entitled to the same tax treatment on the installment obligation as the transferor spouse under IRC Section 453B(g)(2). The rationale is that the transferee will stand in the transferor's shoes.

Nonstatutory Stock Options

A nonstatutory stock option is one that does not meet specific IRC requirements for special tax treatment. Such options may be granted to employees or independent contractors for services. Ordinary income is realized when the option is exercised or disposed of to the extent that the stock's fair market value exceeds the option price. However, under IRC Section 83, the taxpayer can elect to recognize income earlier which would then allow future appreciation to be eligible for capital gain rates. Losses are limited to capital loss rules which are $3,000 for married filing jointly or single and $1,500 for married filing separately.

Formerly, stock options were always taxed to the employee spouse (the person who earned it) based on the assignment of income doctrine and not under IRC Section 1041. However, Revenue Ruling (R.R.) 2002-22 now provides that nonstatutory stock options and nonqualified deferred compensation are considered property subject to IRC Section 1041. As a result, the transferee spouse is taxed at ordinary income rates when he or she exercises the options and the employee spouse is not taxed.

Stock options are difficult to value because of future market fluctuations. Therefore, it is preferable not to transfer stock options but instead to agree to distribute net after-tax proceeds after the stock is sold. This will result in a true fair market value being realized without speculation as to future performance of the stock.

Tax Credits Regarding Children

The following credits may apply to some taxpayers:

- *Child Tax Credit.* This is a credit that the spouse who claims the child as a dependent can get on the tax return. The credit is equal to $1,000 per child under the age of 17.
- *Dependent Care Credit.* This is a credit for a maximum of two children for child care in a two-parent household where both parents are working or in a one-parent household where the single parent is working. The credit is equal to the first $3,000 of expenses for one child and $6,000 for two or more children. The credit range goes from 20 percent to 35 percent based on the spouse's adjusted gross income (AGI).
- *Adoption Expenses Credit.* This is a credit for the costs associated with adopting children. Qualifying expenses would include adoption fees, attorney fees, court costs, social service review costs, and transportation costs. This also includes

children adopted overseas. The spouse can claim the credit in the year qualifying expenses were paid or incurred if they were paid or incurred during or after the tax year in which the adoption was finalized.

- *Education Tax Credits*:
  - *Hope Credit.* Here you hope your child gets the credit! Only the first two years of college are covered (freshman and sophomore years only). The maximum amount is $1,800 per year calculated as follows: The first $1,200 of expenses is covered at 100 percent, and 50 percent of the next $1,200 of expenses is covered, or $600. This credit phases out based on income limitations.
  - *Lifetime Learning Credit.* This credit is a flat 20 percent of an amount up to the first $10,000 of expenses. You cannot claim this credit if the child is already getting the Hope Credit. This credit is typically used by individuals after the first two years of college. Juniors and seniors would typically try to qualify for this credit. The lifetime learning credit is also available for those seeking new job skills, or maintaining existing job skills through graduate training or continuing education. This credit is also subject to income limitations.

Rattiner's Tax Planning Tips

1. A transfer of property between spouses pursuant to a divorce does not create a taxable event for either spouse under IRC Section 1041.
2. There are no gift tax implications between spouses if the transfer is in support of marital support rights; qualifies for the marital deduction; is made under a divorce decree; or is made under a written agreement, and you are divorced within a specified period.
3. The recipient spouse keeps the same tax basis for property transferred from the transferor spouse.
4. When dividing up property, always calculate the net cost through an after-tax scenario.
5. Filing status is determined as of the last day of the calendar year (December 31).
6. You are liable for 100 percent of the tax liability, whether it is yours or not, when you file your taxes with the status married filing jointly.

7. Filing as married filing separately keeps the liability issue separate between the spouses.

8. Head of household should be used as the filing status for a divorced spouse who maintains a household for dependent children.

9. If you are planning to sell your house as the recipient spouse, you may want to do it during the divorce process in order to take advantage of the $500,000 exclusion.

10. Divorce qualifies as an unforeseen circumstance. That means if you sell the house within a two-year period, you may be able to exclude part of the capital gain.

11. You don't have to worry about the capital gain exclusion from a home sale where you transfer the sale to the other spouse as part of the divorce.

12. Tax deductibility of divorce costs must tie in to investment and/or tax advice received.

13. If you retain a rental property from the divorce and wish to exchange it for another more expense property, you can do it under IRC Section 1031 and defer the capital gain.

14. If you claim a child under the age of 17 as your dependent, you may qualify for the $1,000 per year child tax credit.

CHAPTER 7

Retirement Plans

Dividing up retirement plans can be a source of contention for divorcing parties. That's because these plans make up a huge chunk of the balance sheet. Retirement plans are probably the second-largest asset of value behind their primary residence, for most spouses.

Retirement assets generated during the marriage generally tend to fall under marital property and are thus subject to the famous marital split. Retirement plan benefits earned prior to marriage generally stay as separate property.

There are many retirement plans a spouse can have. They can fall under qualified, personal retirement, and nonqualified categories. They could be found through existing employment or from prior jobs that spanned many years. For an older couple getting divorced to have multiple retirement plans is not uncommon.

There are eight critical elements to think about when dividing up retirement plans:

1. What the employee spouse is entitled to due to vesting schedules and other issues.
2. Type of retirement plans to divide.
3. Rules pertaining to withdrawing and rolling over funds inside and outside of a qualified domestic relations order (QDRO).
4. Valuation of retirement benefits.
5. How much of the valuation you are entitled to receive.
6. Whether to accept the retirement benefits or an equivalent amount of other assets.

7. Protection of your retirement benefits if your ex remarries or dies.
8. Discovery of overlooked or hidden retirement plans.

Vesting Rules

An often overlooked concept when analyzing retirement benefits is the vesting of a participant spouse's benefits. Vesting means the benefits are guaranteed to you, the participant spouse. That means you actually own the benefits and are entitled to receive them at retirement or when you leave your employer. Since the benefits are guaranteed to you, you always own a portion of the benefits that you contributed yourself.

The importance of the vesting schedule shows up when considering employer contributions. You can find the vesting schedule of your retirement plan in the employee handbook, retirement plan summary or other official document of the employer. The general rule is the longer you are with the employer, the more you have vested. At some point, you become 100 percent vested, which is when you have been with the company for greater than a specified period of time.

Two types of vesting rules exist. One is called a *cliff* vesting schedule, which guarantees the employee participant employer money after a certain period of years. The other vesting schedule is called a *graded* vesting schedule, which means you earn a minimum percentage of benefits after the completion of so many years and for each year you remain with the employer. The vesting percentage grows and ultimately becomes 100 percent.

Vested benefits are always considered marital property. States treat nonvested benefits differently at divorce. Some states consider them separate property, which means that you don't have to divide them at divorce. However, some states consider them marital property, which means you have to account for them and include them as part of the final settlement. This could mean paying your ex benefits that you don't even own yet!

Furthermore, if you change jobs you could end up losing those benefits forever and ultimately would have paid your ex monies that you never will realize and receive. If you think you will be let go from your employer, or will be moving to another employer, try negotiating those nonvested benefits with the ex. As the ex, however, always look to the value of the accrued benefit in the account, rather than the vested benefit, because that will represent the larger amount.

Types of Retirement Plans

There are many types of retirement plans you need to become familiar with. Descriptions of many of the more common ones appear in this chapter. A distinction is made among qualified plans, personal retirement plans and nonqualified plans. Once you are familiar with the benefits and disadvantages of each plan, then valuing and dividing up the assets of those plans becomes easier.

Qualified Plans

Qualified plans (QP) are generally employer-based plans. These include defined benefit plans and defined contribution plans.

Defined Benefit Plans.   In a defined benefit plan, the employer promises a retirement benefit or pension to the employee when the employee spouse reaches retirement age. The payment amount is either preset under the terms of the plan or determined by a formula that takes into account age, years of service, or both. Generally, defined benefit monies become available when the participant spouse retires. When you get divorced, all you can do is decide what percentage of the payment each spouse will ultimately receive.

Here's how it works. The employer sets up a master account for all employees and bears the investment risk on this account. The benefits accrue while you work for the company, and when you retire you either get a lump-sum distribution or a monthly payment.

Individual employees do not have their own accounts or make any of the contributions. If the numbers don't work out in the defined benefit plan as projected, the employer must make up the difference. For this reason, the number of defined benefit plans has dropped dramatically over the past 25 years.

Typically, a defined benefit plan pays a retirement benefit based on a formula that multiplies a percentage factor, say 1.5 percent, by the total number of years you worked for the company. The resulting percentage is multiplied by the average salary you earned during your final or highest-paid years with the company. Under this formula, an employee who worked 30 years with a company and had a final average salary of $60,000 would be entitled to a pension benefit of $27,000 a year or 45 percent of the final salary. Benefits could also be paid out as a flat amount or adjusted according to the maximum annual benefit.

Since the defined benefit plan is based on age and years of service, the older you are, and the longer you have worked at an organization, the larger your annual contributions can be. That is because you have a shorter time horizon to accumulate funds. With a defined benefit plan, you will know what benefit you will receive, but the contributions are based on what you are entitled to at retirement. That's why the contributions will be larger for an older person with the defined benefit plan.

Defined Contribution Plans.   In a defined contribution plan, the employer pushes the onus of investment risk onto the employee. That is why these types of plans are more popular now than defined benefit plans. With a defined contribution plan, a certain sum of money is put away on behalf of each employee spouse. It is deposited into a separate account established in the employee's name. The employee owns this individual account and knows what the account balance is at all times. Since the employee carries the risk, the employee must do a good job of managing that money.

With a defined contribution plan, the contribution the employee makes is defined, but the benefit is not since it is based on the amount contributed to the plan. The employee spouse knows that an amount of money will be received at retirement. However, the exact amount is unknown and may increase or decrease depending on the value of the investments. The value of the defined contribution plan can be determined as of the date of divorce, because it is possible to distribute the money right then and there. That's because it has a present as opposed to a future value.

Contributions to the plan can be made by you, your employer, or both. Gains or losses to the account will adjust your account. Forfeitures (monies given to current employees from those employees who left the firm before their pensions were vested) may also be rolled into your account at the discretion of the company. The benefits you ultimately receive will depend on the contributions made to the plan by you and your employer and on the investment returns you achieve on these contributions.

Unlike the defined benefit plan where the employer makes good on the funds if the account is short of the intended target, the defined contribution plan's benefit is based on how well the employee invests over time. No particular benefit level is promised to the employee when that person retires.

Generally, defined contribution plans are called *participant-directed* plans since they allow you to allocate your investments among a variety of options. Contributions are made with pretax dollars, and earnings are exempt from federal taxes until you begin withdrawing the funds.

Defined contribution plans are generally simpler, more flexible, and less expensive for an employer to administer than are defined benefit plans.

Anytime pensions or other retirement benefits are at issue, both spouses should become informed and familiar with the opt-out feature of these plans. In this case, a participant worker can either receive a reduced pension to provide a survivor's benefit for the nonparticipant spouse or elect to take full monthly checks after retirement during the participant spouse's remaining lifetime.

Under the Retirement Equity Act of 1984, a worker may not opt out of survivor benefits without the knowledge and agreement of the spouse. Therefore, a participant spouse needs the written permission of the nonparticipant spouse or ex-spouse if a pension was split at divorce before survivor benefits may be waived.

401(k) Plans—Your Own Funding towards Retirement. A 401(k), or traditional 401(k) plan, is a qualified profit-sharing or stock-bonus plan under which you can contribute monies according to government guidelines to fund your own retirement. This cash-deferred arrangement allows you to grow tax-deferred monies earned inside these accounts and allow for these monies to be a direct reduction in taxable income in the year you make the contribution.

Employers set up 401(k) plans when the employer wants to shift the investment burden over to the employees and minimally fund the policy. Younger employees stand to reap the biggest benefit since they have many years until retirement and can continue to defer tax on these monies until funds are withdrawn.

Employees age 50 and over can make an additional catch-up contribution. Employees are always 100 percent vested in any monies they put into the plan. Any employer contributions are not vested until the employee has satisfied the vesting schedule.

A 401(k) plan can also be created under Roth rules. Roth 401(k) plans do not provide for an immediate tax deduction, but do allow all earnings to be distributed income-tax-free, assuming those monies have been held in the account for five years. The preceding discussion of traditional 401(k) plans also applies to Roth 401(k) plans.

403(b) Plans.   A 403(b) plan, also called a traditional 403(b) plan or a *tax-deferred annuity* (TDA), is a tax-deferred employee retirement plan that can be adopted by certain tax-exempt organizations and certain public school systems. Employees have accounts in a TDA plan to which employers contribute or employees contribute through payroll deduction, similar to a 401(k) contribution.

A nice feature with the 403(b) plan is that in addition to the regular catch-up provision afforded qualified plans (such as 401[k] plans) and IRAs, a special catch-up provision exists if you have underfunded your 403(b) plan and have been an employee for at least 15 years with the organization. In this case, the employee can make an additional $3,000 per year contribution for up to five years.

A 403(b) plan can also be created under Roth rules just like a 401(k) plan. Roth 403(b) plans do not provide for an immediate tax deduction, but do allow all earnings to be distributed income-tax-free, assuming those monies have been held in the account for five years. The preceding discussion of traditional 403(b) plans also applies to Roth 403(b) plans.

Federal Civil Service Plans.   Rules that apply to dividing corporate pension plans do not apply to government pension plans. The Civil Service Retirement System (CSRS) covers civilian employees of the federal government employed before December 31, 1983. New hires after that date are covered under the Federal Employees Retirement System (FERS).

Spouses who are basic members of CSRS are not covered by Social Security. All members of FERS and former CSRS members now in FERS or reinstated into CSRS are covered by Social Security.

Also, both programs offer defined benefit and defined contribution plans. As stated previously, defined benefit plans have their own formula for the determination of benefits. Defined contribution plans in FERS are individual accounts in which the spouse would receive a periodic statement.

Employee contributions are required in FERS defined contribution plans. The amounts are deducted automatically from the spouse's pay. Appropriate payroll taxes (Social Security and federal and state taxes) are subtracted from pay.

Postal Service Pensions. Spouses of postal service employees are covered either in the CSRS or FERS as previously described. For spouses covered by CSRS, an allowance will be made by the court for the absence of Social Security.

Military Pensions. The Armed Forces Retirement System covers members of the U.S. Army, Navy, Marine Corps, and Air Force. Because of the landmark 1981 U.S. Supreme Court case called *McCarty v. McCarty*, military pensions are not to be treated as marital or community property. Therefore, these plans do not fall under traditional Employee Retirement Income Security Act (ERISA) plans. Instead, they follow the federal statute of the Uniform Services Former Spouses' Protection Act (USFSPA). These plans are administered under the Department of Defense.

This ruling gave rise to a group called Ex-Partners of Servicemen for Equality (EXPOSE), whose mission has been to organize a nationwide lobby for federal legislation to guarantee that divorced wives of current or former servicemen can receive an equitable share of the assets accrued during marriage under a military pension.

The law does not guarantee military spouses a definite share of the pension benefits, but leaves it up to the court of each state to award a maximum of 50 percent of the disposable retirement pay and related benefits such as medical care. Therefore, the interpretation and implementation of this federal law will vary by jurisdiction of individual courts and various states.

Military pensions are defined benefit plans. Therefore, there are no employee contributions. Only those military members who serve the full 20 years are entitled to receive a pension. Division of military pensions falls under each state's own rules, whether common or community property. Each state views military pensions as a divisible asset.

Personal Retirement Plans

Personal retirement plans (PRPs) differ from qualified plans (QPs) in several ways. Personal retirement plans have less stringent government reporting requirements (per ERISA rules) than qualified plans. With a PRP, the employer does not have to file an annual employer tax return called the Form 5500, whereas with a QP they do. You cannot borrow from a PRP plan, whereas you may be able to borrow funds with a QP. A PRP does not qualify for ten-year income averaging, whereas a QP may. PRP plans provide for immediate vesting (i.e., as soon as contributions are put into an employee's account, they belong to that employee), whereas with a qualified plan there may be a vesting schedule that forces the employee to wait until the monies become the employee's. That is set by the employer in advance. Also, a PRP may be creditor protected up to a limited amount, whereas QPs are always creditor protected in full.

Personal retirement plans include individual retirement accounts (IRAs), simplified employee pension plans (SEPs), and savings incentive match plans for employees (SIMPLE).

The Traditional IRA. If you have earned income (wages, self-employment, and/or alimony), you can contribute to an IRA. A traditional IRA is a type of retirement savings arrangement under which IRA contributions, up to certain limits, and investment earnings are tax-deferred until withdrawn from the IRA. You can contribute to the maximum amount each year, and if you are over age 50, there is a special annual catch-up provision that can be added to the maximum contribution.

Anyone can make a traditional IRA contribution, regardless of whether you are covered by a qualified plan. The requirement is that you have earned income to use towards the contribution. Believe it or not, alimony is considered to be earned income. My rationale is, just ask anyone who is receiving it—they've earned it!

The key issue, however, concerning traditional IRAs is whether it can be deducted on your tax return. Here's the way it works:

If you are not covered under a qualified plan from work, you can deduct your IRA contribution regardless of your income. If you are covered under a qualified plan, then income limitations may restrict you from deducting the contributed amount.

A special rule exists whereby if one spouse is covered by a qualified plan and the other spouse is not, then a deductible contribution can be made if the adjusted gross income (AGI) is less than that year's threshold.

The Roth IRA.   To encourage people to put money aside for the future, the government offers tax benefits to retirement savers. Usually, it's done with pretax dollars. However, in 1997, the government provided an alternative—a way to save on an after-tax basis and still grow tax-free. That alternative is called the Roth IRA. Since then, Roth accounts have also been expanded into many other types of account, such as the Roth 401(k) and Roth 403(b) plans previously discussed.

The Roth IRA is the opposite of the traditional deductible IRA. With a traditional IRA, you may deduct contributions within limits and only if you satisfy certain requirements, but all withdrawal limits are fully taxable. With a Roth IRA, you receive no up-front deduction for annual contributions. But, if you meet the tax law rules, you may withdraw money from a Roth IRA tax-free. You'll owe no tax on the account's investment earnings if it's considered a qualifying distribution. To be a qualifying distribution, two requirements must be met:

1. You have had the Roth IRA for five tax years.
2. You take the distribution on or after the date you reach age 59½, due to your death or disability, or for qualified first-time homebuyer expenses up to $10,000. The expenses can be for you, your spouse, your child, your grandchild, or an ancestor of you or your spouse.

Any other Roth IRA distributions are taxable to the extent of your account earnings. Unless an exception applies, any distributions prior to age 59½ will be subject to the 10 percent early distribution penalty tax in addition to the taxable amount. Unlike traditional IRAs where distributions must begin by age 70½, distributions under a Roth IRA do not have to begin until the holder's death.

Lastly, you may roll over an existing IRA into a Roth IRA as long as your AGI for the year does not exceed $100,000 in 2009. Beginning in 2010, there will be no income threshold, so any spouse regardless of income can roll over traditional monies into Roth accounts. To determine whether converting to a Roth is right for you, ask your CPA, financial adviser, or Certified Financial Planner (CFP).

Just like with traditional IRAs, eligible spouses may contribute to Roth IRAs up to the stated maximum each year. However, these amounts represent the maximum amount that can be contributed to all IRAs. Lastly, eligible Roth IRA contributors can make full contributions as long as their adjusted gross income (AGI) does not exceed the maximum threshold for that year as well.

You need to designate a beneficiary when you open an IRA. This could be your spouse, estate, another person, or a group of people. Don't take this lightly, since your choice of beneficiary can affect the beneficiary's tax liability and who you ultimately want to receive your property.

Simplified Employee Pension Plans.   Simplified Employee Pension Plans (SEPs) are employer-sponsored plans under which plan contributions are made to a participating employee's IRA. These contribution amounts are usually higher than the IRA contribution.

If you are self-employed and earn the maximum amount that you can use towards an IRA contribution, you can put away as much as if you had a defined contribution plan. Therefore, the limits are much higher than what you can put away under a SIMPLE or IRA plan. Also, if you have a slow earnings year, you may be able to skip future contributions, whereas in most qualified plans you cannot do that. All qualified plans (except profit-sharing plans) require annual contributions. That could be an exhaustive drain on cash. However, the flip side is that if you continue to miss making contributions, then you will be lacking in retirement monies come retirement age.

Savings Incentive Match Plans for Employees (SIMPLE Plans).
SIMPLE IRAs are employer-sponsored plans under which plan contributions are made to a participating employee's IRA. Tax-deferred contribution levels are higher than for IRAs but probably lower than SEPs. SIMPLE plans also provide an employer with the

flexibility to decide whether to make contributions annually. Lastly, as with qualified plans, SIMPLE plans provide for catch-up provisions for individuals over age 50.

Nonqualified Plans

Nonqualified plans are mainly deferred compensation plans, whereby you agree to defer part of your existing compensation to a later date. This reduces your taxable income for the year. Monies are not taxed to you until you begin receiving distributions (like other retirement plans). However, the monies remain with the employer until you begin receiving distributions. Also, you are a creditor to the company, and if the company should default, you have to line up with all the other creditors against the company to claim your monies. So don't do this if your employer is not in good financial health.

You need to declare in advance of earning your salary or other compensation how much you want to defer and when you plan on taking the money. You can make changes every year to your earlier decisions.

Most nonqualified deferred compensation plans are designed to provide key employees with additional retirement benefits over and above qualified plan limitations. This serves as an enticement in hiring and retaining key employees to help with the business.

Contributions to retirement accounts are a family asset and could have gone into the family bank account or been used to pay down family debt.

457 Plans. A 457 plan is a nonqualified plan for government employees. These plans receive the same favorable tax-deferred tax treatment on employee contributions as do traditional 401(k) and 403(b) plans.

A 457 plan also has a favorable catch-up provision. In this case, in the three years prior to the year (and not including the year) of retirement, you can double your contribution for each of those three years (up to annual guidelines). In addition, you can take advantage of the catch-up provision for individuals over age 50.

Social Security. Social Security benefits are generally not considered marital property and are not divisible at divorce. However, if you were married to your ex for ten years or more, then your ex will be entitled to a portion of your Social Security benefit upon his or her retirement age. Furthermore, your benefit will not be affected by whether your ex is receiving a benefit based on the amount you are entitled to collect or whether you have begun collecting benefits.

If you are of normal Social Security retirement age (currently age 66), then your ex can receive 50 percent of your benefit. If your ex is age 62 (early Social Security benefits) and you are of retirement age to begin collecting, then your spouse can get a minimum of 37.5 percent of the benefit. For every month that your ex waits, that benefit is increased. Full retirement benefits will be paid at age 67 for those taxpayers born in 1960 and thereafter.

In addition, if the ex collects as a result of your death, he or she is entitled to 100 percent (or essentially your full retirement benefit). Now that can present a moral hazard! Lastly, ex-spouses who worked at least ten years are entitled to their own benefits. Of course, your ex can collect only the higher of the two and not both. Otherwise spouse swapping would gain even more popularity!

To apply for benefits under your ex's record, you will need the ex-spouse's Social Security number, date and place of birth, and parents' names. For more information, call (800) 772-1213 or visit www.ssa.gov.

Understanding Qualified Domestic Relations Orders

The Retirement Equity Act of 1984 dealt specifically with the distribution of private pension benefits upon divorce. It required the use of a qualified domestic relations order (QDRO) to transfer retirement assets without any income tax consequences to either party.

A QDRO is a court order that provides specialized instructions to a plan administrator as to how to pay to a nonparticipant or nonemployed spouse (such as a divorced spouse, child, or other dependent), who is also called the *alternate payee* (someone other than the named beneficiary in the pension plan), all or a portion of a pension plan benefit after the divorce becomes final. Therefore, your ex will be considered the alternate payee on all the documents resulting from the division of your retirement plan accounts.

These instructions specifically tell the administrator that a certain portion of benefits are to be paid to an alternate payee. And if the monies are to be paid to this person, under current law this amount(s) can be divided and taxation deferred until a later date. A QDRO will therefore be used to divide the pension plan as a marital asset, or to pay alimony or child support including missed payments. If the retirement account is not going to be divided, then obtaining a QDRO is not necessary.

Also be aware of the tax consequences when dividing retirement benefits pursuant to a QDRO. Instead of sending one check to the retired spouse, tell the plan administrator to send two checks, one to you and one to your ex, so each of you can each pay your respective share of income tax. If a QDRO is not necessary, you can reduce your tax liability through the use of a marital settlement agreement or divorce agreement to specify how the benefits are to be paid.

A QDRO is needed to divide pension plans, including defined benefit plans and defined contribution plans. It is also needed for division of profit-sharing plans (such as 401[k] plans), savings and thrift plans (after-tax 401[k] plans), and employee stock ownership plans (ESOPs), and for 403(b) plans. However, QDROs do not apply to personal retirement plans such as IRAs.

All QDROs need to include the name, current address, and Social Security number of the participant spouse and the alternate payee spouse, and the exact name and the amount of benefit available, including the form and timing of the payments from each plan.

If the participant spouse is cooperative, obtaining the required information should be relatively easy. However, if the nonparticipant spouse is dealing with a hostile participant spouse, alternative measures will have to be employed. Sometimes the plan administrator will take sides with the participant, which will require an all-out fight.

Plan administrators can take up to 18 months to approve the order. During this time, the court may order that the spousal shares be kept separate so that the spouse pension holder cannot withdraw or borrow any of those funds that would be considered part of the ex's allotment.

There are three reasons for using a QDRO:

1. The value of the retirement plan is so large as to make an offset impractical, in which case the QDRO may be the other alternative.
2. At times when the court is presented with two experts with different present values, the judge may decide to divide the plan by way of a QDRO.

3. To simplify the allocation of marital property, the spouses may wish to take the retirement plans out of the pool of assets by dividing the plan benefits by a QDRO and distributing the remaining assets equally. This helps free up more liquid assets in order to create a balance in the later distribution of the marital assets used by the spouses in their daily lives.

Many mistakes are made while performing the QDRO. Probably the most common are the following:

- Not having the retirement plan reviewed and the QDRO approved in advance.
- Not searching for prior plans from previous employment.
- Failure to specify whether the nonparticipant spouse will share in the growth or loss inside the account, such as interest earned, dividends received, and gains and losses.
- Limiting the share of benefits to vested portions only.
- Using a standardized form and filling in the blanks as compared to personalizing it.

Inquiries to the Plan Administrator

If the plan administrator is out of state, consider a telephone deposition, video deposition, or Internet deposition. If you retained an outside expert, have that person take these depositions or study the results of them. Key items to ask the administrator about include:

- Participant's account or benefit statements from the date of the marriage.
- Summary plan description.
- Current QDRO procedures.
- Distribution policy and forms.

If the plan administrator is not cooperative, pursue the threat of litigation (but only if it can be carried out). If this is done, only work with an attorney who specializes in ERISA matters. In a worst-case scenario, you can have the attorney see if the plan is indeed in compliance with ERISA or whether there are issues of disqualification of the plan by the IRS. This surely will make a plan administrator somewhat nervous.

Valuation of Retirement Plans

Now that you have a handle on the many types of retirement accounts in the marketplace, and the need for a QDRO to help divide certain retirement plans, the next step in the process is how to value each.

Valuing retirement assets depends on the type of retirement plan you're valuing. With certain retirement plans, like defined contribution plans, these numbers are easy to value based on the statements the individual receives each month. However, with defined benefit plans, it is much more difficult because there is no real value until that person retires. There may be a vested balance based on formulas derived in the plan, but how much can be counted in the divorce settlement may be a difficult value to ascertain.

Some retirement assets can be valued and divided using the services of outside CFPs, actuaries, business valuation specialists, or others. As previously stated, some plans require that additional hoops be jumped through and require supplementary documentation through the use of a QDRO in order to avoid the tax consequences of splitting up these assets.

Many times the purpose of valuing a pension is to offset the value against other assets of the marriage so that the participant spouse can retain all or most of the pension benefits in exchange for giving up the other assets. This perspective is often lost in the process. The attorney, financial adviser, CPA, or other involved party needs to alert the court as to which plans can or cannot be divided with a QDRO.

Use Exhibit 7.1 to make a complete listing when valuing your retirement plan assets.

Methods for Dividing a Pension

There are three methods for dividing retirement accounts:

- *Buyout method.* With this method, the participant spouse purchases the interest of the nonparticipant spouse by ultimately keeping the pension interest and provide the nonparticipant spouse with an equivalent amount of assets. Also called the *immediate offset* method, this can be accomplished either by providing a lump-sum payment to the nonparticipant spouse

Name of Asset	Current Value	Rate of Return (%)	Date Full Benefits Begin
Defined Benefit Plans			
Company retirement plan—yours			
Company retirement plan—ex			
Defined Contribution Plans			
Company retirement plan—yours			
Company retirement plan—ex			
Personal Retirement Plans			
IRA 1—yours			
IRA 2—ex			
IRA 1—yours			
IRA 2—ex			
SEP—yours			
SEP—ex			
SIMPLE—yours			
SIMPLE—ex			
Nonqualified Plans			
Yours			
Ex			
Other			
Yours			
Ex			

Exhibit 7.1   Valuation of Retirement Plan Assets

or by giving that person an equivalent amount of marital assets from other sources. Because a dollar amount must be known, under this approach, the value of the retirement accounts must be determined in advance of the final divorce decree. The benefit to this approach is that each spouse is completely free of the other with regard to receiving retirement dollars in the future since it is all taken care of now.

- *Wait-and-see method.* With this method, the pension assets are on hold until a future date and then are split at the date of retirement. That date is when the monies are ultimately received by each spouse. The upside is that each spouse shares in the risk while the monies are accumulating, so that if something happens and the numbers are not where anticipated, both spouses' distributions are adjusted accordingly. The downside here is that the spouses will continue to be drawn together and may have possible contact with each other until the monies are ultimately divided up. A valuation is not needed here (unlike the buyout method). Rather, all that is required is that the future benefit be known to each spouse.

- *Reserved jurisdiction method.* This little-used method asks the court to wait and delay until a later date before valuing and dividing the pension because there are too many unknown variables at this time, thus making an accurate current valuation unlikely. Examples include the receipt of stock options that become vested at a later date, bonuses to be paid dependent on other factors, and other sources of compensation that cannot be determined until later on. This approach is worthwhile if you don't want to hastily value a retirement number and find out that it is completely without merit.

Determining How Much of the Valuation Is Your Share

Once you value the retirement assets, then you need to figure out what percentage of that amount you are entitled to. For example, if you have been in a 21-year marriage and have worked at your company for 30 years, your ex will not be entitled to the entire pension. A quick and easy way to figure that out would be to use the following formula:

Marital Portion = Years participated in pension during the marriage/Total number of years participating in pension at the date of the divorce

In our example, 21 would represent the numerator and 30 would represent the denominator, resulting in 70 percent of the pension benefit being considered a marital asset and entitled to a split.

Bear in mind that other factors can be thrown into the equation, such as cost of living adjustments, future appreciation, whether distribution is deferred until a later date, or some other factor.

Using Retirement Assets to Buy Out or Balance Out Equity

Let's consider how the buyout method of dividing a pension is probably the best solution to providing each spouse with a workable asset. For example, assume that the parties to a divorce have a few assets to divide. These include a house valued at $500,000, automobiles at $50,000, personal property at $200,000, after-tax investments of $200,000, and a pension valued at $750,000. In order to equalize the balances, the spouse with the pension benefit may have to give up most if not all of the other assets to even the playing field. In this example, the spouse with the pension would only receive approximately $100,000 of the remaining assets. This would then allow the spouse with the pension to keep all of his or her pension rights.

A more difficult scenario would be the following. Assume that the pension benefits were valued at $210,000 by one expert and $250,000 by another. Although the difference is rather small (when compared against divorce fees), the judge or the parties may decide to split the difference or call in a third expert that both parties can agree upon.

Another solution would be for the court to simplify the division of property by using a QDRO. Using a QDRO results in the awarding of one-half of the plan to each party when each party retires. In these cases, the financial hardship is lessened at the time of the divorce as only the more liquid assets are allocated evenly to each party. If multiple retirement plans exist, not all of them have to be divided through a QDRO. The bottom line is that each party receives half of the overall value.

This approach is clean and simple. Each party receives an equivalent amount of dollars according to what works best for their scenario.

Your Ex's Remarriage or Death and Your Vested Pension Benefits

Sometimes if an ex-spouse remarries and a QDRO is not properly drawn up, it could spell disaster. That's because under federal tax law, retirement benefits are automatically paid to the surviving spouse, which is now the new spouse. If you are the former spouse, you will need a provision in the QDRO to name you as the alternate payee, which again is the person entitled to the retirement benefits after the participant worker spouse's death.

Inclusion of this clause essentially states that you will remain the surviving spouse for these retirement benefits only, regardless of whether your ex dies or remarries. This way you will be protected and ensured of receiving the retirement benefits you had agreed to at the time of your divorce.

Discovery of Retirement Plans

Attorneys can do a great service for their clients if they uncover each and every type of retirement plan accrued during the marriage. The importance of discovery in both the valuation of retirement plan benefits and QDRO-related issues is another aspect of the process that shouldn't be overlooked. Here are some of the issues to consider in order to uncover these plans.

Frozen Plans

Plans that were previously offered and then frozen when ERISA came along were usually subsequently converted to annuities and paid in addition to the current plan benefits. These plans, while not showing outwardly on the books of the employer, nevertheless are legitimate plans that should factor in the division of property.

Overlooked Plans

Many times if a spouse has contributed to a 401(k) plan, it is assumed that that is the only available plan. In fact, many defined benefit plans go unnoticed. Since defined benefit plans pay out a monthly benefit and don't provide a statement of benefit accruals, it sometimes can be very difficult to find these types of plans when evaluating that spouse's overall retirement benefits. Many times larger companies will have both defined benefit and defined contribution plans.

Discovery Questions

The starting point for the attorney of the nonparticipant spouse should be to ask for a listing of all past employers of the participant spouse and a list of all retirement plans associated with each employer. This helps determine the value of the retirement plan, which can then be offset against the family's other marital assets or used to begin developing a QDRO. If the participant spouse has been with various employers a short period of time (generally before vesting occurs), it's probably safe to assume that no retirement plans existed with that employer.

The next step is to develop a nongeneric questionnaire requesting the plan administrator to list all possible plans that the participant may have had an interest or accrued benefit in while working at the employer. The key to this approach is to determine the value of the benefits that were accrued during the marriage.

Dealing with defined benefit plans is very different from dealing with defined contribution plans. While a defined benefit plan may be the most difficult to get clear answers about, use the following questions to help identify the potential benefits that can be associated with this plan.

Rattiner's Planning Questions for Defined Benefit Plans

- At what age (early, regular, or late retirement age) can any retirement benefits be received from the plan?
- Are there cost of living adjustments associated with the plan?
- Are there any situations in which the participant can opt for an earlier benefit?
- Can the spouse receive the present value of the future benefit payment stream now or at retirement?
- Can the benefit be distributed in a lump sum as opposed to a monthly benefit?
- Is the spouse vested in this plan? If not, then when would the employee become vested?
- Do any supplemental retirement plans exist in addition to the regular plan?
- Are there any subsidized benefits associated with the plan?

If you must wait until a later date to receive the present value of the future stream of benefits, then you may be able to value it as of today and treat it as a lump sum for valuation purposes.

If you are the nonemployee spouse, your spouse's attorney might try to convince you to estimate the value and then accept a fixed monthly payment schedule that corresponds to the value. Don't do that. Make sure the actuary creates a formula for the court order using the factor first described in this chapter (age and years of service) so that you get your full share of the pension benefit when the participant spouse retires.

With a defined contribution plan, it is an easier fit for you to value since statements are provided to each employee and each employee owns his or her own account. You can assess monies contributed before, during, and after the marriage and thereby know an exact amount to divvy up. That is not true for a defined benefit plan. Use the following questions to help identify the potential benefits that can be associated with this plan.

Rattiner's Planning Questions for Defined Contribution Plans

- When did the spouse begin contributing to the defined contribution plan?
- Identify the amount of employer and employee spouse contributions.
- Separate the earnings from the contribution levels.
- When (the earliest date) can the spouse begin receiving distributions?
- Is the spouse vested in this plan? If not, then when should the spouse become vested?
- Are there any loans against the balances in these plans?

Uncooperative Plan Participant Spouse

You will not always get a warm, receptive spouse on the other end. In addition, the plan administrator, who should remain neutral, might feel an obligation to protect the employer's worker in these situations.

You should not take the word of the participant spouse. The nonparticipant spouse's attorney should work with the participant spouse's attorney and explain the importance of understanding the valuation of these assets as a marital asset and what can happen if that participant spouse does not comply. Noncompliance can result in depositions, interrogatories, expert fees, and reliance on the court to impose sanctions for costs including attorney fees. Courts can impose fines for noncompliance.

If one party was planning for divorce, then that participant spouse could have hidden assets prior to the divorce process. If the participant spouse is a frequent traveler to foreign countries, the possibility of offshore accounts may exist. You can find this out by examining tax returns or 1099s from the past few years to determine if any foreign tax credits were taken.

Double Payments

Don't let your ex's attorney double-count the retirement assets. What I mean is don't let your ex include his or her portion of the retirement benefit amount as part of the property settlement and then also use those monies in the calculation of alimony. This double-dipping can also happen when valuing a closely held business. (See Chapter 8.)

Common Mistakes Pertaining to Retirement Plans

Now that you have a handle on the many types of retirement plans, valuation, and division of plans, let's make sure nothing goes wrong for you in this area. The ultimate responsibility for making sure bad things don't happen to good spouses rests with your attorney.

Unfortunately, not all attorneys are schooled in the valuation and tax sides of financial transactions, so outside help is warranted. If you use someone other than an attorney to help you through the divorce process, then following the process with the professional of your choosing. Use the checklist in Exhibit 7.2 to identify and ensure that some of the more common errors are uncovered during the process.

1. Has the attorney identified all past and present retirement plans?	Yes	No
2. Does the attorney understand the differences among all the types of retirement plans that you or your ex possess (i.e., qualified vs. personal vs. nonqualified plans and/or corporate vs. government plans)?	Yes	No
3. Was a QDRO obtained during the divorce process and not afterwards?	Yes	No
4. Has your attorney stepped up to the plate and either prepared the QDRO or is on top of someone else preparing the QDRO?	Yes	No
5. Has an outside party been hired to help value the retirement accounts?	Yes	No
6. Does the value of the retirement plans ask for accrued benefits as opposed to vested benefits?	Yes	No
7. Does the value of the retirement plans include all the activity within the retirement account, such as gains and losses, interest and dividends received?	Yes	No
8. Has the attorney noted what will happen if the parties die during the process?	Yes	No
9. Has the attorney acknowledged and completed the issues necessary for continuation of medical care coverage for the nonparticipant spouse?	Yes	No
10. Did you walk away from the divorce comfortable with the approach used by the attorney and others as to the way the calculations were made in the division of retirement plan assets?	Yes	No

Exhibit 7.2   Retirement Plan Mistakes Checklist

Rattiner's Planning Tips

1. Always know how you want to divide up the marital retirement benefit plans before you go to the negotiation table.
2. Vesting represents the guaranteed portion of the retirement benefit the employee spouse is entitled to receive.

3. A defined benefit plan is an employer-sponsored plan whereby contributions are actuarially determined and are made based on a variety of factors, such as age and/or years of service. The contribution amount can vary but the benefit received from the plan is defined actuarially.

4. Defined contribution plans are based on limits that can be added to an employee participant's account. The amount contributed to the employee's account is limited by IRS annual guidelines, but the value available at retirement is not known until then. Many factors can affect the value at retirement, including investment earnings, employee and employer contributions, and possibly employee forfeitures.

5. A 401(k), 403(b), or 457 plan allows the employee participant spouse to defer some of his own earnings towards building a retirement nest egg.

6. A QDRO is a court order that provides specialized instructions to a plan administrator as to how to pay to a nonparticipant or nonemployed spouse or other individual (such as a divorced spouse, child, or other dependent), who is also called the alternate payee (someone other than the named beneficiary in the pension plan), all or a portion of a pension plan benefit after the divorce becomes final. Your ex will be considered the alternate payee on all the documents resulting from the division of your retirement plan accounts.

7. Qualified plans, such as defined contribution and defined benefit plans, need QDROs for a nontaxable division of retirement assets.

8. Personal retirement plans, such as IRAs, SIMPLEs, and SEPs do not need QDROs, but care should be given to the tax issues of dividing these types of plans.

9. IRAs, SEPs, and SIMPLEs do not have the same favorable tax issues as qualified plans.

10. Nonqualified plans, such as 457 plans, are not affected by discrimination issues since they do not have to be uniformly offered to all employees. As a result, they are not creditor protected.

11. Social Security benefits are available to exes who were married for at least ten years. Benefits can range from as low as 37.5 percent to as high as 100 percent of the worker spouse's benefit.

12. You need to be comfortable with your decision on how to divide up retirement benefits. It may make sense to keep the entire benefits and provide your ex with a comparable amount in other assets.

13. Key items to ask the plan administrator concerning a QDRO include the participant's account or benefit statements from the date of the marriage, a summary plan description, current QDRO procedures, and distribution policy and forms.

14. Make sure all past retirement plans have been disclosed through the discovery process.

15. Don't double-dip retirement plan assets as a future source for alimony.

16. Provide for yourself as a "surviving spouse" beneficiary on your ex's plan if your ex dies or remarries.

17. Make sure you look at the accrued benefits (not just vested benefits) when valuing retirement plans.

18. Make sure you engage the services of an actuary, pension benefit specialist, or other individual to help sort through the retirement plan options and to value the plans.

CHAPTER 8

Valuation Issues

Property Division Issues

There are many property interests the spouse can hold. These serve as the basis of divorce settlements for the state in which you principally reside. These laws may supersede other laws.

There are two different sets of laws that determine how property gets divided: *common law* and *community property law*. The goal is essentially the same under either system, namely, to fairly divide property that the couple owns together. Let's take a look at the differences.

Common Law versus Community Property

All states are divided into either common law or community property (except Alaska which has both). Parts of these laws dictate how the division of property is to be made between a husband and a wife in the event of a divorce. Here's a quick history lesson.

Common law originated in England and is based on statutory and case law according to changes in customs and usages. The English settled this country primarily on the East Coast, which is why most common law states are located in the eastern portion of the United States.

Community property has its origins in French and Spanish law. The French settled this country through Louisiana and the Spaniards came to this country through the Western part of the United States, which is why many of the western states follow community property laws.

Equitable Division: Common Law States

In common law states, courts are supposed to apply equitable distribution standards to divide property equitably or as justice requires. These laws give judges more latitude and property awards tend to vary greatly, although a 50/50 split is considered the norm.

Equitable does not mean *equal.* For example, let's assume a marriage has acquired only two assets: a $600,000 business that the husband has run alone and a $400,000 house shared together. Upon divorce, it is possible (hopefully not probable) that the judge can award the husband the business, since he was the main person involved, and provide the wife with the house to sort of equal out the distribution. That can be considered as equitable although definitely not equal. Forty-one states have equitable distribution laws.

Equal Division: Community Property States

Community property represents a unified or undivided interest in property. It follows the premise that marriage is an equal partnership and that all property acquired during the marriage (whether assets or income) are split equally, 50/50, regardless of who actually earned it.

Community property is grounded in the concept of equality. Because a marriage is a community consisting of two marital partners who, through their joint labors, industry and efforts, contribute to the prosperity of the marriage, both spouses possess an equal right to the property and its benefits.

The same principles apply to debt. Therefore each married spouse owns an equal, undivided interest in all of the property accumulated utilizing either spouse's earnings during the marriage.

For example, let's say that my spouse works 80-hour weeks and makes $200,000 per year. I, meanwhile, stay home and drink beer and watch football 24/7. If we end up divorced (you can probably see this coming), under community property laws it's as if we had each earned $100,000. Like I might quit that job!

There are certain exceptions to these rules. Property acquired before the marriage, or through gifts or inheritance received during the marriage, retains its separate property status if you prefer. However, if any of your separate property is commingled, or can no longer be traced as separate, it will be assumed to be community property. In addition, in some states, if you buy separate property, such as a house, then get married and pay for the expenses of the property (i.e., mortgage, taxes, utilities) as a marital asset, under community property upon divorce the law will state that there were joint contributions from both spouses toward the upkeep of the house, and some portion of the house will end up as community (marital) property. It may not be 50 percent but it could be substantial.

The rationale for enforcing community property laws is that if you enter a marriage with property in your own name but both parties contribute to take care of that asset, then both of you should enjoy the benefits of the ownership if you split up.

Nine states are considered to be community property states: Arizona, California, Idaho, Louisiana, Nevada, New Mexico, Texas, Washington, and Wisconsin. In addition, Alaska allows residents and nonresidents to enter into community property agreements permitting in-state property to be treated as community property. In these states, only property that was accumulated during the marriage will be divided, with a few exceptions, and the property will be divided equally at 50/50, asset by asset whenever possible.

Be aware that while all of these states are listed as community property and share common features and definitions, each state operates their community property laws somewhat differently than the other. Therefore, there is no one common set of community property laws that each state must adhere to or that crosses state lines if you move from one state to another. Although the fundamental aspects of community property laws are similar in the different states, many differences have evolved because of refinements of state legislatures.

Wages, income, and bonuses are community property and are considered credit obtained during the marriage. Therefore, homemakers are not penalized for not working outside the house. Claims of "I earned all the money" therefore are not relevant since it is assumed that each spouse contributed to the household income.

There are various odds and ends you should know about under community property:

- If one spouse takes money belonging to the couple's community property and pays off a separate debt, then the community property will be paid back that amount when the parties split.

- If one spouse receives a financial settlement or award as a result of a community property activity (i.e., that spouse receives an award from a lawsuit brought about as he was driving his kids to school and had his car hit by another driver), then the entire award will be considered community property.
- Community property regimes vary slightly from state to state. In other words, there are nine separate community property laws, not one set of laws to which nine states adhere. So make sure that you understand the specifics of your home state.
- Community property does not have an automatic right of survivorship. When the first spouse dies, one half of the value of the property will pass through the probate process for retitling, per the direction of the decedent's will or the state intestacy (dying without a will) law. Each spouse's one-half interest will also be included in their own federal gross estate.
- Community property status can be dissolved through death, divorce, or by agreement between the spouses. Specifically, one spouse can gift his half of the community property to the other spouse, thereby creating separate property owned entirely by the spouse who receives the property. Because there is an unlimited deduction for gift taxes, gift tax liability would not be created. However, this type of gift tax may occur when a couple moves from a community property state to a common law (separate property) state in which the couple intends to remain. Otherwise, community property once created retains its community property status. Further, any property acquired utilizing the earnings of either spouse, subsequent to the couple's move into the community property state, is considered community property.
- Community property owners receive a full 100 percent step-up in value at death from each spouse's half, as opposed to common law where the heir receives a 50 percent step-up in basis (the decedent's share only). This creates a new tax basis that is higher than the old one. This is called community property with right of survivorship.

General rules to remember are "once community property, always community property" (even if the couple move to a common law equitable distribution state), and "once common law, always common law" (even if you move to a community property state) except in the following situation. In five community property states, a quasi–community property system is recognized for a couple moving from a common law state to a community property state. Quasi–community property is property that would be community property had the couple been living in the community property state at the time of acquisition. Quasi–community property is treated just like community property at the death of either spouse, or at the time of divorce. Before either one of these occurrences, the quasi–community property is treated as separate property. The five quasi–community property states are Arizona, California, Idaho, Washington, and Wisconsin. That means if you move from a common law state (i.e., New York) to a quasi–community property state (i.e., Arizona), then your property takes on the characteristics of the state to which you move (Arizona), which is a community property state.

Separate Property

As stated previously, property acquired alone by a spouse prior to marriage, or received as a gift or inheritance during the marriage, is considered to be separate property. Separate property is not subject to division by the court (with few exceptions). In certain situations, a married couple can own property as separate property even within a community property state. In these cases, this property would not receive a new tax basis on both halves at the death of the first spouse.

If the separate property appreciates and taxes are paid jointly by the couple on their income tax return, then a gray area exists. Many times the appreciated portion of the property can be considered marital property while the original separate property remains just that. If you truly want to keep it separate, you'll have to take additional steps.

For example, let's assume that your ex received a $2 million inheritance and invested it, earning 5 percent per year for a total income of $100,000. If you file a joint tax return and pay taxes on the $100,000 jointly, then the appreciation in the asset can be considered to be a marital asset under community property law. To avoid that scenario, figure out what the tax liability is on the property. In this example, let's assume it's $15,000. The ex would then write a check to the community property account for $15,000 from the ex's inheritance account to cover the tax liability on that money. This way, keeping it separate and having the ability to trace the tax liability directly to the ex, should keep the $100,000 of income as continued separate property.

Common Law Marriage Issues

Couples who act like they are married, hold themselves out to the world as married, and intended to be married are considered legally married. Examples of this type of behavior include filing joint tax returns, referring to each other as "husband" and "wife," and using the same last name.

If you live in one of the states that recognize common law marriage and you meet these criteria, then you are considered legally married and must get a divorce to end your marriage. Before entering into this type of relationship, visit with an attorney who is an expert in this area.

Example

The following 15 states plus the District of Columbia have recognized or still recognize common law marriage:

Alabama
Colorado
District of Columbia
Georgia (if created before January 1, 1997)
Idaho (if created before January 1, 1996)
Iowa
Kansas
Montana
New Hampshire (for inheritance purposes only)
Ohio (if created before October 10, 1990)
Oklahoma
Pennsylvania (if created before 2004)
Rhode Island
South Carolina
Texas
Utah

Closely Held Business Valuation

If you have built a business with joint funds while married, you will have to determine what part of your business will be considered marital property. If separate funds were used, that gets to be a tricky scenario. In either case, if the value of the business appreciated, the likelihood is that the increase in value will be considered marital property.

To determine whether your business should be considered marital property, you'll need to address these issues:

- Was the business established before or after the marriage?
- Did it grow substantially during the marriage?
- If the business did grow, was it due to the fact that your ex was a stay-at-home spouse who did not work full-time in the business?
- Was separate property from either spouse invested in the business?
- Was it a joint business run by both spouses?

The conclusion is that if any part of the business is designated to be marital property, then a value must be placed on it.

If you are the business owner, you won't want your ex to take any part of the business. That means you will have to come up with other assets in an equivalent amount to trade for the value of the business. You may have to raid other joint or separate assets, such as money you have put into a pension plan, and then you'll have to roll over a portion of that entire plan to your spouse. If you don't have other assets, you will have to face the fact that you might have to borrow money or possibly sell out your portion of the business. And there may be no market to sell the business when you need to do it.

Whatever you decide to do, the one thing you will almost certainly feel is that the business belongs to you. Period! Any business owner can attest to that. You will not want your ex to receive anything business related. You may also feel that it is not part of the marital estate. The courts, however, will not be as kind and will refuse that position.

For example, I knew a successful financial planner who lived and operated a business in a community property state and was married for 20 years. After his divorce, his wife received 50 percent of the business even though she never stepped foot in the business during that 20-year marriage. Because he could not afford to pay her out right away, she initially owned 50 percent of the business after the divorce and all decisions related to the business had to be made jointly. Talk about ugly! It took him two years to secure a loan to buy his entire business back. He's still paying for it many years later.

So how do you go about the process? First things first: Obtain a copy of the business tax returns. You'll see the business structure and the income and expenses of the business interest. That should help with the flow of the valuation. The difficulty you'll face in valuing your business is that there are many ways to accomplish this. And unless you owned the business prior to marriage as separate property, it will be counted as part of the final settlement.

Most of the divorced spouses I've interviewed ran small businesses. Few ran larger ones. Big businesses usually require audits, which are easier to value, but those are few and far between. We'll just focus on the smaller ones. As a sole proprietor, one-person LLC, or S Corporation, essentially you are the business. You can make the argument that if it weren't for you, there'd be no business. And most people would agree with you, even the business valuators. For example, if you get disabled or die, there is no business. I had that experience myself. But the business valuators don't value the business in that way.

In fact, the problem with the business is that it can get double-dipped if your lawyer is not on top of this. Here's why. Your ex will get credit for a percentage of the business interest (assume 50 percent) as part of an equitable distribution and then will also be entitled to take part of your earnings or income for support! Heck, why not give that ex the entire package! Therefore, it is counting twice against you.

Don't enter into the relationship with the business valuator/appraiser without understanding the fee that will be charged and exactly what you will get in return for payment. Taking this action does not mean that you should blindly hand over all your books and records to the business valuator/appraiser and expect this person to figure it out, leaving you out of the loop. Qualified professionals should be able to explain their recommendations and assessments in terms you can understand. They should be willing to decipher the alternatives available, explain why certain decisions are recommended, lay out the risks involved, and answer your questions fully. If you are uncertain about the validity of the appraisal, get another opinion.

To get comfortable with this huge undertaking, I recommend that you interview different business valuation firms and determine the method they use to value the firm. Unfortunately, I did not do this. I knew the business valuator beforehand and figured he would be fair and timely. Well, sometimes things don't work out as planned. It would have been a good idea to get references from other clients who went through the process with that firm. In some cases you'll find out that the business valuator does not understand the type of business you had and will derive a number without really understanding how it works.

It's probably a good idea to have your attorney present during the questioning, both before you hire someone and during the valuation process, for good reason. If you go with your attorney, any information exchanged between you and the business valuator will be considered privileged (confidential) information. Without the attorney, you lose that privilege.

There are various methods that business valuators can use. One is the fair market value method. Under Treasury Regulations, this is what a willing buyer and seller can agree upon as the final price, based on how comparable businesses have been valued. Since many businesses are not identical and are uniquely tailored so that they don't look and feel like other existing businesses, this can be tough to do, as it is hard to find comparables. My business, one of Certified Financial Planner (CFP) educational training, definitely fits into that category. There are not many people who do this full-time for a living.

The downside with this approach is it's based on what the business would sell for in cash. Most businesses do not sell for cash. Most are financed. Business valuators will also typically look at the accounts receivable and the debts of the business when considering fair market value. As with my business valuator, there can be an element of subjectivity included in business valuation as well.

There are many types of businesses and each one may require a different approach in valuation. When a business has limited assets but constant cash flow, as is typical of a professional practice, capitalized earnings is the favored method to use. Conversely, when a business such as a manufacturing or retail enterprise has a large amount of capital tied up in assets but a more limited cash flow, the focus generally should be on the market value of the assets. Other types of businesses have a balance between assets and cash flow, and for these, calculation of value should be by an excess earnings method. IRS Revenue Ruling 59-60 deals with methods of valuing closely held corporations such as a professional practice.

Furthermore, in a divorce you are not actually putting the business up for sale nor are you able to find a willing buyer and seller. The Treasury Regulations also state that neither party should be forced to buy or sell. In a divorce situation, this is definitely the case—in fact, nothing out of the ordinary is to be done by the person running the business. But in a divorce, you or your ex is essentially selling one-half of the business. What makes it difficult is that the two parties do not have the same knowledge of your business.

An alternative approach that is probably safer is to look at the business's future earning capacity and ask what the likely amount of earned income will be in the future. That is also risky but probably a better denominator than seeing what it has earned in the past. Historical information is always outdated the moment it is released. It's sort of like saying that just because a mutual fund earned 20 percent last year doesn't mean that the same fund should expect to earn 20 percent this year. Either the fund will or it won't. Assuming it will earn something different in the future is a safe bet. I had that issue when, during and after 2008, the financial sector had its worst beating since the Great Depression. Unfortunately, the new conditions were not factored into the final valuation. When I asked why, I was told that the future is pure speculation and that the valuators have no knowledge of what will really happen in the future. In this case, you may be valuing the business interest much higher (or lower) than the projected income assumed.

Another approach for valuators is to look at sales of comparable businesses. There are books and computer programs available that can also assess the value of similar types of businesses. These formulas are generally expressed as multiples of gross revenues, operating income, and other factors and sometimes can be taken from general rules of thumb. Sometimes business brokers can lend a hand based on what they have seen in the marketplace.

Still another approach is to have the business valued for tax purposes (which is nothing like valuing for divorce purposes) under Revenue Ruling 59-60. This approach requires the valuator to answer certain key questions about the business. These questions address the type of business, its history since inception, the general economic business conditions outlook and the prospects for your business, the financial condition of the business, its earning capacity, whether large quantities of stock were sold, whether goodwill is present, and the market price of similar type corporations.

Documents Needed

Be prepared to show your business valuator the following documents. If you don't have them, your lawyer can also request these documents from your ex's lawyer, and vice versa.

- Past five years of individual tax returns and documents (Form 1040).
- Past five years of business tax returns and documents (Form 1120S [S Corporations], 1120 [C Corporations], or 1065 [partnerships, limited liability companies, limited liability partnerships]).
- K-1s for 1065 or 1120S.
- Income (profit and loss) statement.
- Balance sheet.
- Listing of shareholders or partners who own a piece of the company.
- Capital accounts of the partners if the business is a partnership.
- Retained earnings statement.
- List of cash accounts and any investments.
- List of aged accounts receivable (money due the business).
- List of aged accounts payable (money the business owes others).
- Business plan and projections.
- Key officers' compensation.
- Key officers' life insurance.
- List of existing contracts.
- List of partnership agreements in effect.

Talk about subjectivity: Goodwill, the increase in earnings or value brought about through repeat business, may be another factor in the valuation equation. To determine whether goodwill exists, questions such as whether you have a steady stream of repeat clients or customers constantly knocking at your door need to be answered. Goodwill can be broken down into *enterprise goodwill*, if it deals with selling product, or *professional goodwill*, if it deals with patronizing the same CPA, CFP, doctor, lawyer, and so on. This is very tough to determine. If you run a service business, then some states may include professional goodwill as part of the marital estate.

Another place where goodwill shows up is when one spouse sacrificed a career either by being an at-home spouse or by working various odd jobs or whatever while the other spouse went to school or obtained professional licenses or certifications. That ex may feel he or she deserves a part of that business because of his or her sacrifice to the big marital picture. Many attorneys will try to view the entire marriage and its components (i.e., business interests) as a complete partnership and thus try to determine a dollar value for the spouse staying home to raise the kids, and split the business as part of an equitable distribution.

Valuation Report

Valuation reports can be oral or written. If the two spouses agree on the business valuation, oral reports would be the best way to go since it ultimately saves both spouses money. If the spouses don't agree, more than likely then a written report will need to be prepared which describes the nature of the business and all the facts and documents relied on to reach the final appraisal. Ultimately, it will be needed for court. Ideally, not having to go to court and having the business valuator testify will certainly save lots of money.

If either of you is unhappy with the business valuation findings, you can opt to get a new valuation or hire an expert to challenge how the business valuator arrived at these numbers. The expert will serve on the witness stand, countering the original business valuator's method, logic, and rationale. Before you make that call, you really need to see what the true differential is and whether it is worthwhile pursuing. Sometimes the dollars are not there to support this challenge or redo. If you are headed for court, then you'll probably pursue this path. As many spouses have found out, spending money on a second valuation should be done only if it is a necessity.

The business valuation report should include the following:

- Full description of the business.
- Method of valuation.
- Name and qualifications of the evaluator.
- Names of relevant documents that were reviewed.
- Full explanation of the rationale for the evaluation.
- Date the business was valued.
- Reason for the valuation.
- Relevant industry standards.

If Both Spouses Work in and Own the Business Together

This is a more challenging concept since in most divorces the spouses want nothing to do with each other after the fact. However, if both spouses are relying on this income as their principal source of revenue, should they divide the business initially, or separate and keep the business intact? That's a tough call. Other issues begin to develop, such as if one spouse takes over the business, then how does the other spouse get compensated for that? Should both of them continue to draw profits or a salary from the business? Should they work out a buyout for the present value of the future interest for the spouse no longer involved with the business? What happens when both spouses, while married, ran personal expenses though the business (like car expenses, travel, entertainment, etc.)? How do you account for that situation? I guess the bottom line is that if you can keep the business afloat and not take it down with the divorce, it may be wise to work out some acceptable arrangement.

States that consider professional practices part of the marital estate at this time include:

- Arizona
- California
- Colorado
- Connecticut
- Indiana
- Kentucky
- Maryland
- Michigan
- Montana
- Nevada
- New Jersey

- New Mexico
- New York
- North Carolina
- Ohio
- Oregon
- Virginia
- Washington

Some courts reason that professional goodwill is personal to an individual and not capable of being divided as an asset. In any case, professional income is always the basis of a support order. The courts won't make a distinction between income from goodwill and ordinary income. So even though it may not count as a divisible marital asset, it will always be counted as income for support purposes.

Stock Redemptions

The rules get much more complicated when dealing with spouses who have interests in a large corporation. Regulation 1.1041-2 acknowledges that depending on the circumstances a stock redemption can be:

- A sale of stock that, if held for more than a year, would result in a capital gain or loss (IRC Sections 302 and 316).
- A constructive dividend subject to ordinary income treatment (IRC Sections 302 and 316).

Interestingly, Regulation 1.1041-2 permits the spouses to decide who has to report the constructive dividend or capital gains created by the redemption. Make sure your attorney and business valuator draft this extremely well and tightly. Unfortunately, Regulation 1.1041-2 only applies to corporations. Partnership redemptions, as we will see next, fall under IRC Section 736.

Partner Liquidations

A *partner* liquidation is similar to a *partnership* liquidation except that cash paid triggers IRC Section 736. Section 736 requires money payments to be characterized as one of the following:

- A distributive share or guaranteed payment (IRC Section 736[a]).
- Payment for an interest in partnership property (IRC Section 736[b]).

This allocation generally is made under the partnership agreement. The total allocated to IRC Section 736(b) cannot exceed the fair market value of the partnership's assets at the time of liquidation.

If there is no allocation provision in the partnership agreement, payments are first treated as coming from IRC Section 736(b) to the extent of the value of the partnership interest. The remainder of the payments are considered IRC Section 736(a) payments.

Under IRC Section 736(a), cash payments made to a retiring or deceased partner are:

- A distributive share if figured by reference to partnership income, thus reducing the amount of partnership income available to the continuing partners.
- Guaranteed payments, if not determined by reference to the partnership income, thus producing a deduction from gross income to arrive at partnership taxable income.

Section 736(b) payments are made when the cash payment is exchanged for the interest of the retiring or deceased partner in partnership property. It is treated as a current distribution by the partnership and not as a distributive share or a guaranteed payment. Liquidating cash payments under IRC Section 736(b) are considered a return of capital to the extent of a partner's basis in the partnership, and capital gain is recognized to the extent of any excess.

The tax status of IRC Section 736 payments provides for the outgoing partner's interest in the partnership assets. Thus gain or loss from such payments is determined under the rules of IRC Section 731 (unless IRC Section 751 applies). Section 736(a) income payments are received in lieu of the retiring partner's interest in current or future partnership income and are treated as:

- Guaranteed payments, if they are not determined by partnership income and are either capitalized or deductible by the partnership and ordinary income to distribute.
- Distributive shares, if determined by reference to partnership income and they are excludable from the continuing partners' income and may constitute ordinary income, capital gain, and so forth to the distributee.

Stock Options

In most states, stock options granted to a spouse while married become part of the marital property. If that is the case, they need to be valued just like any other assets. Stock options are considered to be additional forms of compensation that need to be factored into the entire income package. They are really viewed as deferred compensation since this compensation is tied to the future increase in the value of the company stock. The critical issues that develop include whether to consider the option value as part of the distribution of property and/or whether to include the income as part of support.

Stock options are an employee spouse's right to formally buy company stock at a specified price during a specified time period. They can only be issued to the employee and thus cannot be transferred as part of the divorce settlement. Stock options generally remain outstanding for up to ten years. Employee stock options are subject to vesting. If the employee leaves employment, the vesting period would not be satisfied and all those options not vested would then be forfeited. The vested portion would remain intact. If the stock goes down in value, the employee will not exercise the option since it would create a loss.

There are several types of options but the main two are incentive stock options (ISOs) and nonqualified stock options (NSOs). Incentive stock options are options granted by an employer to compensate key employees and executives of larger corporations to buy stock at some specified time in the future. Incentive stock options generally are not issued to closely held business owners because they get their value when the options are sold and there typically is no readily available market for closely held business owner stock. Nonqualified stock options can be issued to both employees and independent contractors and are designed in any manner suitable to an executive or to the employer with few government restraints.

Said another way, the IRC divides stock options into two categories: nonstatutory stock options, which do not meet specific IRC requirements for special tax treatment, and statutory stock options, which include employee stock purchase plans (ESPPs) and ISOs.

That makes analyzing options more difficult because the higher the stock option valuation, the more the ex receives in comparable assets since the employee has no choice but to keep the option. It's no different than the closely held business owner having to keep the business and include the value of the business on his or her side of the marital valuation statement.

To determine whether stock option valuation is even an issue in divorce, you'll need to answer these four questions:

1. Is the stock option part of marital property? In other words, was it earned and received during the marriage?
2. How is the option valued?
3. When is the option valued?
4. What are the tax consequences when the option is exercised?

Your role here is to come up with a proper valuation to adjust for your ex-spouse's entire compensation package, including stock options, retirement benefits, flexible benefit packages, and other perks given to that working spouse. You'll also need to understand at what date the option is valued. Is it at the hearing date, the date of separation, the date of trial, the date of divorce decree? As we have all seen with major stock market declines recently, the date of valuing stock options is critical. Again, these are very tough questions to answer.

The tax issues can be significant because of the difference between ordinary income and capital gain tax rates upon exercise and sale. Incentive stock options are not taxed as wages when the options are granted or exercised, but they can have alternative minimum tax consequences. Incentive stock options are only taxed when sold under IRC Section 522. Nonqualified stock options, by contrast, are taxed as ordinary income upon their exercise because they are considered to be additional wages. In any event, while the options are accruing there are no tax consequences to the employee. However, under IRC Section 83, the taxpayer spouse can elect to recognize income earlier, which then makes future appreciation eligible for lower capital gain rates as long as certain holding period requirements are met. As with other investments, losses are limited.

Formerly, stock options were always taxed to the employee spouse (the person who earned it) based on the assignment of income doctrine under IRC Section 1041. However, Revenue Ruling 2002-22 now provides that statutory stock options and nonqualified deferred compensation are considered property subject to IRC Section 1041. Thus, the transferee spouse is taxed at ordinary income tax rates when he or she exercises the options and the employee spouse is not taxed.

The problem with stock options is that they are not easy to value. One reason is because of future market fluctuations. Second, unlike wages, where you receive a W-2 and know exactly how much you have earned during the year, stock options are not as clear-cut. To make matters worse, courts also recognize that options can be granted for past or future service and, as such, a value will need to be assigned during the appropriate time period. If there is for the possibility of a huge valuation and income potential being assigned to the stock option, some ex-spouses will tell their employer to hold off on granting them options until the pending divorce is final. Good attorneys will know how to argue either side. As a general rule, it is preferable not to transfer stock options but rather to agree to distribute net after-tax proceeds after the stock is sold. This will result in a true fair market value being realized without speculation as to future performance of the stock.

Stock options are not always black-and-white. There is a huge gray component present. For example, if an option is awarded to you while you and your ex have been separated but it relates to past performance (which is when you were married), is it considered marital property? What if the marriage ends before the options vest? That's also a tough question to answer. I don't know. That's why you need special valuation people to assist you in this area. You'll definitely need to determine when the services were performed to help make that call.

Many attorneys and judges do not know how to value these options. You definitely want to call in an expert to determine the value. You can even have the stock options appraised by an independent appraiser.

Rattiner's Planning Tips

1. Common law deals with equitable distribution, and equitable does not necessarily mean equal. Once common law, always common law.
2. Community property deals with equal distribution of all property in the marriage stemming from assets and income and also all of the debt. Once community property, always community property.

3. There are nine community property states, all following different versions of the community property laws. There is no one size fits all.

4. An exception exists to planning tip 1 if you move from a common law state to a quasi–community property state. In that instance, the property now becomes community property under the rules of the state to which you moved. There are five quasi–community property states.

5. Separate property brought into the marriage, or gifts and inheritances received during the marriage by one spouse, will remain as separate property as long as none of the property is commingled.

6. There are several states that enforce common law marriages. For all practical purposes, it is viewed as being legally married without the piece of paper.

7. Closely held business owners involved in a divorce are usually in a lose-lose situation. If the business is considered to be a marital asset, not only will they have to give up half the value of the business counted as an asset against them, but the future income stream of the entire business gets factored into the equation, resulting in what is commonly called double-dipping.

8. The capitalized earnings method is probably the one most used for valuing professional practices.

9. Make sure you interview your business valuator initially with your attorney present so you can maintain a confidentiality privilege when talking with the business valuator. Without the attorney's presence you will not have that right.

10. Some states do not consider a professional practice a marital asset while others do. Since it is a huge asset, you'll need to research it. See the supplied listing of states that do.

11. Regulation 1.1041-2 permits the spouses to decide who has to report the constructive dividend or capital gains created by the stock redemption.

12. When a spouse liquidates his or her partnership interest, rules of IRC Section 736 apply.

13. Stock options are a difficult type of compensation to value because they are based on many contingencies and it is difficult

to put forth a true value. Appraisers and business experts should get involved in the valuation.

14. Do not forget to include the tax aspects, vesting requirements, and how and when the stock option is valued in determining a bottom-line number. In most instances, as a general rule, it is preferable not to transfer stock options but to agree to distribute net after-tax proceeds after the stock is sold. This will result in a true fair market value being realized without speculation as to future performance of the stock.

9

Redesigning Your Personal
Financial Plan after the Divorce

Once you have completed the divorce process, you will need to regroup. This means that you will need to take a new accounting of where you are financially. Rest assured, you will have no clue where you stand financially when the divorce is finally over, and for good reason. Unforeseen expenses, receiving less than you anticipated, paying off the costs from the divorce, taking on additional responsibilities, planning for new events, and other issues will take most of your money. That is just the way it is.

It is important to take care of these financial matters as soon as possible since most of these issues were probably overlooked during the divorce process. Of even greater significance is the fact that you are somewhat limited (you have an absolutely finite ceiling) as to what you can do going forward since it is all based on future assets and income you either received or were left with at the conclusion of the divorce.

Now reflect for a second. When going through the divorce process, you just try to get by financially. Even though you may have set amounts you pay for bills or support each month, you have legal fees and other legal expenses, perhaps counseling fees, and other expenses you were not counting on having thrown at you constantly. There is no real game plan in place and it was ad hoc living all the way. However, keep in mind that your financial situation going forward will be radically different than what you experienced beforehand. If you do the simple math, it makes sense. Previously there was one household to support; now there are two, and most likely both of you will want to maintain the same quality of lifestyle going forward, even though this may not be at all realistic, so you are not going to be reasonable about the reality of that taking place.

Now you will have to work with what is left and what is anticipated, and begin anew. The only way you will make it work is through the redesign or creation of a new personal financial plan. There is no time like the present to start developing a financial plan. Some readers may never have completed a financial plan; others will need only to modify or tweak their existing plan. One thing is for sure, however: You will definitely need to revisit the issue.

The personal financial plan presents a system that will help take you from where you are now, point A, toward your destination, which is point B. This plan provides the road map, or essentially the blueprint, for your financial success. Too many people I have interviewed told me that they had an ad hoc approach with the money they received from the divorce and now it is running out or, in some cases, has already run out. Development of a plan will give you the guidance you need to take the shortest and most efficient road to get to where you are going. A competent CFP, CPA, or financial adviser can help get you on track. See Exhibit 9.1 for a listing of questions to use when interviewing for a qualified financial planner.

If you are the one paying money to your ex, you will need to learn to adjust. If you are the recipient of money, whether it involves future monthly payments or assets that you can use to your benefit, you may have been given more money than you have ever dreamed of having or are used to spending and accounting for. This planning phase involves learning how to use your money, which is not as easy as it sounds. Again, to accomplish these goals, you will need to redesign your personal financial plan.

Think about it. It may be no different than winning the lottery for some people. To give you an idea, lottery winners tend to go bankrupt three and a half years after winning the lottery, regardless of the amount they won. I had a former NBA player in one of my financial planning classes in Ohio who told me that the average NBA player goes bankrupt six years after he retires—again, regardless of the millions he may have made playing basketball. And, just like with

1. Are you a Certified Financial Planner, CPA, or financial adviser with a background in personal financial planning?

2. Do you have a divorce practice specialty?

3. Do you have a team of professionals with whom you work, such as insurance agents, stockbrokers, CPAs, retirement plan specialists, and attorneys?

4. Do you keep up with all the continuing education requirements that are necessary to keep your licenses active?

5. Can you provide me with a list of client referrals?

6. What is your approach to investing and conserving money?

7. How are you compensated? Is it fee based, hourly, or on commission? Does receiving commissions impair your objectivity or independence?

8. What is your way of communicating with your clients? Is it by e-mail, phone, fax, or some other method?

9. Where do you get your information for making financial recommendations?

10. Are there any judgments filed against you? Has anybody ever tried to sue you? Have you ever been to arbitration? Have you lost any professional licenses or certifications?

Exhibit 9.1   Questions to Ask When Selecting Your Personal Financial Adviser

any newly divorced person who comes into a huge sum of money, if you don't learn how to manage it well, you will be in for a long and ugly haul.

The Personal Financial Process

In this chapter, I describe the financial planning process you need to complete to be successful. It starts with an executive summary of what you should be doing going forward and then gets into the most important technical aspects (disciplines) of developing your personal financial plan.

At the end of this chapter you will find checklists arranged by technical discipline to guide you in what you need to look for when redesigning your personal financial plan. You will be able to use these as an action list of things you need to work on, not just now but well into your future, in making a smooth transition to the post-divorce world.

The New and Improved Game of Life: Executive Summary

As an overview for what is to come, here are some general thoughts on how to plan for the game of life. Life events, as they occur, will awaken you and help guide you toward the realization of your goals and objectives. Many of these financial uncertainties become realities at some point during your lifetime. In fact, you will typically experience at least eight special situations during your lifetime. Some tend to be welcome occurrences, while others inflict panic.

Planning for the Seasons of Life

Here are several basic pointers summarizing the entire financial planning world in only a few pages. The detail follows thereafter.

Start with a budget. Be careful about the pitfalls of excessive credit card spending because it may prevent you from jump-starting your new financial life. Continue paying all your loans. Surplus funds should be invested into a regular savings program. Savings should be 10 percent of gross income. You should anticipate life contingencies by establishing an emergency fund, which should consist of six months' worth of living expenses. Design an investment portfolio with properly diversified mutual funds. Do not skimp on needed health insurance, car, home, or umbrella insurance, or renter's insurance policies, if applicable.

As a newly single person, you probably have no one to count on financially other than yourself. You need to create your own safety net for the long term. Analyze your insurance policies. Health and disability are primary. Life insurance may not be needed if you no longer have any dependents. In case of illness or incompetence, a health care proxy will assist others in making decisions for you, and a durable power of attorney or a revocable living trust will help in case you are unable to run your own affairs. Consider choosing an institution, such as a bank or trust company, to share the responsibility with a friend or relative. A will may become necessary, if for nothing else than to name a guardian for your children. Investment planning becomes more crucial because there is no one else to help pick up the loss of income. This poses perhaps the greatest challenge for single individuals.

Start a savings plan. This includes contributing to retirement accounts, flexible spending accounts, and creating an investment portfolio. The approximate cost and date of retirement can be estimated, affording you plenty of time to get ready. Since life is unpredictable, it is necessary to seek risk protection. Auto, health, and disability insurance should be purchased. If you have not already done so, you should also change the beneficiaries of all pension plans, IRAs, annuities, and living trusts.

If you are buying a home, a significant amount of debt is incurred since this will probably continue to be your biggest purchase. Spend time getting to know the neighborhood. Comparison-shop for mortgage deals. Purchase homeowner's insurance with replacement cost for both dwelling and contents and umbrella insurance to protect the homeowner in the event of future liability claims.

If you plan on restarting a family, you should consider purchasing life insurance. The financial impact on your family upon premature death can be overwhelming. If you remarry or plan to have additional children, revise your will and begin thinking about college funding. College costs have been increasing at a higher rate than inflation. Parents and college-bound children need to learn about new possibilities for college funds and become acquainted with the financial aid process.

If you have young children, a savings program for college is crucial, even if the amount put away each year cannot actually meet projected college costs. If you have children closer to college age, evaluate your current financial position in order to assess what resources, if any, might be used to fund college costs. When the children are young, estimate the amount of money needed to pay tuition bills and dates when these bills will arrive.

If your children have graduated from college and are out of the house, your prime earning years are probably approaching. If you have not already done so, saving for retirement should become a priority and you should set up an automatic deduction from salary. Maximize contributions to 401(k) plans, 403(b) plans, Keogh plans, and other types of deferred savings vehicles. You can always do an IRA if you have earned income or are receiving alimony.

You may elect to downgrade your house to a smaller residence. If you lived in the house for at least two of the past five years, you can exclude up to $250,000 if you are single or up to $500,000 if you remarry. If you lived in the house for less time than that, and had to move for what is deemed an unforeseen circumstance, then you may be able to prorate that gain. Have your CPA, CFP, or financial adviser help you with those calculations if applicable. However, do not be too quick to sell. More and more children are moving in with their parents after graduating college.

You need to be very focused during the several years before you approach retirement. Continue with a similar investment strategy to the one you began years before. Do not become too conservative. Do not completely pull out of equities and go into fixed income. Fixed income accounts do not perform as well as equities over the long haul, because of early retirement trends and increased longevity. Nowadays, it is possible that retirement could total one-third of a person's lifetime. Preserving capital is more important than maximizing return. You should consider formulating an estate plan and have an attorney review all legal documents to ensure that they are in accordance with your goals. Providing effectively for survivors means that you must plan as if you were going to die tomorrow, however unlikely that may be.

Planning for Life's Uncertainties

If you are terminated from your job, extreme worry and preoccupation may result. You probably cannot predict how long you will remain unemployed. The main problem will probably be how long you can stretch unemployment income to pay living expenses during unemployment. This can be calculated through the use of a budget.

Assume that you will remain unemployed between six and nine months and apply for unemployment benefits. If a layoff is imminent, seek a severance package and secure good references. One thing people tend to do is omit or cancel what they consider to be unnecessary items to carry and pay for during a prolonged work stoppage. Be careful. Do not forget to continue your insurance coverage. Your insurance needs never go away, so do not make that one of the first items to go.

To counter the immediate urge to sell off investments to foot the bills, develop a cash flow analysis that provides you with a reasonable idea of how long existing funds will last. This approach will enable you to be calm and orderly when contemplating necessary financial decisions. If the company offers you either a lump sum or a continuation of salary, check the facts. Generally, a lump sum will be better but not always. Before you decide, see if salary continuation will prolong benefits, such as health insurance and funding of a retirement plan. If so, salary continuation will probably be a better deal.

If you get married after your divorce, the question becomes how can you provide for your new spouse and protect the children of your previous marriage? Look at both family's resources and the demands for each. Inquire about when the money will be spent. Take a long-term view. Once it is determined what things need to be paid for, you should start investing in order to meet those goals.

If, in fact, you want the children from a prior marriage to get the bulk of your estate, you can set up a qualified terminal interest property (QTIP) trust for the benefit of the new spouse. This gives your spouse access to all income for life, but upon the spouse's death, the assets will pass on to your children from the prior marriage. If the children are close to the same age as your new spouse, give a portion of the estate to your children at death, with the rest going into a QTIP.

If your new spouse dies first, your financial plan may need revisiting. Take it slowly. Gather important documents, such as the death certificate, insurance policies, and financial account information. With a complex estate your attorney should be contacted. Will probate documents and changes of titles and ownership will need to be filed. Resources must be identified to settle the estate.

If the decedent spouse had a life insurance policy, a choice must be made by the beneficiary as to the disposition of the proceeds. Lump-sum settlements, fixed payments, and annuities are three ways to receive these payments. Do not get pressured into spending the insurance proceeds immediately. Many smooth-talking salespeople will try to get you to buy an annuity with the insurance death benefits or other options that may not be appropriate for your situation.

Depending on your age and situation, you may want to consider taking a lump sum and parking it in Treasuries or cash for six months until you get through emotional and financial hurdles. Credit accounts should be reviewed to ensure either that outstanding debts from the deceased spouse are paid off, if possible, or that as the surviving spouse you do not borrow more than you should. Assess the composition of your assets, such as investment portfolios, as well as the capability of surviving family members to manage these investments. Stability of income may be something of concern to you. However, don't get too conservative with the remaining investments. The period of widowhood could last many years.

Ownership designations on invested assets and disposition of closely held business interests must also be evaluated, as well as whether to utilize the marital deduction, any unused unified credit, or disclaim the property. A federal estate tax return may need to be filed if the estate is over the threshold for passing assets to heirs estate tax–free. State tax laws vary. See a CPA or other qualified tax professional to help you sort through the potential tax ramifications for your state.

Your income tax filing status will change to widow or widower. However, in the current year, as a surviving spouse, you may still file a tax return as married filing jointly and you can still claim a dependency exemption for your deceased spouse. If you, as surviving spouse, have children who qualify as dependents, then your home (as surviving spouse) is your principal residence. If you, as the survivor, provide over half the cost of maintaining your household where your children still live with you, and you have not remarried, then you will be allowed to file a joint return as a surviving spouse for two years after the date of death of your spouse. Retirement projections will have to be revised to account for the changed circumstances.

The most important part of any financial plan involves constant monitoring of life events. It is easy to get off track. Make sure you are logical and rational in your future actions. The bottom line is that you need to make sure that you stay the course.

Take a moment to answer the questions in Exhibit 9.2 to ensure that you have begun planning appropriately. Any "no" or "not sure" answers can point to potential problems you may wish to investigate. If you answer "no" or "not sure" to two or more of these questions, you should discuss them with your CFP or CPA.

Designing the Personal Financial Plan

Now that I have outlined what you need to be concerned about in one quick and easy executive summary lesson, let's get ready to plan! This is where you will begin to develop a financial plan.

Monthly Income and Expenses

1. Do you use a budget?   Yes   No   Not sure

2. Do you have any financial problems that   Yes   No   Not sure
   require immediate attention?

Retirement

1. Are you saving for retirement?   Yes   No   Not sure

2. Do you know what rate of return you need to   Yes   No   Not sure
   maintain your lifestyle and keep ahead of infla-
   tion and taxes?

Children's Education

1. Have you planned for this expense?   Yes   No   Not sure

2. Is the ownership of your education savings   Yes   No   Not sure
   designed to reduce taxes?

Your investments

1. Are they well diversified?   Yes   No   Not sure

2. Are you satisfied with their performance?   Yes   No   Not sure

Risk and Insurance

1. Will your insurance cover your family's needs in Yes   No   Not sure
   the event of death or disability?

2. Do you have an umbrella liability policy?   Yes   No   Not sure

Estate Planning

1. Are your wills current?   Yes   No   Not sure

2. Is your estate designed to minimize taxes and   Yes   No   Not sure
   fees?

Exhibit 9.2   Planning for the Game of Life: A Quick Evaluation

As stated earlier, a personal financial plan provides the financial road map for this long and strenuous journey. The following are the six steps in the financial planning process:

1. *Gather* all necessary data.
2. Set appropriate *objectives.*
3. *Process* all the information into meaningful financial statements.
4. *Develop* recommendations.
5. *Implement* those recommendations.
6. *Monitor* your situation annually.

Gather All Necessary Data

There are two types of data that should be gathered. We will call them *quantitative* and *qualitative* data. Quantitative data consists of the hard facts that you see when reviewing your financial statements and much more. Examples of quantitative information include your last three years of tax returns (because you can go back and amend up to three years of tax returns), your estate planning documents (including wills, deeds, trust documents, living wills, powers of attorneys, etc.), your before-tax information (retirement plans and employee benefit information), your after-tax investments (such as dollar cost averaging and other routine or monthly investments), your charitable gifting strategies, your education accounts, your business documents (including buy-sell agreements and other instruments if you have partners), and other documents from which amounts can be pulled.

Remember, the more information you accumulate, the better! This will ensure that you have taken into account as much critical information as possible. You can never have too much information. The more information you gather, the more representative your plan will be of what you own. Even when in doubt as to its usefulness, just pile it with all the other stuff you have gathered and then review it.

Set Appropriate Objectives

There is a clear distinction between goals and objectives. Goals are open-ended, broad statements. Goals, by themselves, will not do you any good. For example, you may have a goal that you want to be rich! The problem with that goal is how do you define rich? Rich can mean different things to different people. Furthermore, it may have or not have a monetary value. Is your goal to retire at age 60 on $2 million or retire at age 55 on $200,000 of income per year?

Objectives are both definite and measurable. There is a definite time frame and dollar amount tied to each objective. You will learn that each objective will have at least one distinct investment tied to it. Therefore, some objectives with shorter time frames may have an entirely different investment philosophy than other objectives which have a longer time horizon.

Prioritize your objectives. List them in order of importance to you. You will quickly see that you have many objectives and limited resources to achieve all those objectives. And because you will not be able to achieve all the objectives you have listed, make your resources count! Work your way down the list so the ones at the top are the ones you can do really well, and then be surprised if you can ultimately achieve the objectives you have identified which are lower on the list.

Process All the Information into Meaningful Personal Financial Statements

Now that you have gathered all of the necessary data and prioritized your objectives, you need to take that information and incorporate it into meaningful personal financial statements. The statements you should develop which will tie all your financial information together are the balance sheet and the cash flow statement. These statements show an individual's financial well-being.

The Balance Sheet.   A balance sheet represents a financial snapshot in time. It determines your net worth by showing all your assets and liabilities as of today. *Assets* are things you own and *liabilities* are amounts you owe. Assets are recorded at their fair market value (what they are worth today, not what you paid for them). Liabilities are the face amount of the balance owed (the current amount due, which is equal to the difference between the original loan and what has been paid off against the loan). Net worth is the amount of excess equity you own and is determined by subtracting your liabilities from your assets.

When preparing these statements, try to be as realistic as you can. Value your assets at what you would likely get if you were to sell these assets today. All too often, people tend to overvalue what their assets are really worth. Liabilities are not an issue because they are simply the amount owed as of a certain valuation date. Also beware that there may be income tax consequences when you do finally sell these assets at their appreciated value.

Once an up-to-date personal balance sheet has been prepared, you can make plans to increase your net worth. If you are new to your career, do not be discouraged if your numbers are not where you want them to be, such as a low net worth or even a negative one! The important thing is to use your financial intelligence to improve upon it. Periodically checking your net worth helps determine the progress you have made in the financial planning process.

The Cash Flow Statement.   The cash flow statement represents all the inflows and outflows of cash which occurred during stated intervals. They can be computed annually, semiannually, quarterly, monthly, or even weekly. If you pay all your bills in full, then your inflows will always equal your outflows. If you leave balances on your credit cards, then your outflows will exceed your inflows. This is the true gauge of how much money you are saving. The objective here is to minimize your expenses against your income so you can use the difference to fund the specific stated objectives that you identified and prioritized earlier.

Inflows represent all income items, such as wages, self-employment income, interest, dividends, capital gains, rents, royalties, alimony, and other forms of income. Outflows can be broken down into two categories. *Fixed* outflows are recurring expenses that are fixed in amount and payable monthly or at definitive periods. These include things such as mortgage payments, taxes, insurance payments, and other regular expenses. *Variable* or *discretionary* expenses are things that you can control and try to minimize to improve savings. These expenses include items such as vacations, entertainment, dining out, and so forth. Remember, expenses represent payments, and balance sheet liabilities represent balances owed.

Develop Recommendations

Now that you have reviewed your personal financial statements and determined your available resources, you can match these resources against your stated prioritized objectives.

Recommendations must be specific. Like objectives, they must be definite and measurable. That means a dollar amount and time frame must accompany each. Recommendations must represent specific action steps to pursue. Categorize these steps by discipline. For example, separate your recommendations into the following basic categories. If you have other categories as determined by your objectives, then add those as well.

- Cash flow and budgeting.
- Insurance.
- Investments.
- College education.
- Income tax.
- Retirement and employee benefits.
- Estate.
- Charitable giving.

Implement Those Recommendations

This is your action or to-do list. State what the specific recommendations are, again listing them by category. You may wish to seek advice on these recommendations if you are new to developing and implementing a financial plan. Make a list of as many recommendations as are applicable, even though you may not be able to accomplish all of them by virtue of not having sufficient resources to implement them.

Prioritize these within each category by date so you take care of the most important ones first. Then list the person responsible to make it happen. Will it be you, the attorney (estate planning), the CPA (for income tax planning), the insurance broker (insurance planning), the investment/stock broker (investment planning), the financial planner (for any of the items listed), or someone else?

The importance of the implementation list is to make sure those things identified during the recommendation stage do in fact happen. Setting up the road map will ensure that they do. These moves are critical because they will help move you along the journey from point A to point B.

Monitor Your Situation Annually

Things change! Not only can your personal situation change (as you have well experienced), but the economic conditions in which the plan was created may change as well. The purpose of the personal financial plan is to ensure that you stay the course. When things move off the road map for whatever reason, the monitoring process ensures that you get back on track as quickly and easily as possible.

If you have previously devised a personal financial plan, you can see that at that point in time, the plan you chose was representative of the things that were important to you then, and that things have changed since that time. For example, after your financial plan was first implemented, you may have gotten married, had children, been divorced, moved to the suburbs, adopted a dog, bought a station wagon, and so forth. You see where this is going. None of those things were relevant at the time the plan was initially established, so the financial plan needs to be monitored and adjusted, if necessary, to fit your current circumstances. If this is your first experience developing a financial plan, I can assure you that you will look back a year from now and realize that life happens and things change, especially within the first several months after a divorce.

Another factor that can play a major role in your financial plan is the larger economic scenario. Imagine if you were creating your first plan in the late 1970s. Much was going on then: We had double-digit inflation, double-digit interest rates, a poor stock market, and disco! If you adopted a plan that included inflation numbers at 12 percent, when historically they have averaged 3.1 percent over the past 80 years, your numbers would be drastically different than when creating a plan now. And even though minimal change may be required when the economy falters, you need to design a plan that weathers the course in all financial situations.

Life Cycle Analysis

Based on the discussion of the personal financial process that you need to follow very closely, and where you want to end up, the following chart shows you what you should be doing at the different stages of your life.

Ages 20–29 and 30–39

- Have an emergency fund equal to six months of gross living expenses.
- Make sure you always have adequate and continuous

coverage of life, disability, health, homeowner's, automobile, and umbrella insurance.

- If moving between jobs, be careful of short-changing your pension benefits or other deferred compensation arrangements.
- Roll over any retirement benefits into an IRA or to your next 401(k).
- Minimize your income tax bite by maxing out your deductions.
- Contribute regularly to your 401(k) and/or IRA, and any other retirement fund.
- Purchase a home with a 15-year mortgage so that by the time you retire, your housing costs will be under control.
- Write a will.
- Discuss retirement plan benefits with your human resource personnel.

Ages 40–49

- Contribute regularly to your 401(k) and/or IRA, and any other retirement fund.
- Check your Social Security statement annually to ensure that all your wages have been credited correctly. If not, contact the Social Security Administration (SSA) immediately.
- Analyze personal assets, and work out a plan for funding an adequate retirement income.
- Actively manage your IRA and other retirement funds with appropriate emphasis on capital gains–oriented investments.
- Review your will every three years or when moving to another state. Review it with an experienced attorney.

Ages 50–59

- Contribute regularly to your 401(k) and/or IRA, and any other retirement fund.
- Check your Social Security statement annually to ensure that all your wages have been credited correctly. If not, contact the SSA immediately.
- Analyze personal assets, and work out a plan for funding an adequate retirement income.
- Review your retirement income and expense projections, taking inflation into consideration.
- Confirm the beneficiary designations on life insurance policies, annuities, and retirement plans.
- Join the American Association of Retired Persons (AARP).

- Review your will every three years or when moving to another state. Review it with an experienced attorney.

Ages 60-64

- Discuss early retirement offers with a financial planner.
- Collect the documents necessary to process Social Security benefits.
- Determine whether it makes sense to sell your primary residence, taking the tax consequences into consideration.
- Prepare detailed cash flow projections from estimated year of retirement until age 90, taking inflation into consideration.
- Practice living for a month or two under your new retirement income amount.
- Determine the status and duration of ongoing loans and mortgage commitments.
- Determine which activities will keep you active during retirement.
- Consider different retirement locations.
- Inquire about possible retirement entitlements from previous employers.
- Consider long-term care insurance.

Ages 65 and Up

- Live and enjoy life!
- Take care of your health.
- Be active, if health permits.

The Personal Financial Planning Disciplines

When going through the personal financial planning disciplines, one thing is clear: It all begins with cash flow. You need to have a good accounting of your income and expenses before you can move through the process.

Cash Flow Management: It All Starts Here

Cash flow management helps those spouses who live from paycheck to paycheck or who haven't set long-term goals for themselves. What I have found is that spouses accept this approach and practice it as a way of life! Not good!

The lifestyle you choose should be based on available cash and not credit. If you make $50,000 per year, then you should spend less than that and keep the balance for savings. If you make $100,000, the same principle applies. That remaining balance will be the key to meeting your long-term objectives.

Many people underestimate the importance of cash flow management. Effective cash flow management has two primary objectives. The first is to manage income and expenses in order to establish and maintain a reserve of cash or near-cash equivalents to meet unanticipated or emergency needs, including the expenses of sudden illness, injury, or death, or as a cushion for possible loss of employment. The second is to create and maintain a systematic surplus of cash (reserve) directed toward specific types of investments for capital accumulation. Both of these objectives are integral and essential parts of the personal financial planning process and are a prerequisite to the development of a personal financial plan. If you don't focus on these areas, you will find it more difficult to accomplish your goals.

The premise of financial planning is built on cash flow management. It is through this monthly surplus of funds that you can accomplish several financial goals. This surplus of funds will ensure that you have enough cash and other liquid assets to conduct ongoing family operations; maintain an adequate emergency fund to meet unforeseen contingencies; minimize unproductive assets; prevent illiquidity from becoming a problem; and have enough money to earmark toward children's education, retirement, and various long-term goals and objectives.

Cash flow management can help you achieve future financial independence. Achievement of this goal requires regular growth of your family's personal net worth. This is accomplished primarily by adding regularly to savings and investment assets out of current net cash flow. If net cash flow is negative or zero instead of positive, net worth will decline or remain constant and you will slip further away from your goals. If this occurs, you may wish to develop a budget.

The last step in analyzing cash flow is the construction of a cash flow statement. The cash flow statement shows the net change in inflows and outflows over time as determined by your receipts and disbursements. Expenses and income are condensed into general categories for comparison purposes. Examples of inflows on the cash flow statement include salary or self-employment income, interest, dividends, net rental income, and income tax refunds. Outflows include housing, food, clothing, transportation, insurance, taxes, savings, and investments. Analyzing a cash flow statement will help you better understand your spending habits over time as well as identify and achieve your goals. The cash flow statement is in contrast to a balance sheet, which provides you with a snapshot or picture at a given point in time and should be updated annually.

Use the form in Exhibit 9.3 to calculate your cash flow.

	Monthly	*Annually*
Income		
Your net (take-home) pay		
Your spouse's net (take-home) pay		
Investment income (dividends, interest, capital gains)		
Other income (i.e., rent, royalties, Social Security)		
Total Income		
Expenses		
Fixed Expenses—Housing		
Rent/mortgage		
Taxes (property)		
Gas/electricity		
Fuel (home heating)		
Water/garbage/sewer		
Telephone		
Household and yard maintenance		
Other		
Fixed Expenses—Grocery		
Groceries (food and nonfood)		
Meals away from home		
Other		

Exhibit 9.3   Cash Flow Statement

	Monthly	Annually
Fixed Expenses—Car		
Car 1 payment		
Car 2 payment		
Fuel		
Maintenance/repairs		
License(s)		
Carpool/parking		
Other		
Fixed Expenses—Personal		
Family purchases		
Uniforms/work gear		
Dry cleaning/laundry		
Toiletries		
Haircuts/perms		
Other		
Fixed Expenses—Medical		
Medications		
Medical		
Dental		
Optical		
Other		
Fixed Expenses—Insurance		
Home/property		
Auto		
Medical		
Life		
Disability		
Other		

Exhibit 9.3   (Continued)

	Monthly	Annually
Discretionary Expenses		
Eating out		
Memberships		
Vacation/travel		
Entertainment		
Dependent (child) care		
Alimony		
Child support		
Holiday gifts		
Charitable contributions		
Education/school expenses		
Crafts/hobbies		
Dues (union/professional/other)		
Newspaper		
Pets (vet, medications, etc.)		
Allowances		
Other		
Savings		
Savings account/bonds		
Investments		
IRA/pension plan		
Other		
Debts		
Miscellaneous		
Total Expenses from Columns 1 and 2		
Subtract Expenses from Income		
Surplus (deficit)		

Exhibit 9.3   **(Continued)**

Tips for Improving Your Cash Flow.   The following are some tips you can use to improve your cash flow:

1. *Organize yourself better.* Try to keep your records organized, labeled, and in the same location. Purchase a file cabinet and keep all your records in it. Organize it in alphabetical order or categorize by group. Develop a system that makes it easier for you to locate these documents when needed.

2. *Be dedicated.* Dedicate yourself to tracking your cash flow at least annually. In the beginning, you may do it more frequently than what ultimately ends up being your routine, since it will be a new experience for you and will probably take you a little longer. You will also realize things about yourself and your money habits that you never knew before. Once you work out the kinks, you can operate a very efficient strategy for budgeting and ultimately for cash flow management.

3. *Leave home with less cash.* If you don't have the money with you to spend, you won't spend it. You won't be tempted and you'll show greater fiscal restraint.

4. *Kill the credit cards.* Everyone should have a credit card or two for emergencies. Don't rely on them as a crutch or to get you through until you receive your next paycheck—or, worse yet, for an impulse purchase. Interest rates on credit cards are exorbitant. What happens is that when you purchase too much, you tend to pay the minimum balance and make no progress on paying the debt off, so the debt lingers for a very long time.

5. *Give yourself and family members weekly spending money—an allowance.* If all family members spend what they have and no more, future problems can be avoided. Perhaps provide an incentive such as an award to the family member who stays within the budgeted amounts the best.

6. *Make saving a priority expense.* Savings should come before most other expenses. Unfortunately, certain expenses, like the mortgage, rent, insurance, and taxes, cannot be avoided. But try to make savings the next big expenditure. As previously stated, you need savings in order to fund your ultimate long-term objectives.

7. *Refinance your debt during times of lower interest rates.* It may sometimes make sense (not always) to refinance your home

debt, car debt, student loan debt, credit card debt, or other outstanding debt, especially when interest rates have been too high. Refinancing this debt can result in lower monthly payments, thus freeing up money for you to save for long-term objectives.

8. *Give yourself incentives for a job well done.* We keep talking about minimizing expenses to help fund long-term objectives. But this requires hard work. And anytime hard work is involved, you should be rewarded for achieving success. Set realistic objectives, try to come in under your budgeted numbers, and treat yourself to a little bit (not a lot) of the savings as an added incentive. You'll still end up spending less and enjoy some treats not originally earmarked.

Budgeting: There's No Time Like the Present

Budgeting is a time-driven process whereby you analyze the way in which you are currently spending money in order to make spending decisions that would be compatible with the achievement of your longer-term objectives. Income and expenses should be monitored in accordance with your specified plan (budget) to achieve short-term objectives that are in harmony with long-term objectives. Essentially, budgeting is a spending plan of action.

Successful budgeting requires you to stay in control over your actions. It results in a plan you direct for saving and spending household income. If you feel you're in control of your budget, then you'll be more likely to succeed.

To be successful at budgeting, you need to keep detailed records for a set period, like a month or a year, to see where your money is going. The process is tedious and time consuming, but very necessary. The bright side is that by keeping these records religiously, the potential for realization of long-term objectives and financial security is increased significantly.

When establishing your budget, keep the following purposes in mind:

- Set a forecasted amount for each revenue and expense item.
- Identify variances between actual and budgeted numbers.
- Define possible problems in spending patterns.
- Identify opportunities to overcome these problems.
- Realistically plan to improve your spending patterns.

Your budget should carefully balance the various needs of all your family members. Perhaps setting up a personal allowance for each family member can help you accomplish this. When preparing your own budget reconciliation, remember to leave a comfortable margin for discrepancies in your budgeted numbers and for those unexpected expenses that were not even considered in the first place.

Consider the following tips when developing your budget:

- *Design a budget form that is suitable to you.* Budgets come in a variety of formats. Try the one provided with this book or modify it to better suit your needs. You can even use a computerized version through one of the many software vendors available. Some of these programs are integrated with other types of software, such as tax software.
- *Forecast your income.* The budget worksheet will help you identify various sources of income (see Exhibit 3.1 in Chapter 3). Be realistic in estimating your income, particular nonrecurring items (income that is not received on a regular basis). Categorize your income. Be conservative when you estimate— in other words, estimate income on the low side.
- *Summarize past expenses.* Past expenses need to be summarized before you can estimate what your future expenses will look like. Categorize these expenses. Take your time when doing this. Ways you can accomplish this include examining past checking account and credit card statements, and making a list of all cash expenses. Carry a notepad and pencil, and every time you make a purchase, record it. You'll be surprised at how quickly those expenditures add up. After analyzing these records, you may conclude that most of these purchases were indeed impulse purchases that you probably could have done without.
- *Estimate future expenses.* Now that you have forecasted income and examined past expenses, extend these numbers on a monthly basis and look forward 12 months. Again categorize these expenses. Your objective is to budget these future expenses so they don't exceed your income going forward. Your long-term solution will be to minimize your expenses and transfer the excess income amounts into savings. The main caution is to be aware of nonrecurring expenses (those that don't occur on a monthly basis). These can present a problem

when budgeting. Examples of these types of expenses include insurance premiums that are paid six months or a year in advance, IRA contributions, and vacations. Take a monthly average and factor these less frequent expenses into the budgeting process. Put this money away in advance and when these payments come due, just dip into the account that has been housing these future expenses.

Debt Management: A Difficult Task

Ex-spouses will often, after a divorce, use extensive amounts of credit to buy almost any conceivable combination of goods and services. The use of credit has become part of our lifestyle, enabling people to enjoy the use of items before they can pay for them outright. However, the use of credit requires committing future income to pay off the debt. As such, the management of debt is an integral part of financial planning that you need to understand.

Use of debt may be an important tool for you. Debt does have its advantages. For starters, it allows individuals to purchase products on sale, pay for several items together with one check, use goods and services even before they are paid for, and avoid laying out money for an employer or others, thus allowing you to be reimbursed before the bill comes through. Borrowing money also helps establish good credit and more favorable terms and rates. Debt can also be used to purchase an item now with the knowledge that you will be receiving a check at a later date to cover those expenses. In general, debt is best used for large purchases, such as a mortgage for home ownership, where it would be difficult for you to pull together enough cash to purchase the item outright. That is logical and may make sense over the long run.

However, debt does have its disadvantages. Entering into debt (1) requires the payment of interest, which increases the cost of obtaining the item; and (2) entails periodic repayment of principal, which limits the availability of funds for other consumption and savings. Therefore, consumer debt should be avoided as much as possible.

This is particularly true if you are unable to control spending when consumer debt is readily available. In addition, while mortgage interest is deductible for income tax purposes, interest on consumer debt is not. Therefore, any financial benefit of carrying balances on credit cards or financing smaller purchases, such as automobiles, has been reduced. Also, the interest rate you'll pay will be significantly higher than debt secured against your home. Although some situations will require the use of consumer credit for the individual to obtain the needed item or service, consumer credit generally should be used for short-term convenience only.

As a rule of thumb, consumer debt repayments (excluding mortgage payments) should be kept below 20 percent of take-home pay. Although this 20 percent guideline does not include mortgage or rent payments, it does include all credit card payments as well as auto, personal, and student loans. If these debt repayments represent 20 percent or more of take-home pay, the debtor is probably stretched to the limit. Debt repayments should be reduced to no more than 15 percent of take-home pay.

Loan officers often use the following rules of thumb in assessing whether a home mortgage will be offered to a prospective borrower.

- Monthly housing costs (including principal, interest, taxes, fees, and insurance) should be no more than 28 percent of the prospective borrower's gross income.
- Total monthly payment on all debts should be no more than 36 percent of gross monthly income. According to the underwriting guidelines for the Federal National Mortgage Association (Fannie Mae), this includes:
  - Monthly housing expense (including taxes and interest).
  - Monthly payments on installment/revolving credit.
  - Monthly mortgage payments on non-income-producing property.
  - Monthly alimony, child support, or maintenance payments.

And nowadays, with the economy nearly in shambles and credit card companies toughening up their borrowing requirements, your debt should be lower than these recommended ratios. Really, the best way to approach this is to determine what your comfort level is with respect to debt and ensure that you have a sufficient amount of money left over to save for your long-term objectives.

Credit Costs and Regulation.   Do you really know what credit costs? You'd better. There is no such thing as free or cheap credit. Our standing rule is that if it sounds too good to be true, then it is.

Know what you are paying ahead of time. Shop around for lenders. It's no different than shopping for a car, house, or other big-ticket item. Fortunately, there are laws that help in this area.

The Consumer Credit Protection (Truth in Lending) Act enables you to compare disclosure of credit terms so you can make meaningful comparisons of alternative sources of credit. This law is the cornerstone for Regulation Z of the Federal Reserve System and mandates that the finance charge and the annual percentage rate (APR) be given explicitly to the consumer. The finance charge is the actual dollar amount that the borrower must pay if the loan is granted. Costs such as interest and price differential (that is, the difference between the selling price of the item if it is sold on credit and the selling price if it is paid in cash) must be explained to the customer. Items such as points, discounts, service fees, carrying charges, and credit insurance must also be explained. The method used to calculate the APR must be disclosed as well.

The cost and payment requirements for different types of consumer credit vary widely. To manage your finances effectively, you must understand the terms of credit as well as its cost.

Debt Management Tips

- Don't go crazy. Debtors gone wild is not a fun exercise and will get you in the poorhouse. Work within the budget rules discussed earlier. Limit credit card purchases to what you can really afford to pay.
- Shop around. Shopping around will help you set your own terms as to what works and doesn't work for you. If the terms of one credit instrument are not acceptable to you, then look around and find a company whose terms do work for you.
- Review credit card bills. It happens—credit card companies do make errors.

Exhibit 9.4 is a survey to help you understand your basic debt solvency.

Insurance Planning Essentials: Protecting Your Financial Assets

Insurance is the most important financial discipline. You may not hear that from your investment broker, but it's true. And that's because if your insurance needs are not taken care of properly, then

1. Is more than 20 percent of your take-home salary used for credit card payments?	Yes	No
2. Are you charging more each month than you are paying off?	Yes	No
3. Have you received calls from credit card companies because of paying bills late?	Yes	No
4. Do you charge things impulsively?	Yes	No
5. Are you approaching the limit on your charge cards?	Yes	No
6. Do you find yourself paying only the minimum payments on your charge cards?	Yes	No
7. Have you defaulted on a mortgage or rent payment more than once?	Yes	No
8. Are you uncertain about how much money you owe?	Yes	No
9. Are you using the cash advance on one credit card to pay off another card?	Yes	No
10. Is the balance in your savings account shrinking?	Yes	No

Exhibit 9.4   Debt Solvency Worksheet: Ten Basic Questions

all your other financial disciplines might go awry. For example, if your house burns down and you have no homeowner's insurance, you will need to raise sufficient funds to find a place to live. You may have to borrow monies from investment accounts, like 401(k) plans, brokerage accounts, college funds or any other places you can obtain the necessary funds.

Insurance is kind of an ironic type of investment. Think about it: You are purchasing a product you hope you never have to use. In this situation, you may think you have wasted a significant amount of premium dollars. But the real risk is not having proper coverage.

Risk management issues are present throughout our lives and should be a key concern to everyone. Because people don't like talking about insurance, many smart people just ignore the risks inherent in everyday life, assuming that nothing bad will ever happen to them. The reality is bad things do happen to good people, and as the Boy Scouts say, you must always be prepared! Preparation comes through the purchase of adequate insurance coverage.

Have You Reviewed Your Insurance Needs Lately?   Even a well-thought-out financial plan can be ruined if you fail to take the proper precautions to protect your assets. That's where insurance planning comes in. Buying insurance may seem like putting money into something you'll never use. If you're lucky, this will indeed be the case. Unfortunately, you have no way of knowing if you're ever going to use that insurance. All you can do is prepare so that if an unfortunate event does occur, you and your family will be covered. Being properly and adequately insured can mean the difference between financial security and financial devastation.

What Types of Insurance Do You Need?   Many types of insurance are available today. However, not every kind of insurance is right for everyone. There are probably some types of insurance that you don't need at all. It's also possible that there are some types of insurance that you don't have but should consider. Once you've carefully reviewed your policies, you may find that you're over-insured in some areas and underinsured in others. You may want to call in your financial adviser to help you determine the types of insurance and the amounts that are right for you.

So what are some of the basic types of insurance you should consider? Life insurance, disability insurance, and personal liability insurance are three types of insurance that many people need; we discuss each of these in detail here. There are also a few other types of insurance that we touch on briefly.

Life Insurance.   What would happen to your family if you were to die today? Would your loved ones face undue financial hardship, or would they at least have the comfort of knowing their finances were in order? As difficult as it is to think about the possibility of a premature death, life insurance is one insurance need that should never be overlooked. In all likelihood, you already have life insurance. But when was the last time you reviewed or updated your policy to make sure it meets your current needs? Have you changed jobs, been promoted, or bought a new or a bigger home? Has your family expanded? Or have your children grown up and moved out on their own? Any one of these lifestyle changes may signal a need to update your insurance plan. Take the time to review your life insurance needs on a regular basis and make sure that you're adequately covered so that your family will be taken care of in the event that you die.

Assuming you already have some form of life insurance, what type of policy do you have? Is it a group policy through your employer or a professional association, or is it an individual policy that you purchased on your own? Depending on your age, overall health, and risk factors, either a group or an individual policy could offer you greater benefits. Premiums for group plans are calculated based on the average risk of the group; as a result, they can be helpful to higher-risk individuals who would otherwise pay high premiums. Conversely, healthy younger people with few risk factors can generally find better rates and benefits through an individual plan.

Calculating How Much Life Insurance You Really Need. Making sure you have enough life insurance is more important than the type of policy you buy. To determine how much life insurance you need, start by asking yourself the following questions:

- What expenses and debts do you have that would need to be paid upon your death (i.e., funeral expenses, probate costs, educational loans, installment debts, mortgage payments)?
- What is your current income? *Note:* Calculating insurance needs solely on rough rules of thumb (i.e., six or eight times your annual income) may be inappropriate in your situation.
- What is your new spouse's income? If your new spouse doesn't work, would he or she do so if you were to die?
- How many children do you have? Do they plan to attend college?
- Do you have investments, savings, or other assets that survivors could draw on? If these are sizeable, you may need little or no life insurance.
- Would your family receive any income from Social Security? Would that amount be reduced if your spouse was to work?

- Would your survivors need to maintain their current standard of living or could they live comfortably at a lower standard of living?
- Do you have an illiquid estate, such as real estate, that might require cash to pay estate taxes?
- What amount of tax can you or your survivors afford?

Once you've settled on your life insurance needs, you're then ready to select an appropriate life insurance policy.

Term versus Cash-Value Life Insurance. Term insurance offers pure protection. In other words, the policy is worth its face value. Term insurance is often a good choice for young people who want a lot of protection without the expensive premiums of investment-type products. The downside to term insurance is that the premiums become increasingly expensive as you age. However, these policies can sometimes be converted to cash-value policies at a later date.

Those who opt for a cash-value life insurance product usually have a set premium; you pay more in your younger years than you would for a term policy, but your premiums won't increase as you age. In fact, once you've accumulated enough cash value, a loan will be drawn against the cash value to cover the premium and prevent a lapse of the policy. These policies can also be used to help finance a college education, retirement, or long-term care.

Disability Insurance. One asset that most individuals can ill afford to lose is their income. Yet your chances of being disabled at some point during your working years are statistically quite high. In fact, you are four times as likely to be disabled for at least 90 days during your working years than you are to die before age 65. And if you are disabled for at least 90 days, the odds are good that you'll be disabled for at least five years. Despite these frightening statistics, you may have never stopped to think about what you would do if you were to become temporarily or permanently disabled or suffer from a prolonged illness. Such an event could have a devastating impact on your financial situation.

There are two types of disability insurance: short-term and long-term coverage. Short-term coverage generally lasts for 26 weeks or less; once short-term coverage expires, long-term coverage usually kicks in. As with life insurance, your employer probably offers some type of disability coverage. However, the amount offered through your workplace often is inadequate to meet your financial needs and the result would still cause financial hardship for you and your family.

Personal Liability Insurance. The primary purpose of liability insurance is to protect your assets if you're sued for damages as a result of negligence which results in harm or injury to another person. The other reason for liability insurance is to pay defense costs. You may not think this type of insurance applies to you. However, given our current lawsuit-prone society, most people should at least consider liability insurance. Do you serve on the board of directors of a private or public company? Do you own a rental property or a swimming pool or do you have dangerous animals? For these and many other reasons, you may need some type of liability insurance. In fact, as sad as it seems, you should have some form of liability coverage even if you're just coaching your child's baseball team.

So what types of liability insurance are available? There are three primary types of liability coverage: professional liability coverage, comprehensive personal liability coverage, and umbrella liability coverage. In many cases, your homeowner's or auto policies offer sufficient umbrella coverage. Be sure to read exclusions carefully to ascertain whether you need additional coverage.

Other Types of Insurance. Some types of insurance are designed to protect your assets, such as homeowner's or auto insurance, and are absolutely necessary. However, there are other types of insurance that are often already covered in your other insurance policies. As a result, most planners do not recommend these kinds of policies. Some such policies include credit card insurance, hospital indemnity, specific disease coverage, and flight insurance. Our professional planners can help you determine whether the coverage limits of your other policies are sufficient to cover any debt needs.

Long-Term Care. Long-term care is the kind of assistance you need when you are unable to perform daily personal care tasks on your own. The need for this assistance usually arises from a disabling or long-term medical or physical condition. Long-term care services can include in-home care as well as a nursing home setting of community care.

There are a variety of home health care programs that allow older people to remain independent. They rely on other people assisting those persons in need. These include personal care, homemaker services, hospice, respite care, and adult day support centers. If you have to bear the cost of this care yourself, then perhaps you should look for an assisted living facility or residential care facility. These facilities include room and board plus personal care in a supervised environment. If a higher level of care is needed, the individual may have to be cared for in a skilled nursing facility.

What should you know before purchasing a long-term care insurance policy? Here are a few rules of thumb to help you plan. Your policy should not exceed 7 percent of your annual income. If you have significant assets, plan to pay the premiums yourself. Premiums are based on age, so the older you are, the more expensive the premiums will be. If you have serious health issues, it is unlikely that you would be accepted for long-term care insurance. Also, if you have any preexisting conditions, the company may refuse to pay you during the first six months after you buy the policy. Look at the financial rating of the insurance company before purchasing. Rating companies such as Standard & Poor's, Duff and Phelps, Moody's, and A.M. Best rate insurance companies on their financial condition and their claims paying ability. These ratings are available by calling up the company or from your local library.

Cost is another issue. Factors to consider include:

- Your age and your health at the time you apply for coverage.
- The deductible or waiting period you choose before the policy begins to pay.
- The types of benefits you want.
- The daily benefit you want.
- The number of years you want the company to pay benefits.

Long-term care insurance is an issue you should begin planning for sooner rather than later. See my end-of-chapter tips for pointers when evaluating your insurance needs.

Investment Planning: Developing a Game Plan

Now that we have covered the basic financial planning needs, we are finally ready to invest. The key to wise investing is to develop a process and follow through with it closely. While results cannot be guaranteed, you can do much to reduce your risk exposure and hopefully not sacrifice return that you're counting on to help you hit the objectives you set up in the financial planning stage.

Most successful investment portfolios will depend on the strategic decisions you make with your investments. Once that is accomplished, a tactical approach that fills in the details with investments will be needed. We'll talk more about that later, after we look at a five-step plan for investing successfully.

Uncomfortable Realities about Saving and Investing. It's easy to *not* plan ahead for savings. For many young people, concern about funding a secure retirement does not compete with the costly and current realities of purchasing a new home and raising children. By the time they reach their forties, thoughts of retirement start to set in—only to be pushed aside by the costs of college tuition or more concern with buying a more opulent lifestyle. Studies show that people wait until they pass age 50 to focus on funding their retirement. That's unfortunate because the sooner you start to save regularly and invest those savings wisely, the greater your chances of successfully meeting the financial challenges throughout your entire life.

The bottom line is, to accomplish those objectives you set out for yourself, you should save at least 10 percent of your gross income. Given the common financial hurdles that most of us will have to overcome during life, like the erosive effect of inflation, and longer life expectancies, saving 15 percent to 20 percent of your income is preferable. Of course, those who prefer spending to saving will have another option: working three jobs to put their children through college, and flipping burgers at a fast-food joint when they're 75 in order to support their own so-called retirement. Do you really want to be in that position?

Inflation works against your savings. When considering how much money you will need to reach your financial goals, you must factor in the impact of inflation on the cost of living. For example, assuming that inflation averages 3.5 percent per year, your living expenses will double in about 20 years. If you anticipate needing the purchasing power of today's $30,000 in 20 years—for your child's college tuition or for your retirement—you will need, if living costs do double every 20 years, $60,000 at that time.

Therefore, your investment program should assure, over the long run, that your assets provide you with a return that beats inflation. Assume, for example, that inflation for a given year was 4 percent and a certificate of deposit happened to have a 4 percent return for the year. On an inflation-adjusted basis, the CD just kept pace with inflation; it produced a zero inflation-adjusted return. On top of that, if the CD interest also was subject to income taxes, it actually lost ground to inflation after taxes were paid on the interest. If a stock mutual fund rose by 9 percent in a year when inflation was 4 percent, this investment beat inflation handily,

One of the advantages of owning stocks and stock mutual funds is that they have generally outperformed other types of investments when held for at least five to ten years. Remember, the true test of a successful investment is how well it's able to keep ahead of inflation over many years.

Investing for a Secure Financial Future.   Now that we have discussed the uncomfortable elements and the importance of saving and investing, let's find out what you need to do in order to make investing work. There are many key ingredients to successful investing. The following five-step plan can prove beneficial to ensure your financial future.

1. *Know why you're investing.* Everyone invests for different reasons, even if we all share one overall goal: achieving ultimate financial security. Some common investment goals also might include providing an emergency fund for unforeseen events, meeting major expenses—a first home, college education, a daughter's wedding—and, most important, saving for a comfortable retirement. You must be clear about your investment goals in order to achieve them.
2. *Invest for growth. Every* investor needs to invest some money for growth to offset the effect that inflation and taxes will have.
3. *Diversify across investments.* Diversification is key to successful investing. No one investment category and no one industry has consistently outperformed all the others. When choosing particular areas of stocks, bonds, and mutual funds to invest in, don't bet too heavily on what's hot in the current market. Rather, consider what investment classes will continue to be attractive five and ten years from now.

4. *Diversify within investments.* Diversifying among investment classes—holding a certain percentage in stocks, bonds, and mutual funds—is a good start to a successful investment portfolio. Within each category of investment, however, some are going to thrive, and others will not. The best way to protect yourself from the effect of a mediocre stock, bond, or mutual fund is to select more than one to invest in. You may want to hold an international stock mutual fund as well as a U.S. stock mutual fund to take advantage of investment opportunities both at home and abroad.

5. *Take control over your investments.* Perhaps the most important attribute of a successful investing program is to stay in touch with all your investments. Don't rely on someone else to watch over your portfolio and make all of your investment decisions. While professionals can make helpful suggestions, you also should be well enough informed to be able to make the final decision.

Investing is not cheap and is certainly not without risk. If it were, then everyone would be doing a great job with it and making all sorts of money. But before you can be a careful investor, you must understand the parameters that are faced when making investment decisions.

Investment Parameters.   How do you define risk? The most critical component of the investment planning process is the assessment of client risk. Risk involves probabilities that actual future returns will be below expected returns. This uncertainty is created by the volatility in the marketplace.

If you understand this concept of risk, then what has happened to your investment return during the past year will make sense and your disappointment with your investment returns will have been greatly reduced. I think most individuals truly do not know their tolerance for risk. Essentially, how much pain can you take? Given this fact, where do your investment parameters fit in the overall investment planning process?

With a stock market currently on pace to having yet another lackluster finish, how can you tailor your portfolio design to reach your investment parameters? There are six different investment parameters that help us to define our clients: risk tolerance, time horizon, liquidity, marketability, income tax consequences, and diversification. These investment parameters serve as the premise in the creation of an investment policy statement. Let's discuss what they are and how they relate to constructing your portfolio.

Risk Tolerance.   We've all heard the statement that people are risk averse. That's simply not true. People are not risk averse. They are *loss* averse. They want great returns without any risk! The fact of the matter is that if you undertake more risk, then the propensity for reward will be that much greater.

How much risk are you willing to take? It helps if you have been around the block a few times—in other words, if you have been in the market, made money, and then lost that money and received the ultimate wake-up call! From what I gather, older clients tend to have less tolerance for risk simply because their time horizon is shorter. In my practice, males take on more risk than females, singles take on more risk than married people, and those who work for the public sector are more risk averse than those who work for the private sector. Some of my readers have probably used a risk tolerance questionnaire as an objective means of measuring risk tolerance to help you select the right portfolio design for you. But is that really enough?

Time Horizon.   As a general rule, if you have a long time horizon, you'll generally require less liquidity and can usually tolerate more risk, whereas individuals with shorter time horizons don't have the time to overcome riskier investments. For longer time horizons, the concern is one of purchasing power risk rather than volatility risk. If you have a shorter time horizon, say less than five years, don't invest in equities because you do not have the time to ride out a possible market downturn. If you have one year or less, then short-term accounts like money markets are best. Make sure you always tie back to your objectives. For example, if you have two children, ages 12 and 10, and college funding is a priority, select a time horizon between 10 and 12 years. Anything beyond 10 to12 years would not be warranted.

Liquidity versus Marketability.   People often get these two terms confused. Liquidity means the ability to convert an asset into cash without significant loss of principal. That differs from marketability, which states whether there is a readily available marketplace to buy, sell, or exchange an asset. Generally, assets are more liquid if many traders are interested in a fairly standardized product. For example, Treasury bills are a highly liquid security whereas real estate and venture capital are not. Liquidity provides you with the opportunity to change your mind by correcting any errors that were made relatively easily and cheaply. Therefore, as your circumstances change, adjust your investments to stay in close harmony with your changing short-term objectives.

If you have shorter time horizons, keep more of your money in liquid types of accounts, such as money market accounts. For example, if you are looking to fund college relatively soon, have a fair amount of those costs in liquid accounts.

Older individuals have increased liquidity needs. For example, a 60-year-old may need a higher reserve to fund unanticipated medical or long-term care concerns. Wealthy individuals need liquid funds to pay tax liabilities. You need to know, in the event of liquidation, which part of the portfolio will have to be sold first.

Marketability generally provides no liquidity. For example, your primary residence is marketable. You could sell it today if need be, but if you did, the chances of getting anything close to fair market value would be pretty slim.

Tax Considerations.   Virtually all investment decisions have some degree of tax concerns. However, always remember, think substance over form. You really need to answer the question, does the investment transaction make good economic sense? For example, if your goal is to lower your income tax liability, understanding the IRC rules will assist you in making a decision on when to invest in a given scenario. If you are approached with a real estate deal designed to produce losses to lower your income taxes, care must be taken. If your income is over $300,000, you would not do the transaction since real estate losses for the small investor get phased out beginning with adjusted gross income (AGI) over $100,000 and are completely eliminated when AGI exceeds $150,000. It may make sense as a good deal, but not in helping you to achieve the objective of tax minimization. Finally, investing in retirement accounts over after-tax accounts still provides more leeway to shelter and reduce current taxable income.

Diversification.   Nowhere like the present can we see the importance of diversification. Clearly the approach of the 1990s was "Stocks rule," and having only stocks in a portfolio was very shortsighted. It just doesn't work like that anymore. Just like a properly balanced meal, a properly balanced portfolio, consisting of an asset allocation of stocks, bonds, and cash as the core food groups, makes the most sense. Real estate and other types of investments may be warranted as well.

Diversification leads into asset allocation. A solid approach to asset allocation is to tie in to your objectives. The two areas of focus should be capital *accumulation* and capital *distribution.* In the beginning of your investment career, you will be in the capital accumulation mode. If you have a longer time horizon, your answer as to the best way to build the nest egg is through the growth of capital. Stocks tend to be a better investment choice than other types of investments because of higher historical returns. You should have no immediate need for the money and can therefore take on greater risks in exchange for these higher returns.

If you are in the distribution stage, make preservation of capital and current income your primary objectives. However, capital growth through stock allocation should not be discarded during this stage (just reduced perhaps) since the retirement period could extend as long as one-third of your lifetime. In addition, although bonds have historically produced the highest current annual income of any financial asset, bond interest income doesn't increase over time. Considering inflation, real interest income actually declines. Stock income has historically grown at the rate of inflation. Over a ten-year period, dividend income from stocks will generally exceed interest income from bonds.

Sometimes, you will need to make a trade-off between taxes and diversification needs. If you are a small business owner and have most of your wealth concentration in the equity of your small business, or if, as an employee, you purchase substantial amounts of your employer's stock through payroll deduction plans during your working life, then your portfolios may contain a large amount of unrealized capital gains. In addition, the risk position of such a portfolio may be quite high, because it is concentrated in a single company. The decision to sell some of the company stock in order to diversify your portfolio's risk by reinvesting the proceeds in other assets must be balanced against the resulting tax liability.

With the volatile marketplace setting all sorts of reality checks, the inherent issues surrounding your investment parameters play an even larger role. Through this exercise, you will understand the risks and rewards pertinent to successful achievement within the investment planning process.

What Are the Risks of Investing?   Risk is concerned with the uncertainty that the realized return (what you really receive) will not equal the expected return (what you hope for). There are no sure things in life and investing certainly falls near the top of that list. Investing encompasses many risks. That's because investing isn't a sure thing. As we have learned recently, stock and bond prices do not always go up and in many cases they can go down by significant amounts.

Risk can be broken down into two components: systematic and unsystematic. Systematic risk means that there is no way to reduce or eliminate this type of risk. As a result, if we do undertake that kind of risk, we expect the marketplace will reward us for doing so. This risk stems from the loss of **purchasing power** through inflation, **reinvestment rates**, fluctuating **interest rates**, fluctuating security prices in the **marketplace**, and losses from changes in the value of **exchange rates**. The acronym I use representing the first letter in each of the bold items is "PRIME." These sources of risk are not affected by the construction of a diversified portfolio.

Unsystematic risk means we can minimize the risk, diversify away from it, or even eliminate it. These risks encompass business risk (being in the wrong sector), financial risk (having too much debt), default risk (determining the likelihood that the company will continue as a going concern), and regulatory risk (either from the U.S. Government or a foreign government). In any event, redirecting your investments can help alleviate these risks and the marketplace will not reward you with additional return for choosing to undertake these risks.

An understanding of these risks is paramount before you can even consider investing. You may want to consult your CERTIFIED FINANCIAL PLANNER® (CFP) to help you assess the risk you would be comfortable with when designing your investment platform.

Asset Allocation.   Asset allocation means not putting all your eggs in one basket. Diversification is the key. Asset allocation can have many meanings and include significant issues depending on the type of investor you are.

Some of the more important issues that carry out the diversification process include determining the tax status and after-tax implications of investments in a given asset class, your individual motivations, personal circumstances, and cyclical and secular market outlook. Also pay close attention to the timing and magnitude of intergenerational income requirements, the ability to tolerate and be adequately compensated for bearing risk or loss, absolute and relative performance goals and benchmarks for measuring returns, the influence of one or more concentrated investment positions, personal holdings and collectibles, and meaningful financial liabilities such as mortgage debt.

While asset allocation can provide true benefits, some drawbacks also exist. For starters, by diversifying across major asset classes, if one asset class is a hot segment, then you will not participate in potentially huge price advances of specific asset classes.

Understanding Basic Asset Classes: An Investment Primer.   Sorting out and understanding numerous investment alternatives is actually easier than you may think. Let's start by examining the four main categories of investments.

1. *Cash and cash equivalents.* These are interest-earning securities with maturities less than one year after their issue date. Common examples are CDs, savings accounts, cash surrender life insurance, and Treasury bills. Cash equivalents are investments considered to be of such high liquidity and safety that they are virtually as good as cash. In addition to CDs and money market accounts, other cash equivalents are money market mutual funds and Treasury bills.
2. *Fixed income investments.* Fixed income investments, or bonds, represent lending money to a corporation. There are three main categories for bonds: U.S. obligations, municipal obligations, and corporate obligations.

   Backed by the "full faith and credit" of the federal government, Treasury bonds and notes are considered the safest bonds. Next in safety are municipal bonds. While they aren't guaranteed by Uncle Sam, they are backed by state and local governments or by specific revenue sources. And although cities and towns can default, or fail to pay their debts, they very rarely do. (Defaulting would seriously impair the issuer's credit rating.)

Least secure are corporate bonds. Why? These bonds are usually only backed by the company that issues them, so their degree of safety is directly related to the company's health. If a firm goes bankrupt, the bonds can become worthless.

3. *Stocks.* Most people think of *stocks* as a synonym for investments. Yet, paradoxically, many Americans never take advantage of stock ownership because they consider them too risky. But they should try them, because stocks can provide both regular income (in the form of dividends) and inflation-beating appreciation (increase in value over time).

4. *Real estate.* Owning real estate is perhaps the most complicated form of investing. Evaluating a property's potential for income, appreciation, and its tax ramifications is very difficult. On top of that is the need to monitor—and if you buy the property yourself, manage—the property once it's purchased. Some people opt for passive real estate ownership through a limited partnership, which considerably simplifies the process of real estate investing. But it in no way safeguards your investment from real estate slumps. The easiest way to participate in the real estate market is to buy shares of real estate investment trusts (REITs), but returns may be far less than you could attain by buying individual properties.

Allocating Investments. Investing effectively is crucial to your financial success. Therefore, you need to develop a plan that will help guide you both in deciding on the types of investments to make and in reviewing your investments periodically. *Periodically* doesn't mean every day; the danger of daily review is that you'll become so concerned that you'll end up making investment changes too frequently. Rather, if you establish sensible criteria now, you will be able to invest wisely without needing to spend an inordinate amount of time worrying about your investments.

The four steps to allocating your investments are:

1. Decide how much of your money should be invested in stocks and how much in interest-earning securities (bonds and short-term securities).

2. Once you know how much of your portfolio should be in each investment category, you need to determine how to purchase the securities you want. You can buy individual stocks and interest-earning securities yourself, or you can take advantage of professional management by investing in mutual funds. You may well want to use some combination of both approaches.
3. For each investment category, determine what types of investments would be appropriate for your portfolio objectives and comfort level.
4. Finally, you need to select and purchase the actual securities— such as a particular stock, bond, or mutual fund—that will work to achieve your investment goals.

Nine Tips for Investing in Bonds

1. *Seek expertise when necessary.* Investments in bonds that you are unfamiliar with, perhaps foreign bonds, should definitely be made through a mutual fund with management specializing in these areas.
2. *Keep an eye on price volatility.* Since interest rates can fluctuate widely over the course of a year, price volatility is a factor that must be taken into account in planning and selecting bonds. Generally speaking, the longer the maturity date, the more volatile the price of that particular issue.
3. *Ladder maturities.* Laddering, or staggering, the maturities of bond investments is a tried-and-true strategy. Rather than investing in a single issue or in several issues with roughly the same maturity, you should opt for a variety of maturities— some short-term (less than 3 years), some intermediate-term (3 to 10 years), and some long-term (10 to 30 years). That way, if there is a significant change in interest rates, you will have avoided placing a heavy, and perhaps incorrect, bet on a single maturity. Simply stated, laddering maturities reduces the risk in any bond portfolio. Don't forget to set some of the maturities to coincide with when you may need the money (for instance, to meet college tuition bills or to provide money during your retirement years). If you invest in bond mutual funds, you can follow a similar laddering strategy by spreading your money among money market and short-term

bond funds, intermediate-term bond funds, and long-term bond funds.

4. *Compare interest rates.* Interest rates vary among types of bonds, both within the same investment category and between alternative categories. For example, if you shopped around a little, you might discover that the rate paid on CDs at your local bank is not as good as it might be. Over the past several years, interest rates on tax-exempt bonds have been very attractive compared with the after-tax returns on Treasury securities and corporate bonds.

5. *Don't chase yield.* While shopping for yield is a virtue, chasing yield is a sin. A bond investment that pays 10 percent interest when other bonds of the same type and maturities are at 6 percent is trying to tell you something. This probably is a junk bond (high-yielding, highly risky type of bond that has a low, speculative credit rating) or similarly risky investment. Don't be fooled. Always remember, the higher the yield, the higher the risk.

6. *Diversify.* Unless you have only a very small amount of money to invest, don't concentrate your interest-earning investments in a single or very few securities. Select several different issues and several different categories of investments or mutual funds.

7. *Keep maturities relatively short.* Even though longer-maturity interest-earning investments usually have higher yields than shorter-maturity investments, many experts contend that there is usually not enough of a difference to justify the greater risks in concentrating on long-maturity bonds. Remember, the longer the maturity, the more the value of the bond will fluctuate in reaction to changes in interest rates.

8. *Use mutual funds for investing in unusual bonds.* If you want to invest in foreign bonds, chances are you won't have the time or ability to track the market as closely as a smart investor needs to do. By investing in a foreign bond mutual fund, you can diversify the bond portion of your portfolio and, at the same time, take advantage of the professional manager's foreign bond expertise.

9. *Consider the tax effects.* You may be able to increase your investment returns by carefully examining the tax effects of alternative interest-earning investments. While some are fully

taxable, interest on Treasury securities is federally taxable but exempt from state taxes. Municipal bond interest is exempt from federal taxes and may be exempt from state taxes. It is important to keep in mind that the federally taxable securities should be purchased for your tax-deferred retirement accounts. Tax-favored investments like municipal bonds should be purchased for your personal investment account.

Stocks.   This section is designed to help you make an informed decision about stock investing. It explores such areas as what stocks are, their advantages and risks, how you can tell if they're the right investment for you, and how you can select and purchase them.

Why is investing in stocks so important? If you are not investing in today's stock market, you risk falling short of realizing your financial goals. Why? Stocks have consistently proven to be the best inflation-beating vehicle for long-term investors. And if your investments aren't beating inflation, you're losing ground to the ever-increasing costs of living.

How Stocks Are Classified.   There is a wide variety of common stock investments. Some pay dividends; others don't. Some have relatively stable prices; others are more volatile. Despite this variety, most common stocks can be classified into one of the following categories.

- *Growth stocks.* Investors buy growth stocks for capital appreciation. Because many companies have to finance their growth and may be involved in expensive research, most or all of their earnings are reinvested in the company for future expansion. Thus, growth stocks have the potential for increased market value, and they pay little in dividends. Therefore, prices of growth stocks are usually more volatile than those of other stocks.
- *Income stocks.* Income stocks are bought for current income because they tend to have a higher-than-average dividend yield. Companies whose stocks fall into this category are usually in fairly stable industries (for example, telecommunications and utilities), have strong finances, and pay out

a substantial portion of their earnings in dividends. Many of the stocks are considered total return stocks because they offer the opportunity for both dividends and capital appreciation.

- *Blue-chip stocks.* Blue-chip stocks are considered the highest quality of all common stocks because they are dominant companies that have the ability to pay steady dividends in both good and bad times. For example, all of the 30 stocks that compose the Dow Jones Industrial Average are blue-chip stocks. These companies hold dominant positions in industries that generally are not as vulnerable to cyclical market swings as are other industries.

- *Cyclical stocks.* Cyclical stocks are shares in companies whose earnings tend to fluctuate sharply with their business's cycles. When business conditions are good, a cyclical company's profitability is high and the price of its common stock rises; when conditions deteriorate, the company's sales, profits, and market price fall sharply. For example, when interest rates are high and business conditions slow down, the housing and steel industries suffer tremendously. The timing of ownership is crucial to successful investment in cyclical stocks.

- *Defensive stocks.* In contrast to cyclical stocks, some companies are considered recession resistant. They sell products or provide services whose demand does not fluctuate with business cycles. Examples include food, cosmetics, and health care stocks.

- *Small company stocks.* Small company stocks, also known as small cap stocks, are stocks of companies that typically have a total stock market value of less than $500 million. These stocks are usually traded on the over-the-counter (OTC) market. Historically, small company stocks have outperformed larger company stocks—but they are more volatile because smaller companies usually have less stable and predictable earnings, and/or they may have insufficient assets to weather a business downturn.

- *Speculative stocks.* In a sense, all common stocks are speculative, since they offer a variable return rather than a fixed return like a bond. But some stocks are more speculative than others. A speculative stock is subject to wider swings in share price—down as well as up—so it's riskier. For example, hot new issues, high-flying glamour stocks, and penny stocks are speculative stocks.

Tips for Investing in Stocks.   There are no guarantees for stock investment success, but there are many ideas that may prove to be helpful to you. Here are ten of them:

1. *Never buy stocks indiscriminately.* Many investors buy stocks haphazardly simply because they have money to invest. This is a very bad practice; make investments only when you have a good reason to buy them.
2. *Select a promising industry.* At any given time, most industries in the economy are either on an upswing or a downswing. When choosing a stock, start by selecting a promising industry with a good future outlook. Then look for a company within that industry whose prospects look the most promising.
3. *Diversify.* Try to own stocks in several different industries. The danger of too many eggs in one basket can't be overemphasized. However, overdiversification is also unwise. It's easier to keep track of 5 to 10 stocks than it is 25 stocks. You generally can achieve excellent diversification with about 10 well-chosen stocks.
4. *Buy low and sell high.* You don't necessarily have to be a contrarian to condition yourself to buy stock when a company's share price is down and sell it when the price is up. Stocks can gain when prices are low, and major selling opportunities come when the stock is hot (everybody wants to own it) and prices are high. This is the famous "buy low, sell high" rule. It is recommended that you use caution when following this or any other stock market strategy.
5. *Stay abreast of market trends.* Look at the general trend in the market. A stock that already has risen in value might be a good candidate for continued gains if the market is still rising. Conversely, a stock that does not respond to a general market rise might turn out to be a candidate for selling.
6. *Use stop-loss orders to protect against loss.* Potential losses can be effectively limited by using stop-loss orders (not available on over-the-counter stocks), which fence in gains by restricting the effects of a market downturn on your stocks. Stop-loss

orders also can be used to force you to sell. For example, say you buy a stock at $12 per share and it rises to $18 per share. You might put a stop-loss order in at $15 per share to lock in a gain. The risk of this strategy is that you might get left behind at $15 per share if the stock falls to $15 and then resumes rising, but this may be less risky than a loss due to a sharp decline.

7. *Buy value.* Companies with strong finances (not too much debt) and solid earnings growth are consistently better long-run performers.

8. *Buy low P/E high dividend stocks.* Many successful long-term investors use the investment strategy of purchasing common stocks of companies with relatively low price-to-earnings (P/E) multiples and relatively high dividend yields. The logic behind this is that the stock price is depressed (a low P/E multiple), and hence, the stock is being purchased when no one else wants it. This is in itself a good strategy as long as the company has no major long-term problems. Moreover, when the stock price rises, the company probably will attempt to maintain its high dividend yield by raising its dividend. Investors, therefore, get the best of both worlds: rising stock price and higher dividend income.

9. *Buy stocks in companies with strong dividend payment records.* Consider stocks in companies that have a consistent history of paying generous dividends. In a bear market (in which stock prices have declined), these companies tend to decline less in price than companies that pay no dividend at all or pay dividends erratically, since investors are confident that the dividends will keep coming, through thick and thin. Some companies have paid annual dividends for more than 100 years.

10. *Rely on your own experience and judgment.* Often, looking for successful companies to invest in doesn't require that you go to Wall Street. Investment ideas can come from your own observations of how things are selling on Main Street. This commonsense strategy (on Wall Street, it's known as *real economics*) has been used by some of the most successful investors and money managers for years. The next time you go to the mall, keep your eyes open for new investment opportunities.

Retirement Planning: How to Prepare Yourself for a Successful Retirement

Retirement is really a passage from one journey to another. To make the most of retirement, you should consider retiring *to* something, not retiring *from* something. Retirement should represent the next stage of your life. And since this stage can last 30 or more years, it is imperative that proper planning start now to ensure that your ultimate dreams come true. Therefore, take the time now to begin your future journey. It is never too early to begin the process.

Unfortunately, it is true what people say: Most of us tend to spend more time planning our two-week summer vacation than we do planning for our retirement. The more you determine what you want, the easier and quicker you'll reach your passage for your retirement years.

Critical Issues You Face During Retirement.   To begin thinking about your retirement financial picture, you must answer tough questions relating to longevity, running out of money, inflation, income, volatile stock market, and estate issues.

Longevity: How Long Will Your Retirement Dollars Last?   The life span of the typical American has increased dramatically over the past few decades, largely as a result of advances in health care and nutrition. Years ago, the length of time one spent in retirement was minimal because people did not have the longevity they do today. Nowadays people are living longer than ever before. In fact, spending one-third of your lifetime in retirement is not uncommon. So now the challenge is to plan not just *to* retirement but *through* retirement. This makes it more difficult since this was not what we had in mind when we first decided to put away funds for retirement.

Running out of Money: Your Biggest Challenge.   Because of this increased longevity, running out of money represents your biggest challenge. This problem occurs more than you think. Many older individuals will outlive their savings and will be forced to live on amounts provided by the government and/or their employer, such as Social Security and possibly an employee pension. People age 85 and older are twice as likely to be living under the poverty level as those between the ages of 65 and 74.

Most of us tend to underestimate our life expectancies and overestimate the amount we can safely spend during retirement. This will result in not having sufficient funds to last during retirement.

Inflation: How Much Will Your Living Expenses Increase over Time? You'll need to prepare for the challenge of inflation. Inflation refers to the fact that $1 saved today does not equal $1 called upon in the future—when we need those funds. Historically, inflation has averaged 3.1 percent since 1926. Of even greater uncertainty are the unknown future factors that could have a devastating effect on your resources. Just look at the late 1970s and early 1980s when inflation averaged double digits for many years. The unpredictability of future living costs poses significant challenges and complications during the planning process.

Income.   How much income is really enough? Can you really oversave? Can you outlive your income? These are tough questions, with no easy answers. The good news is that people tend to need less money to live on during their golden years. A good rule of thumb is that people tend to spend approximately 80 percent of their current living expenses during retirement. Another way of saying the same thing is that retirees need about 80 percent of their before-tax income earned in the final working years. However, as with any rule of thumb, it is not a one-size-fits-all solution. The amount you accumulate will be specific to your needs.

The actual level of income you will need during retirement will depend on many variables. These could include your income before retirement, your age, your health, and your newfound lifestyle. You could be spending more money instead of less. Changing habits and patterns of retirees will dictate most of what is yet to come. Therefore, plan on spending more than you would normally anticipate.

Volatile Stock Market.   What happens if you are planning on beginning your retirement during an unfortunate period? For example, suppose you were to begin retirement during the latter half of 2008 with a stock market that has not seen the likes of its volatility since the Great Depression! Most of us assume we will have a certain amount of dollars available at retirement, but that may not always be the case. The latter half of 2008 definitely threw most of us for a loop! Therefore, having a proper allocation of investments, while not providing an absolute fix, will go a long way toward helping us.

Estate: How Much Will You Leave Behind for Your Heirs? This is really a retirement question. Leaving assets to your heirs will also dictate what you can afford to spend during retirement. Because most retirees will need to draw on their accumulated savings and investments, their desire to leave behind an estate for their children or other family members, and/or to provide gifts to religious institutions or other favorite charities, poses a direct conflict with their retirement objectives.

You will find that you can't have your cake and eat it too! With a limited amount of financial resources, care must be taken in determining what you can spend on yourself and family members during retirement versus what can be given away or left behind to others. This is a decision you alone are faced with.

As you can see, the challenges we face can be mounting. Proper planning and a desire to take charge of your own financial intelligence can go a long way in being prepared for the inevitable—with the uncertainty in which we all live.

Five Common Retirement Planning Mistakes People Make. Now that we know what challenges lie ahead, we need to do everything we can to address them intelligently. Unfortunately, too many of us don't do the little things we should in helping get to our chosen destination. We have the ability to control many of the issues we need to achieve success, whereas the challenges we face are beyond our control.

The following is a brief explanation of some of the mistakes we make when planning our own retirement.

Not Taking Advantage of Contributing Towards Your Retirement Plan, Such as a 401(k) or 403(b) Plan
As they say, there is no time like the present to begin saving! Max out your account if you can. This is one of the few remaining pretax benefits you can get since it is a direct offset against your total W-2

(wage) income. So not only can you reduce your taxable income each year, you will see the overall effects of compounding your annual investment. For example, look at the effect of compounding by maxing out your 401(k) in the following situations:

Age	Annual Savings	Growth Rate	Future Value at age 65
25	$16,000*	8%	$4,144,904
35	$16,000*	8%	$1,812,531
45	$16,000*	8%	$732,191
55	$16,000*	8%	$231,785

*Note that the maximum 401(k) contribution can change every year so maxing out your 401(k) should result in you putting away more than the number stated here.

Furthermore, if the company matches some or all of your contribution, the increase in your account can be astronomical. Please see Chapter 7 for a more detailed explanation of retirement plans.

Neglecting to Prepare Retirement Income and Expense Projections During Your Working Years. This is critical; otherwise, you won't know whether you are saving enough to cover expenses during retirement. Let's look at an easy chart I use with clients that can help you gain control over the situation.

The beginning balance is the money you have accumulated during your working years. Additions represent things like pensions, Social Security, other income, and investment income. Withdrawals include things like basic and discretionary expenses as well as taxes. The beginning balance plus additions less withdrawals give you the ending balance.

The ending balance for one year is the beginning balance for the following year. If these balances decline to zero at an age earlier than your life expectancy, then you need to rethink your long-term retirement strategy. I'm using a hypothetical situation as an example of the way you should set this up. You can see that this hypothetical client will run out of money at age 72.

Age	Beginning Balance	+ Additions	− Withdrawals	= Ending Balance
65	$500,000	$50,000	$100,000	$450,000
66	$450,000	$55,000	$110,000	$395,000
67	$395,000	$60,000	$120,000	$335,000
68	$335,000	$65,000	$130,000	$270,000
69	$270,000	$70,000	$140,000	$200,000
70	$200,000	$75,000	$150,000	$125,000
71	$125,000	$80,000	$160,000	$45,000
72	$45,000	$85,000	$130,000	$0

Expecting Social Security to Cover All Your Needs at Retirement.   Social Security was created as part of FDR's New Deal and instituted in 1937. Its purpose was to supplement a worker's retirement at age 65, which was supposed to be primarily funded with employer retirement dollars, such as defined benefit plans. Unfortunately, too many people believe that is still the case and are disenchanted when that doesn't work and they don't have the monies necessary to retire in the manner they would like.

There is also the thought that Social Security won't even be there when you are ready to collect. I wouldn't be too concerned with that. It will be there in some way, shape, or form, but may not be recognizable as it is today. The bottom line is this: Don't rely on someone else or some other entity to fund your retirement. Do it yourself!

Accepting an Early Retirement Offer from Your Employer Without Thinking It Through.   All too often, people can't wait to leave their jobs. The fact that the employer will front-load money is even that much more of a bonus. Many people do not make the proper calculations to determine whether the money will be sufficient to retire on, or whether it can be used as a partial retirement amount if you have a desire to go back to work. For example, let's say you are 55 and wish to accept your employer's early retirement offer. Assuming your salary is $80,000 per year, and you were getting 5 percent annual pay increases, and you anticipated working another ten years, here's how the numbers would look:

$80,000 payment (PMT)

10 more years till regular retirement (N)

5 percent growth rate for pay raises (I)

Present value (PV) = $617,739

What this means is you need to receive a retirement package of at least $617,739 (not counting insurance and other fringe benefits you currently receive) to equal the payout you would get over the next 10 years! I would venture to say that most people never look that far ahead and only receive a fraction of the proper amount. If you are concerned about these types of calculations, have your Certified Financial Planner (CFP) assist you.

Failing to Take Out Required Minimum Distributions (RMDs) after Age 70½. With the exception of 2009 only, individuals are required to take out a required minimum distribution (RMD) from their retirement account by April 1 in the year in which they turn 70½. Failure to do so will result in a penalty of 50 percent of the excess distribution that should have come out. Since this distribution represents income (not previously taxed at an earlier date during your working years), you must add this amount to all your other income streams. And since it is taxed at ordinary income rates, it can push you into a higher income tax bracket.

How Much Income Are You Likely to Need from Your Personal Investments? Based on the preceding scenarios, maximizing our retirement investment income can be a struggle. We now have to weigh all these factors together and determine an overall game plan on how to tackle this issue. Much of how you proceed will be determined through the amount of risk you are willing to take, your time horizon till retirement, how liquid and marketable you want your funds to be, the income tax consequences of your actions, and by creating a properly diversified portfolio to weather the unforeseen storms. See my end-of-chapter tips for strategies when evaluating your retirement concerns.

Estate Planning

Estate planning is the process of organizing your financial and personal interests, in accordance with prevailing laws, so that *your* wishes are met with a minimum of inconvenience and expense to your family. Estate planning also can assure that your estate incurs the minimum possible estate tax.

Effective estate planning need not be complicated. It has several straightforward objectives, including:

- Minimizing the problems and expenses of probate; avoiding potential family conflicts, where possible; and passing on your estate in accordance with *your* wishes.
- Providing your spouse with as much responsibility and flexibility in estate management as desired, consistent with potential tax savings.
- Providing for the conservation of your estate and its effective management following the death of either or both spouses.
- Minimizing taxes at the time of death as well as estate taxes after death.
- Avoiding leaving the children too much too soon.
- Providing for adequate liquidity to cover taxes and other expenses at death without the necessity of a forced sale of assets.
- Providing for estate management in the event of the incapacity of either spouse.
- Organizing all important papers affecting your estate plan in a location known to all family members and reviewing them at least annually.

Most estate planning objectives can be accomplished by hiring an attorney. You will just be responsible to provide that attorney with your thoughts and concerns. Much of this information can be determined during the financial planning process.

Where There's a Will, There's a Way.   A will is a document that specifies how to divide property, names a guardian and executor for your estate, passes through probate court, and alerts creditors of your death.

It can be changed by amending it with codicils, and can be handwritten (holographic) or recited from an oral transcript (noncupative).

You don't need a will to pass property along. Property can be passed by titling it a certain way (i.e., such as joint tenancy with right of survivorship) and placing it in various instruments, or in a trust. See Exhibit 9.5 for guidelines to follow when preparing a will.

The following ten items should be included in a will:

1. A statement that the document is a will.
2. A statement revoking all previous wills.
3. Your full name and location of principal residence.
4. Specific transfers of property to the named beneficiaries.
5. Instructions for dividing the balance of the property.
6. A list of trusts, including the names of selected trustees and successor trustees.
7. Names of guardians and alternate guardians for minor children or special-needs relatives.
8. Designation of what monies are to be used to pay death taxes.
9. Names of the executor and backup executor.
10. Signature and date. The will should be signed in the presence of all of the witnesses.

Exhibit 9.5   Guidelines for Preparing a Will: 10 Item Will Preparation Checklist

Letter of Instructions.   A letter of instructions is not a legal document like a will. In some ways, it can be more important than a will. Here, you have a lot more flexibility in both the language and content. Your letter is a good place to make your true desires known, specify what you want to happen after your will is executed, and include those items not addressed in the will. Essentially, you will state your personal wishes and final comments, but your heirs will be very grateful if you include details about important financial matters.

The letter of instructions plans out exactly what should be done. For example, you would start out with a section on the "First Things to Do." This could include contacting acquaintances and organizations, including Social Security, the bank, and your employer; locating your life insurance policies; and making arrangements with a funeral home, which include providing your lawyer's name and telephone number, the present details of your wishes, and any arrangements you have made; providing the funeral director with specific facts about you; and calling the newspapers to convey obituary information, including the location of the cemetery and funeral parlor.

Your investment information should be included as well. For your stocks, provide the companies, name(s) on certificates, number of shares, certificate numbers, purchase price and date, and location of certificates. For your bonds, gather the names of the issuer, issued to, face amount, bond number, purchase price and date, maturity date, and location of certificates. For your mutual funds, give the companies, name(s) on account, number of shares or units, and location of statements and certificates. For your other investments, list amounts invested, to whom issued, maturity date, issuer, and other applicable data, and location of certificates and other vital papers.

For your primary residence, list information about the home. Include in that the name(s) listed on the deed, address, legal description, other descriptions needed, lawyer at closing, and locations of pertinent documents including statement of closing, policy of title insurance, deed, and land survey. Concerning the mortgage, include the date taken out, amount owed now, method of payment, and location of payment book or statements. If there is life insurance on the mortgage, list the policy number, location of policy, and annual payment amount. For property taxes, include amount and location of receipts. Regarding the house, include initial buying price, purchase closing fee, other buying costs (real estate agent, legal, taxes), and home improvements. List improvements, what each consisted of, cost, date, and location of bills; and for renters, provide lease location and expiration date.

For funeral instructions, specify whether *or not* you would like to have either of the following done: donate organs, public viewing; you can also specify a maximum cost of burial. State whether your remains should be donated or cremated. Also specify what type of service should be performed and where the graveside service should be conducted. Specify where memorial gifts should be given or whether to omit flowers; if prearrangements have been made with a mortuary, give details.

Understanding Trusts: It's as Easy as A-B-C. The ABC trust arrangement is designed to enhance family wealth by minimizing estate taxes after the death of both spouses. The ABCs stand for the following: The type A trust is the *marital* trust or power of appointment trust; type B is the *bypass* trust, also called the exemption equivalent or *credit shelter* trust; and type C is the *qualified terminal interest property* trust, or QTIP.

The marital trust allows for the passing of an unlimited amount of property to the spouse. A bypass trust is designed to contain property that sidesteps or bypasses the surviving spouse's or beneficiary's estate. Where one spouse has most of the assets, those assets should then be transferred to this poorer spouse to try to provide sufficient assets so he or she has ample assets to fund the bypass trust. A QTIP trust is a trust that qualifies for the marital deduction as made by the executor on the decedent's estate tax return (Form 706). The key point here is that the QTIP qualifies for the marital deduction even though its property neither passes to nor is controlled by the surviving spouse.

Using the A-B Trust Arrangement

The A-B trust uses one trust, the A trust, as a marital deduction and a second trust, the B trust, as a bypass trust. The A trust contains the assets subject to the marital deduction. The B trust is intended to take advantage of the unified credit against estate taxes. The credit equals the exemption equivalent (maximum amount allowed by law) of assets that will be held in the bypass trust. By not using the B trust, you would be wasting an opportunity to successfully rid your estate of up to the maximum allowable amount.

If you want to achieve zero estate tax after the first death and to provide the surviving spouse with the powers over all or none of the other assets, you would then help them place the remaining assets into the A trust. The key benefit of this planning is that the surviving spouse can have access and benefit (though restricted compared to an outright ownership of the assets) without those assets being later taxed in the surviving spouse's estate.

Here's how it works. John and Jane Smith have been married for 40 years. Both are U.S. citizens. John and Jane decide to set up an A-B trust. Assume John dies first. After his death, the assets bypass Jane and go to a named beneficiary. Upon Jane's death, she gets to pass the maximum amount of property to any beneficiary estate tax–free. The family successfully passes the maximum amount of property, thus saving a significant amount of estate tax. A side note is that Jane has the right to receive the income and assets of the B trust if those assets are needed for her support. Also, an unlimited amount of property can pass to Jane. Thus, property is not subject to estate tax at the death of the first spouse.

However, the assets remaining in the A trust will be included in Jane's estate because Jane has a general power of appointment over these assets at the time of her death. A general power of appointment allows the spouse, Jane, the right to take the property of the trust for herself, her husband John, or others, or to give the trust property to her estate. The general power of appointment, as the A trust's name indicates, qualifies for the unlimited marital deduction if it can be exercisable by the surviving spouse, Jane, alone and under all circumstances. Practically speaking, this is accomplished by including this power in Jane's will. Therefore, the right to appoint Jane must be unconditional.

Some rules exist for general power of appointment trusts. This trust:

- Must provide the surviving spouse with all of the annual income.
- Provides a power which can be exercisable only by the surviving spouse during life or at death, or both where it can be exercisable in favor of the spouse or the spouse's estate, or the creditors of the spouse's estate.

Where Do Qualified Terminal Interest Properties Fit for Divorced Spouses?

For a recently divorced spouse, using a qualified terminal interest property (QTIP) trust is critical. QTIPs would enter the picture if a marital deduction would be created with an amount in excess of the exemption amount at the death of the first spouse (which is funded within the B trust), but for which a general power of appointment in the surviving spouse would not be warranted.

QTIPs are common when dealing with multiple marriages whereby the decedent wants to benefit his or her own children from those earlier marriages, and not benefit the current spouse's children, since property left outright to the surviving spouse can be directed to his or her own children and not to the decedent's children. From a planning technique, the QTIP is valuable because the decedent can control the assets long after he or she has left this earth.

The benefit received by the executor in deciding whether some or all of the property should qualify for the marital deduction is that with this added flexibility, he may determine if there is a tax benefit to be gained by paying tax on the first estate.

Since annual income must be provided to the surviving spouse, it is important to fund the trust with income-producing assets.

Rules for QTIP Trusts

QTIPs:
- Must provide the surviving spouse with all of the annual income.
- Cannot give anyone a power to appoint any of the property to anyone else while the surviving spouse is alive.
- Require the executor to make some or all of the property qualify for the marital deduction.
- Must include in the survivor's estate the portion of the assets elected to pass tax-free under the marital deduction.
- Allow the transferring spouse to direct who receives the trust property upon the death of the recipient spouse.
- Are possible only if the decedent was a U.S. citizen or resident.

For example, non-income-generating real estate or small business owner stock, which pays little or no dividends, would not be appropriate properties to be placed into the trust. The reason is that the surviving spouse must be given an interest that is supposed to produce income consistent with its value.

What you should look for is for the surviving spouse to be given the power within the will or trust to convert non-income-producing property into income-producing property. The flip side of QTIPs involving small business owner stock exists when a family member, other than a surviving spouse, is active in the business. The QTIP provides for that other family member.

As a result, the QTIP trust is generally favored by attorneys and estate planners alike, over the general power of appointment trust, because:

- The decedent retains control over the disposition of the QTIP trust assets upon the death of the surviving spouse.
- The QTIP provides more flexibility in that the executor can make a partial election or a full election to utilize a marital deduction for a QTIP trust, even if the entire trust could qualify for the election.
- The executor is given a chance to clean up mistakes made by being given a second go-round to make changes between the date of death and the filing date of the return, which is when the election must be made.

The general power of appointment trust may work better than the QTIP if:

- A trust is desired to provide stability of management.
- The surviving spouse desires to make lifetime gifts from the trust.

Making the Election. Since the QTIP trust qualifies for the marital deduction, as stated previously, the executor for the decedent spouse must elect to take the marital deduction. This is done on the Federal Estate Tax Return (Form 706). As a result of the executor's election, the assets in the QTIP trust eventually will be includible in the surviving spouse's estate. Once made, the marital deduction election is irrevocable.

Potential Funding Problems. Funding a QTIP with inappropriate assets may create all sorts of problems. If the QTIP is funded with unproductive assets, such as closely held business stock that has not paid prior dividends, or poor real estate that generates no cash flow, it may not be able to satisfy the surviving spouse's annual income requirement. Without careful planning, the marital deduction can be lost since the surviving spouse must be provided with an annual income. Another problem arises when the trust assets by their nature do not permit total income distribution on an annual basis.

Planning Your Inheritance. Those who expect to inherit a significant estate should ask their benefactor to create a trust for their benefit, preferably a spendthrift trust. A trust fund set up for an individual is a private transaction which can protect the principal from one's creditors (and from those of your descendants), from creditors of your estate, and from becoming marital property available for a divorce settlement arrangement. Moreover, your parents, grandparents, and ancestors can bequeath up to the maximum IRS amount which can be sheltered from future transfer taxes in your estate and that of other descendants. If you expect a large inheritance, you can even be trustee of these types of trusts as long as you do not have unlimited discretion to make distributions of trust principal to yourself.

The Generation-Skipping Transfer Tax.   Use of the generation-skipping transfer (GST) tax can also substantially reduce the overall wealth transfer tax. Know that the GST tax is an additional tax over and above the estate tax. The GST was traditionally used as a device to save federal gift and estate tax by keeping property out of the taxable estates of the members of the intermediate generation. The beneficiary could be trustee, have all the income, invade the principal for needs, and control the distribution of the property as long as the beneficiary did not have a general power of appointment. Now, the GST tax considerations of such transfers must also be considered.

Rattiner's Financial Planning Tips Checklist

Use the following checklist of action items to gain control of your new post-divorce life. It will teach you how you should approach these complicated and often overlooked areas to ensure that you have not omitted any critical issues when planning for the next chapter of your new life.

Insurance Pointers

1. When reviewing your life insurance policy:
    a. Separate long-term needs from short-term needs.
    b. Recalculate needs regularly.
    c. Review ratings of existing carriers.
    d. Review reasons why current insurance was purchased.
    e. Determine how original needs have changed and identify new needs.
    f. Review beneficiary designations.
    g. Review policy riders and options.
    h. Review each policy's features.
    i. Compare your current health if debating whether to switch policies.
    j. If it's a term policy, evaluate conversion and renewability features and feasibility.
    k. If it's a permanent cash value policy, evaluate the true cost of insurance with the value received.
    l. Determine whether it makes sense to gift one of your life insurance policies.
    m. Determine whether it makes sense to name a charity as a revocable or irrevocable beneficiary and establish a wealth replacement trust.

   n. Determine whether it makes sense to establish a charitable trust to own the life insurance.

   o. Evaluate the effect of current life insurance ownership on its value in the estate.

   p. Determine if any incidents of ownership exist for insurance that is intended to be outside the estate.

   q. Determine if beneficiary designations of any policies owned outside the estate will cause inclusion within the estate.

2. When reviewing your health (a) and disability (b through h) policies:

   a. Inquire whether you opted for the best type of medical coverage based on your family situation.

   b. Determine the monthly disability needed.

   c. Determine whether sufficient coverage exists under your current policy, or was the existing coverage purchased many years ago when you were earning a lower salary.

   d. Determine whether the policy provides a definition of *own occupation*.

   e. Determine whether the policy is noncancellable and guaranteed renewable.

   f. Determine whether a provision for residual and partial disability exists.

   g. Determine whether a guaranteed insurability rider or cost of living adjustment (COLA) rider has been added.

   h. Determine whether the elimination period is appropriate.

3. When reviewing long-term care insurance:

   a. Identify qualification triggers for benefit eligibility. The use of activities of daily living (ADLs) and/or physician referral is preferred.

   b. Compare existing policy triggers to current products. Consider replacement of policies requiring prior hospitalization.

   c. Determine levels of care provided. Avoid policies that do not cover all levels of inpatient care. Evaluate your needs regarding home care versus inpatient care.

   d. Review elimination period and relate to other resources for coverage.

   e. Review benefit level relative to current costs and other available income.

    f. Review benefit period relative to your family history.

    g. Compare premium histories of guaranteed renewable policies.

4. When reviewing your homeowner's insurance coverage:

    a. Ensure whether coverage is adequate to replace dwelling only. The replacement cost and the value may be two very different numbers.

    b. Is the proper form of insurance in place? A homeowner's policy on a property currently being rented out is not acceptable.

    c. Determine the last time you reviewed the cost of the coverage.

    d. Determine whether you have replacement cost coverage or actual cash value (ACV) coverage.

    e. Determine whether the policy contains an inflation-adjustment rider.

    f. Determine whether personal property coverage is adequate based on assets owned.

    g. Determine whether replacement cost protection on personal property exists.

    h. Determine whether you understand the limitations on high-value items.

    i. Determine whether you have floaters for all high-value personal property.

    j. Determine whether an HO-15 rider exists.

    k. Determine if disaster coverage is necessary and appropriate.

5. When reviewing your liability coverage:

    a. Determine whether current policies include adequate coverage for you.

    b. Determine whether current coverage is enough to qualify you to obtain an umbrella policy.

    c. With your current circumstances, determine whether your umbrella policy is sufficient and cost-efficient.

    d. Determine whether you have any high-risk assets, such as a swimming pool, that would warrant additional or special coverage.

6. When reviewing your auto policy:

    a. Consider whether state-mandated levels are met and whether they are adequate.

    b. Consider the deductible relative to other assets.

    c. Determine whether it would be appropriate to remove collision coverage on older vehicles.

    d. Determine whether all owned vehicles are included on the policy.

7. When reviewing business insurance:

    a. Determine whether coverage is appropriate.

    b. Determine whether insurance agents have been performing an adequate job of discovering all of the pertinent exposures.

Investment Management Action Plan

1. Summarize all of your investments.
2. Determine how your investments are allocated, in total, among the three investment categories: stock, fixed income, and cash.
3. Factor in your objectives when designing the right allocation of your investments.
4. Put savings first. Save on a regular basis.
5. Constantly monitor your portfolio. Don't be rash in making changes.
6. Substance over form. Make sure the investment merits outweigh everything else.
7. Taxes should be a secondary reason to invest.
8. Don't time the market. Long-term buy and hold will usually work best.
9. Use mutual funds as your primary investment vehicle.
10. Don't chase returns. Keep with your long-term strategy and don't deviate from your long-term objectives.

Retirement Strategies

1. If your savings program will not result in a sufficient amount to fund your retirement lifestyle, there are basically four courses of action:

    a. Save more.

    b. Earn more (a higher investment return on the retirement savings fund).

    c. Retire later.

    d. Retire in a more modest lifestyle.

2. Wherever possible, you should be saving through a tax-deferred vehicle such as a qualified plan or a personal retirement plan, such as an IRA, SEP, or SIMPLE.

3. In determining your retirement savings need, use appropriate assumptions for investment rate of return, inflation rate, years till retirement, and years during retirement.

4. Retirement plan funds should be maintained in tax-deferred accounts to maximize the benefits of tax deferral. Consider alternate sources of funds needed during the pre-retirement period, so that retirement plan balances will not be eroded.

5. Review beneficiary designations on all retirement plan accounts to ensure that they are consistent with your goals.

6. Keep retirement planning in view as short-term decisions are being made regarding the use of income and assets.

7. Review your retirement projections periodically; revise the analysis periodically and in the event of material changes in your situation (change of employment, divorce/marriage, death of spouse).

8. As you approach retirement, plan on incorporating the stretch (multi-generational) IRA to enable the retirement funds to grow tax-deferred as long as possible.

9. Fully analyze any projections made by other professionals when projecting a pension maximization or other recommendation.

10. Monitor your investment return; compare it to assumptions that were used to build the retirement fund. If your investments are not realizing the expected return, you may need to shift your investment allocation or modify your retirement lifestyle.

11. Monitor your expenses compared to projections; modifications in lifestyle may be necessary.

Estate Planning Issues

1. In considering any gift or estate strategy, analyze the basic aspects of any particular property being planned for use in the strategy.

2. Where spousal transfers are involved, always check the citizenship of the transferee spouse.

3. Where necessary, be willing to pay a small tax to achieve an important personal objective.
4. Be sure to have a will, even if the plan you have in place will avoid probate completely.
5. It's wise to establish a durable power of attorney and the medical proxies available under state law.
6. It's a good idea to file your will and other estate documents for safekeeping with the appropriate court.
7. Consider all charitable giving techniques that would enhance current income.
8. Review all indications of domicile and try to consolidate domicile as much as possible.
9. Avoid seeing probate and revocable trusts as an either-or proposition.
10. Use joint ownership arrangements sparingly as an estate planning technique.
11. Estimate estate liquidity needs and identify sources of liquidity.
12. If life insurance is to be purchased as a source of liquidity, avoid even initial ownership by the insured.
13. It's best not to use joint, mutual, or reciprocal wills, and/or joint trusts.
14. Compile a family tree, clarifying relationships and identifying critical dates (e.g., marriages, births, deaths, gifts, etc.).
15. Construct a net worth statement for yourself, extrapolating from that the degree of planning appropriate.
16. Identify items that would be classified as income with respect to a decedent in a prospective gross estate, and attempt to determine how best to handle those items.
17. Make sure you understand the planning limits imposed by spousal rights in community property states and common law states.
18. Determine the estate plan that you currently have (even if it is all intestacy).
19. Don't allow the generation-skipping transfer tax to discourage you from making transfers to grandchildren or others until the exemption is fully utilized.

20. Consider carefully what plans are in place for the disposition of pension plan benefits and whether different dispositions should be explored.
21. Assess the adequacy of provisions for minors and dependents, and make changes as needed.
22. Where there is a closely held business interest, determine definitively how the succession in interest is to be achieved, whether by a buy-sell agreement or through another technique.
23. Survey the postmortem elections that might be available to your particular estate and adopt strategies that will preserve the availability of these elections.

Now that you have a brief idea of where you should be in your post-divorce stage of life, please take a few minutes to complete this checklist. Any "no" or "not sure" answers can point to potential problems you may wish to investigate.

CHAPTER

10

Afterward

THE 25 STEPS TO FUTURE SUCCESS

Now what? You've gone through the divorce process, attained your ultimate goal, so I'll say it again: Now what? Are you happy? Are you sad? Are you indifferent?

When I was going through the divorce process, I always thought to myself, how will I react when it is all said and done? I imagined that I would be interviewed on television, and the interviewer would ask me, "Jeff Rattiner, you just got divorced. What are your immediate plans?" Then I would look into the camera and respond, "I am going to Disneyworld!" After that, I figured background music would be played from the musical group The Who, with the song, "I'm Free." Then I'd blast the song so the world could hear, and throw a big party! But when push came to shove, I did quite the opposite.

Everyone has their reasons for wanting a divorce, but the real deal is bittersweet. I mean, after all, you married this person. There must have been something there initially. While you were reciting your wedding vows, the chance of divorcing was not on your mind. You never thought this would ever happen to you. But as I stated in Chapter 1, unfortunately, the person you married is not the same person you are divorcing.

Recap

What have we learned from these 10 chapters? You've acquired this piece of paper at a cost to you of only $50,000, give or take. Some people I have spoken to gave me a figure of $200,000 or more.

Ouch! The paper states that you are not legally married anymore. What a bargain! You're happy that you can go on with your life, but sad at the destruction that has taken place. Irreparable damage from things that can never get fixed or undone has developed and could cause you future reason for concern. But you are now free to move about the cabin!

When speaking with many interviewees who have gone through the entire divorce process, 90 percent of them tell me they wish the divorce process would have worked out differently. They were very disappointed throughout every aspect. They were sorry that they dragged the process through their high-powered attorneys and sorry for the misery they caused the other spouse and their children. When everything was said and done, they didn't see their sense of justice confirmed. They didn't get what they bargained for. They ended up with nothing, just a big legal bill. But worse yet, those future monies once earmarked for the kids were no longer available, as many people find out the hard way.

Many rational spouses getting divorced will try to work out proposed settlements to expedite the process and come to a quicker, more efficient close. I tried to do that three times, but to no avail. And in all the cases in which I conducted interviews, all of the participants stated that they would have received more had they taken any one of a number of proposed settlement options.

But again, it's not really about the money for most people. Remember, money can be made back at a later date. These soon-to-be-divorced spouses are not thinking clearly or rationally. It is all being fought in the heat of battle sparked 100 percent by emotion. We all know that you can't come to rational decisions in a heated rage. That's why you have always heard that if you need to make an important decision, take a few days to mull it over, and then come back to it when you have a clear head. Important decisions need to be made in an unbiased thought process. The same thought process applies here in divorce.

Going through the legal process makes winners of both lawyers and their support team (see Chapter 1) because no one can really declare victory. Who wins what? What is there to win? How do you measure what you won? You are basically resigned to the issue of "How much did I lose?" It's sort of like going to Las Vegas. If you didn't lose much, then you consider your experience to be that of a winner! What is true and proven is that both spouses lose (again, see Chapter 1). That's a definite! Not only that, the parties who lose are footing the bill for everyone involved in the process. What's wrong with this picture?

Even though it's over, you'll still have certain things that never go away. The children will always be there and your relationships with family members and friends may continue as beforehand. Lastly, if the ex was difficult to deal with before, he or she can continue to be difficult going forward. You can count on that!

The Next Phase: Chapter Two

There are new things to think about going forward. There's a lot of mending to do, a lot of soul searching to experience, a lot of fences to rebuild, a lot of changes to make, trying to turn negative horror stories into positive experiences. And most of all, now that you have received your walking papers, you have to create a brand new life for yourself. Create "you" as the new brand. That's part of the fun. A new confidence bursts through at the seams, waiting to get started on the next phase of your life, chapter two. New experiences, new challenges, and new opportunities will evolve. This may be the first time you can experience those things that are truly important to you in an independent setting.

But before you can go out there and do your thing, you need to gain closure to some very important things that tend to get overlooked when everything is said and done—the post-divorce game wrap-up. You need to take care of many overlooked items and adjust accordingly. As the great philosopher Yogi Berra said, "It ain't over till it's over!" But a more accurate description pertaining to divorce might be, it ain't over even when it's over!

I have compiled a list of 25 items—13 financial and 12 nonfinancial—that you need to understand to protect yourself and minimize potential problems going forward.

Financial Planning Responsibilities That Need to Be Followed Up

This section describes what you need to do with regard to updating financial documents. There is no time like the present to get started on making these changes. Unfortunately, more men forget to do what I am about to explain than women. Don't procrastinate. The law books are filled with cases resulting from arguments between current and former spouses about a person's intent to leave money or property to one or the other. Do yourself a favor and make sure you are clear about your intentions after your divorce.

Read the Divorce Decree Carefully, Hopefully One Last Time

Stand back for a bit but then go back and reread the divorce decree you just purchased. Review the entire court order to make sure it says what you expected it to say and that you understand it all.

If you do find a mistake, you'll need to act. The type of mistake you view will dictate your future action, if any. If it is merely a typo, as I say to my students, you need to punt—essentially, move on. It's not worth belaboring. The single-word accuracy here is irrelevant and not worth creating waves over. However, when reviewing the agreement, if you notice that there are things included that you did not agree to, or something you agreed to is not stated correctly, then you need to take immediate action.

Contact the person who drafted the agreement right away. This is probably your lawyer or mediator. If your divorce was uncontested, contact your ex to make sure he or she agrees with your assessment of the changes. If you both see eye to eye on the discrepancy, you can both approach the court together and ask them to remedy the mistake. Then speak to your attorney regarding the next step. Amending the final agreement against the wishes of the ex can be tricky and costly.

Make sure, when you are rereading the divorce decree, to mark down all that you are responsible for going forward. This could be a substantial list. Then highlight those changes and record them in a journal or diary where they are easy to access, maintain, and remember. You are ultimately responsible for whatever shows up in the divorce decree.

Things you want to take notice of include future payments, where to send or receive the payments, canceling of all credit cards, which assets you did receive, notifying people and organizations of your changed situation, and other terms so you don't give your ex ammunition to take you back to court. And sometimes when you don't think you are giving your ex reason to act, you can still end up back there for something you did, such as pulling money out of a retirement account in a different manner than the ex thought was right. You might see the ex file a motion, pay legal fees, then withdraw the motion simply because there was nothing for him or her to gain from the situation. The bottom line was no change.

Obtain Certified Copies of the Divorce Decree

Once you receive your divorce decree signed by the judge stating that you are no longer married, you'll need to receive certified copies of the decree so you may follow through on certain transactions, including moving retirement dollars to the ex, changing titles to real estate, changing beneficiaries on the insurance policies, and so on. *Certification* is the official seal of approval from the court clerk that shows the document is an accurate and official copy of what the judge has signed. Either your lawyer can provide you with a copy or you can run down to the county courthouse, see the court clerk, pay a minimal fee, and have the copies certified with a special seal stamped on it by the court. The seal is raised, which marks it as an official copy.

Make New Deeds for Real Estate

Many times the attorney will require you to do this before everything is signed, sealed, and delivered. For example, if you are transferring the primary residence to your ex, the ex's attorney will require you to sign the deed of transfer before the divorce decree becomes finalized. Many times this is necessary if you are going to buy the ex-spouse out or vice versa, and this gives you the ability to refinance the house in order to accomplish this objective. The bank or mortgage company will not allow you to refinance with the ex's name still on the deed without making him or her liable on the mortgage. As stated in Chapter 6, there are no tax consequences with the transfer of the real estate to the spouse pursuant to a divorce under Internal Revenue Code Section 1041.

Have the lawyer prepare the deed. You shouldn't do it yourself because you will risk not getting it recorded properly. The real estate transfer is usually done through a quitclaim or grant deed.

A quitclaim deed is a deed that simply transfers to the new owner (called the *grantee*) whatever interest in the property may be held by the person signing the deed, without warranty. It conveys only such rights as the grantor has. The signer of the deed (called the *grantor*) makes no warranties or guarantees about the quality of the grantor's interest in the property, whether or not there are any liens against the property, or whether anyone else may claim any interest in the property. A quitclaim deed is most often used in non-sale transactions relating to divorce.

A grant deed is a form for the conveyance of interest in real property. A grant deed implies certain warranties. It implies the grantor has not previously conveyed any title to the property to another. It implies the property is, at the time of the conveyance, free from any liens allowed to be placed on the property by the grantor or grantor's agent.

Transfer Car Title

You'll need to make sure each of the titles from your cars is transferred to the appropriate spouse. You can probably do this online or go down to the motor vehicle bureau and do it in person.

One thing I found out when doing this is if you had a car loan that was paid off a while back and the Department of Motor Vehicles (DMV) did not record that there is no longer an outstanding loan on the car for whatever reason, you will need to obtain proof of the satisfaction of mortgage statement from the lender in order for the DMV to remove the loan payee's name from the title and thus transfer the title to you, who in turn can then transfer it to the right spouse. It can be easy, but if the prior lender merged with another lender or went out of business, that could be an issue. It may also be an issue if you do have the paperwork and it is located in one of hundreds of boxes you have piled up during the divorce.

Update Insurance Coverage and Beneficiary Information

You need to look at all your existing insurance policies and ensure that the appropriate new beneficiary is named on each one. Policies can include life, disability, health, homeowners, automobile, and umbrella (liability). Resist the temptation to purchase new policies until you understand what coverage you now have. Many insurance agents may view you as live bait, knowing your situation has changed, and offer to find a policy that suits your needs, even if there are no new needs.

Also, to ensure that all coverage for the following types of insurance has been done correctly, ask the insurance agent for a copy of your declaration page for each policy. This is a one-page synopsis of the coverage you have—the amounts, the insureds, the beneficiaries, if any, and all the other specifics as it relates to the issuance of the policies.

Life Insurance. You should have a primary and secondary (contingent) beneficiary listed on your policy. Typically, you probably had your ex as the primary and children as your secondary beneficiaries. It is important to change this. It is just a matter of filing a simple change of beneficiary designation form with the insurance company.

Here is a real-life client example from my tax practice. I had a male client who owned a $2 million life insurance policy naming his wife from his first marriage as the beneficiary. We'll call her wife number one. He ended up getting divorced and married wife number two. He named wife number two in his will as the sole heir to receive the proceeds from this life insurance policy. He never bothered to change the original life insurance policy.

Well, he died, and guess who ended up with the $2 million death benefit? You guessed it—wife number one did. Why? Because life insurance policies pass by contract law and contract law always supersedes a will. That's why it is imperative to change the beneficiary designations as soon as possible. But to be fair, wife number two did receive a consolation prize. She got to pay the $10,000 funeral costs. So each spouse did end up sharing in the event.

Imagine if an angry first wife knew she was still the beneficiary on her ex's life insurance policy. She'd make a quick call to 1-800-MOBSTER and the rest, as they say, is history.

On the flip side, you may choose to continue to list your ex as the beneficiary. There are many reasons for that, many of which are unfortunately ignored. If you are the payer of alimony and you die, then monies earmarked for your children's college education or other children's things you may have been responsible for will not be available. Or if the ex is concerned about the lack of child support and alimony because of the payer spouse's early death, the life insurance policy protects the payee spouse in this event and ensures that sufficient life insurance is purchased as a contingency plan.

Also, the payee spouse may want to obtain coverage if the payer spouse has a pension benefit that is supposed to go to the payee spouse, for fear of losing out on the benefit if the payer spouse dies too early. The amount purchased would be calculated as the lump-sum present value needed to cover the payer spouse's obligations if that spouse were to die today. The death benefit would be paid at the payer spouse's death to the payee spouse. If invested conservatively, it should provide for enough funds to pay for those expenses earmarked until the payer spouse's obligations are completed.

As a practical matter, it makes sense for the payee spouse to own a policy on the payer spouse. There is definitely an insurable interest here, as previously discussed. Remember, there always has to be an insurable interest present for life insurance to be purchased on a particular person. The rationale for this is that if the payer spouse owns the policy and problems arise down the road, the payer spouse can simply cancel the policy and the payee spouse is therefore left unprotected.

Lastly, if the life insurance policy is a requirement in the divorce decree and the payer spouse owns the policy, the payee spouse can send a letter along with a certified copy of the divorce decree to the insurance company demanding he or she be notified of changes to the policy or that you notify the company on a regular basis to determine the current status of the policy. If you didn't get a letter or it wasn't a requirement from the court, ask your ex to provide that information to you and keep you in the loop.

Disability Insurance. You can make the same argument for disability. If the payer spouse becomes disabled, he or she may not be able to fulfill the obligations required per the divorce decree. The payer spouse needs a policy to complete the financial responsibility.

Health Insurance.   If your ex works for a company that employs 20 or more employees, then COBRA benefits will be available to you. In the event of a death or divorce (perhaps one and the same!), the worker's health insurance coverage benefits can still be extended and made available to you for up to 36 months from the respective date of the worker spouse's death or divorce.

There are very strict timelines for signing up for continued coverage so you'll need to get moving on this ASAP. Verify that the plan administrator has been notified of COBRA election by the nonemployee spouse.

Homeowner's Insurance.   Contact your homeowner's insurance company and make sure the policy has only your name on it. If you have moved, also make sure the proper address is on it.

Automobile Insurance. Contact your automobile insurance company and make sure the policy has on it only your name and other dependents for whom you may be responsible. Also ensure that you are listed as the only owner of the car. If the car was transferred into your name alone, you should have a new policy issued.

Umbrella (Liability) Insurance. Contact the umbrella insurance company to ensure that you are the only one listed on it. Also, if you have other properties, make sure all your properties are listed on this policy. This coverage extends to all properties you own.

Update Your Retirement Plan Beneficiary Designations

A good place to start is by looking at all the retirement plans you've listed on your financial statement to the court. This would span all your working years. These include qualified plans like defined benefit and defined contribution plans; personal retirement plans, like IRAs, SIMPLEs, SEPs; and nonqualified plans, like deferred compensation, rabbi trusts, and supplemental executive retirement plans. See Chapter 7 for a description of what these plans cover.

Make sure to change all the plans on which you have listed your ex-spouse as your beneficiary. Contact your plan administrator, human resource personnel at your place of employment, or other places where retirement plan assets may be located. Lastly, have someone check the forms you complete to ensure that you did it right. Never take anything for granted.

Update Your Retirement Plan Accounts

Just because you have done your part to divide your retirement plan assets pursuant to your divorce decree doesn't mean it has actually happened. You need to verify that it has. If it was a qualified retirement plan, make sure the court enters a qualified domestic relations order (QDRO) and make sure it is filed and given to the retirement plan administrator so those funds can be divided in accordance with the QDRO. This could be for the lump sum available in the defined contribution plan, or for future pension plan distributions from the defined benefit plan.

If a QDRO was part of your divorce decree, make sure the order actually gets written, signed by the judge, and made a part of your court file. The QDRO is separate from the order that says you are divorced. This is easy to overlook, especially if the court order doesn't say who is responsible for obtaining the QDRO.

Usually the spouse who is supposed to receive the benefits takes the lead in obtaining the QDRO. Further, if you are the non-employee spouse, it's in your best interest to take charge even if you are not required to, just to ensure that you don't lose those pension rights down the road. If the benefit you are receiving is a pension, once all the paperwork is completed, you do not have to do anything else until the pension benefits are to be received. This could be many years down the road. Lastly, make sure you get a certified copy from the court.

QDROs are not necessary for the splitting of personal retirement account assets, such as IRAs, SIMPLEs, and SEPs. But you do have to make sure that the split actually occurs. You cannot have the account name changed, a check written to you, or even a retirement check endorsed over to you. It must also go through proper procedure. One of the issues often overlooked is that the payer spouse just hands over the money to you and claims to have fulfilled their obligation. The problem with that approach is that you could pay tax on the money received if it is not rolled over to you properly and you may incur an early withdrawal tax penalty of 10 percent. Again, make sure you have someone sign off on the roll-over to ensure that it is done correctly.

Update your Estate Planning Documents, Including Wills, Trusts, and Powers of Attorney

I'd say *minutes* after the divorce, update your will. That may be a little exaggerated, but any will that says you are married can be trouble down the road, especially if it stated that your property was to be left to your ex. If you made a new will before your divorce was final, it may be automatically revoked in short order when the judgment has been entered. You still need to make a new will even if you do want to leave something to your ex (i.e., your handgun). The will needs to say that you are a single person and should show that your intentions have been restated.

If you hold any separate property in trust, you may have already taken the property out of the trust due to the divorce. Review the trust document and amend it if necessary or check with the lawyer who prepared the trust.

If you signed a power of attorney that would give your ex power over your finances if you were unable to take care of your own financial well-being, make sure you destroy it. The same rationale goes for your health care directive or living will if you named your ex.

Confirm that All Bank Accounts, Brokerage Accounts, and Stock Certificates Are Separated into Your Own Name

You should have closed all your joint bank and brokerage accounts, as directed in Chapter 2. But you should still revisit the issue just to make sure. Just contact the bank in writing and instruct them to do so as per the terms of your divorce decree. Send along a copy of your divorce decree and provide clear instructions as to what needs to be done. You should also send a copy of this communication to your ex.

If you are holding actual stock certificates, you'll need to send the certificates back to the transfer agent with endorsements by both you and your ex on the back. Again, include a copy of the divorce decree calling for the division and a letter of clear instructions for the transfer agent to issue new stock certificates and where they should be sent.

Confirm that All Credit Cards, Other Obligations, and Possessions Are Separated by Having Your Ex Removed from the Accounts

You should have closed all your joint bank accounts, again as mentioned in Chapter 2. Send a copy of the divorce decree to notify all creditors, including credit card companies, credit unions, credit card agencies, or other places where you have outstanding credit. Legally, your creditors can look to you to pay the joint debts or your ex-spouse's debts until things are finalized. What you are accomplishing here is putting your creditors on notice about the change in your credit card status.

If your settlement agreement makes your spouse responsible for some of your debts, take steps to have those debts transferred into your spouse's name. Close any joint safe deposit boxes and post office boxes that you have, and open new ones.

Lastly, obtain a copy of your credit report now that everything is basically behind you. If there are inaccuracies, contact the credit card agency and write a letter disputing those charges. If done within the appropriate timeline and in accordance with their guide-lines, the agencies will have to make the necessary changes.

Keep Meticulous Records

As the payer spouse, make sure you have a full accounting of all the payments you make to your ex. These include alimony, child support, or other items that you are responsible for paying. Keep copies of all canceled checks. Keep a calendar of all payments paid or received. Just keep all the records in a separate envelope or folder. If you cannot prove you paid for something, then you might as well accept the fact that you didn't.

Keep records of all your children's doctor visits, insurance claims, insurance payments, and insurance denials, and your payments to providers or to your spouse for the children's care.

If you are co-parenting, keep a journal record of how visits with the other co-parent went, and if there were any specific problems you encountered during the process. This will help in solving future disputes.

For your income taxes, make sure you have all the Social Security numbers for the children you are claiming as dependents and for your spouse if you are paying alimony.

If you are the payee spouse, keep a running account in a permanent place. If you cannot prove what you received, the court might not believe you when you testify about what you did not receive. It is easier for both parties, and sometimes required by law, to have payments automatically deducted from the payer spouse's account.

Remove Personal Assets

If you still have remaining personal property in your ex's basement or at your former residence, then ask your ex when you can come by and pick it up. Prepare a listing of those items so you can do the transfer in one clean swoop. Not doing that immediately can create confusion down the road as to who owns what.

Name, Address, and Work-Related Changes

If you are changing your name back to your maiden name or perhaps some other name, you'll need to follow up to make sure that all of your official documents reflect your new name. If you change your name because of the divorce, get your driver's license and Social Security card changed as well as other permanent information.

Notify your children's schools of any new addresses of both parents for mailing records, as well as all relevant agencies and companies. Alert them that the divorce is final. Notify the IRS of a change in address by filing Form 8822; also notify your state authority.

For work, contact human resources and change your W-4 from your employer to ensure that you no longer need to take an extra exemption for your spouse.

Other Critical Issues That Need Your Follow-Up

Your Children

Again, as stressed throughout this book, it's all about the kids. And your responsibilities are towards those kids. Now you may think that just because you are divorced from your ex, you'll never tango with that person ever again. Unfortunately, the dance does not end. You'll always have an attachment with the ex-spouse because of the kids. So just accept it.

If your children are young, shuttling them back and forth between homes will involve working with your ex. The best thing you can do is to comply with the court order as is, without asking for changes and exceptions.

Until your children reach adulthood, the court has the power to make decisions about child custody, visitation, and support. As time passes, you'll develop a standardized routine. Changes that need to be made with the ex can hopefully be accommodated. You'll also notice that your parenting plan will adjust accordingly since kids are very unpredictable and their needs will change a lot during the time you have shared custody with your ex.

You should keep the ex in full communication about the kids since things will constantly change. Examples would include changing days for sports practice, band, babysitters, and so on. Never assume just because the changes will work for you that they'll also work for your ex-spouse. Remember, as stated earlier, if you assume anything you are likely to be wrong. This also gives you an excuse to practice the high road.

If there are significant changes, you may need to go back to court to address them. Examples would be going from joint custody to solo custody with visitation rights, more time with the children since you have a new job that doesn't require a lot of traveling, and so on. Start the discussions with the ex, maybe get a therapist involved, but if that doesn't work, then you'll need to go to court.

Moving Away

What happens if you (the noncustodial parent) move away due to a job change, transfer, or some other issue? Or what happens to the custodial parent if you both share custody and are not allowed to leave the state or move to a different area?

For some noncustodial parents, your intent to move can be construed as a declaration of war. It sends a message that the other parent will not be able to enjoy the same relationship with the children as they enjoyed before the divorce.

If you are the custodial parent and decide to move, you should understand that even expressing a desire to do so, such as filing a moving petition with the court, will probably make your ex furious. Do not take this lightly.

Expect the noncustodial parent to fight back in any way possible. That parent may not allow you to move without protest and you can probably expect an unfair fight. Expect that parent to raise arguments that it is not in the best interests of the child to be moved from his or her surroundings. The ex will probably threaten to file a motion to reduce support, especially if you are moving in with someone else, or may even try to challenge your fitness as a parent.

As the custodial parent, if you have a legitimate case to move, such as you are unemployed and you now have the opportunity to work, even though it is a logical reason, it still may be challenged by the noncustodial parent.

Modifying Child Support

Circumstances change and after your divorce, as the payer spouse, you might want to lower the amount you are responsible to pay, such as the support obligation, because you're temporarily out of work or you find yourself facing extra ongoing expenses like a chronic illness or caring for a parent. If you're receiving support, an increase in your spouse's income or in your expenses might justify an increase in support.

Either way, try to resolve it with your ex so you don't have to go to court. Don't stop paying your financial obligation in the hope that things will work themselves out. With no communication, they never do. You can always use a mediator again to help you both sort through the issues. Remember, to change an order, you have to do so with another order.

If your spouse tells you it's okay to miss payments, still get it in writing. This way, if your ex has a change of heart, the courts won't have a field day over it.

If you can't work it out with your ex-spouse, then the next step is court. You need to show that something beyond your control is interfering with your ability to continue to make those payments at the level you were paying beforehand.

If the payee spouse moves in with a new fling, the child support payments may be affected since the courts will now say that the payee has other sources of income, so the amount being received as child support can be reduced.

Your Kids and Post-Divorce Syndrome

Even after the divorce, your children may still have issues and conflicts they need to resolve. The children may still think the divorce is their fault or somehow they had a part in it. That's understandable but you need to nip it in the bud.

Your children will always need two parents. Period! Unfortunately, many people I speak to don't practice this and continue to blame an ex for the divorce, for the changes in their lifestyle, or for things that are likely to occur down the road. Now this doesn't mean you can't stress out over it, if need be, with the children. But you can talk about things with the kids without going into detail or exaggerating the facts to make your point.

What it does mean is that you should not be bitter in front of them or in blaming mode towards your ex all the time. Never tell the kids that your ex is a bad parent, doesn't care about them, or anything else that is not taking the high road. Every child needs a mother and a father. Period!

Down the road you may see your children revisit many of the issues you struggled with and agonized over, and you may feel like you are recreating the divorce scenario. That's because your children may need information one, two, three years or more down the road simply because they are processing the information differently now and are ready to accept closure on what transpired years earlier. Divorce is always a very stressful time for the children.

As I keep quoting the great philosopher, Yogi Berra, "It ain't over till it's over." Just because the divorce decree is signed as of a specific date doesn't mean the actual divorce ends completely at that date, for anyone. For some children, it may never end. Others tend to come to grips with the situation much sooner. It is important for you to realize that there is no right or wrong answer in any of this. The only important thing is full acceptance by all those involved and trying to minimize the disruptions to the children's life, and your own, wherever possible.

Modifying Spousal Support

Courts are reluctant to modify spousal support for the payee spouse unless you can prove you gave up your right under duress or prove that something unfair existed when you signed the agreement. If your income decreases because your job changes or if you lose your job, you may still be able to petition the court for more money. Finally, if you can prove your spouse is making more money now than at the time of the divorce decree, you may be entitled to share in that improved scenario. You can check your state's child support web site and do the calculations yourself to see if it is worthwhile to go back to court and modify the child support amount.

As the payer spouse, if you can prove that the payee spouse just landed a high-paying job and will be earning more money now, the courts may reduce what you have to pay. Or if you can prove that the payee spouse is now living with someone else, you can argue that the payee spouse has more household income and does not need as much from you going forward.

Dating Again: Helping Your Kids Cope

Now you must turn a greater amount of attention to yourself. After all, you are divorced and beginning the next chapter of your life. There are many ways to go about the dating process. The fact that you don't go to singles bars and don't meet people in meat-market settings is no longer an excuse.

After spending many years in marriage, some people reenter the dating field with trepidation. Many wonder if the game has changed. While the Internet may have increased the number of opportunities you have to meet someone, basic human interaction has not changed. Besides Internet dating, joining groups or teams, participating in activities, blind dates, your gym, dancing lessons, spiritual activities, and other creative activities will work to help you meet people. It takes a while to make the transition from married to single, but the roadblocks you encounter are just temporary. You'll ultimately get to where you are going.

So therefore everything should be happy, right? Not necessarily. If you have children, this will always present a challenge no matter what age they are. I have seen it become an issue for children, teenagers, and even 50-year-olds! The bottom line is that no child wants to see their parent being replaced—or, in baseball terms, to have their parent put on irrevocable waivers!

How your children accept the new "replacement" depends on how you approach it with them. It should always be a slow and gradual process. You should not introduce your friend to your children as a replacement for the other parent, but rather as a companion for you. You should also value your children's opinions and ask them how they like or dislike your friend. The children may have legitimate concerns that need to be addressed early. Many times if the children don't appear to like the person at first, they may come around and soften their stance over time. "Everybody needs somebody sometime." Good song. Your children have to know that you are lonely and need companionship, too.

So should you not date because of the children? One person I interviewed said that the man she began dating after the divorce made her feel whole again, something she hadn't felt in many years. Should she not exercise her chance at happiness again because of her kids' negative reactions? I don't know the answer to that.

Some people view the opposite sex as taboo, the cause of all their problems, and have no interest in dating again. Others state that they want to find someone because they don't want to grow old and lonely. Forcing yourself out of desperation will present more challenges than the good that it can bring. You may end up over your head with the other person's problems and issues. While both responses are normal, taking one extreme or the other can be hazardous to your health! You need to find a proper middle ground, and that can take many years to do.

Perseverance will pay off. Don't settle on the first person to come your way. Keep your standards the same as they have been and look for those persons who have the same interests as you and can relate to the same experiences and pleasures as you do. There are more people out there in these situations than you think. What I found out in my own life is that when you least expect something to happen, then one day it does happen.

Some view dating someone right away as rebound dating. They say that your first relationship after a divorce is all about the gap and wounds you are trying to close after the divorce. Some say it is a meaningless relationship but you need it to move your life forward after you're ready to begin getting serious again. Others truly find their bliss and live happily ever after.

I offer some words of caution no matter what road you choose. Be discreet initially. Don't force your new love interest into your children's lives too soon. Studies have shown that you should wait a year before making that happen. Don't force your date, boyfriend, or girlfriend on your kids right away. The children will get to know him or her over time.

You probably will be ready for dating long before your children are ready to accept someone new into their lives. Just wait it out in terms of introducing that person to your children. Another interesting thought is, don't be surprised if your ex has a hard time with you dating again. I would say to exercise the same caution that you are applying with your children. Don't introduce the partner to your children or even to your ex (if you are still talking with your ex) until you are serious in your relationship.

In any event, I would say it is probably better if your children or your ex hear *from you* that you are dating again, and not from someone else. The same is true if your ex is dating someone else. Your gut reaction may say, "Good—I suffered, let someone else suffer too!" But deep down, it could be an emotional time for you since you were involved with that ex for many years and the thought of that person being with someone else can leave a bittersweet taste for you. If it does bother you, you can talk about it with friends, but never belittle the person, give your ex a hard time about it, or act out other destructive mechanisms. You also may find that in time you will grow to like that person and not resent him or her. Always take the high road with it.

The other often overlooked reality is that if you or your ex becomes serious with someone else, that person then enters the fold. What's more, he or she can help with daily routines, like picking the kids up from school or being around for them when they come home from school. The kids ultimately will get used to that person being around.

Cohabitation Agreements

If you are living with someone again after the divorce, you're better off protecting yourself with a strong front. "Better safe than sorry" should be your motto.

The cohabitation agreement should state how things will work between the two of you. It should cover how household expenses are to be paid, what happens in the event of various contingencies, and how all joint debts should be divided while alive and even after death.

It should cover assets brought into the relationship but acquired prior to both of you living together. In other words, property brought into the relationship remains separate property both during the relationship and after it ends; property acquired by you separately during the relationship remains separate property, while things you buy jointly are considered to be joint property. If you and your live-in roommate own property together, the cohabitation agreement should also specify who should receive what property if you break up.

To help protect both parties, you might even want to consider buying life insurance on the other to help with the buying out of others (i.e., children) in the event of your partner's death. This way an equivalent amount of money can pass to the decedent partner's children instead of forcing you into selling the asset to pay that comparable amount to the children. The rationale is that it will enable you to provide the beneficiaries with an equitable sum that the decedent partner wanted to ensure was received by those heirs, and you can then keep the property that the two of you were sharing while the decedent partner was alive (i.e., house, car, boat, and so forth).

This approach allows the dollars to work out equally and not have the descendants force you to sell the property so they can liquidate it and receive that part of the proceeds they were entitled to receive. It also gives you peace of mind knowing that the decedent's heirs cannot attach themselves to the property now that you own it outright after the decedent is gone.

Prenuptial Agreement

Here's an executive summary of what you should remember. Fool me once, shame on you. Fool me twice, shame on me! If you are fortunate enough to come into another relationship again, as they say, you need protection. Protection is found in the form of a prenuptial agreement. You want to protect the assets you've earned during your lifetime, even if for no other reason than that you want to protect your children's inheritances. Just look at the numbers—65 percent of all second marriages end up in divorce.

A prenuptial agreement is a document that lets you and your spouse-to-be make your own decisions about which of your state's marital property and support laws will apply to you and which won't. Examples found in the prenuptial agreement include your giving up your right to spousal support, or agreeing to keep your property separate so that if you do divorce, your spouse is not entitled to ask for any of your assets.

As you start to contemplate marriage again, it may start to hit a little too close to home, or you start to remember too much from your last experience to be trusting again or to go into it blindly. If you don't believe me, just ask Paul McCartney.

I found it interesting talking with several females whom I interviewed for this book, who all reiterated the same thing. They stated that the woman has a hard time with this type of agreement because the process seems very businesslike. No woman wants to enter a relationship on a contractual basis. What if the contract is not renewed down the road? The woman is entering into a legitimate business contract and is viewing the romance and love as having been removed from the relationship. The woman wants to enter the marriage as a commitment that will last forever; so does the husband, for that matter. But that may not be in either of their cards down the road.

A prenuptial agreement must provide for full disclosure and is designed to avoid fraud. In a nutshell, with the prenuptial agreement, you must reveal your entire poker hand face-up on the table before the hand is over and show the other person what you have. If you hide any assets and this is discovered after the fact, the prenuptial agreement will become null and void. Ouch!

You must then incorporate all of the terms into the final agreement, stating that if the relationship does not work out, then this is what I walk away with and this is what you walk away with from the end of our relationship. The prenuptial agreement cannot be used to promote a divorce and cannot be signed under duress.

Prenuptial agreements came into existence to make sure that the soon-to-be-spouse who is giving up rights understands the agreement that he or she is entering into and does not feel forced into creating and signing it. You should each have a lawyer present to ensure that your rights are being represented.

A prenuptial agreement might seem unromantic, but if you remember from your own divorce, your marriage ended in a very unromantic way, certainly much different than how it started. See this agreement as a precaution that in the event of your second marriage failing, you'll be in a better position. That's because all of the assets and income items have already been predecided and the divorce should go much quicker and more smoothly.

"Better safe than sorry" should be your motto. They say if you want to prevent war, you take all the necessary precautions ahead of time to ensure that you don't go down that path. The United States followed that approach successfully during the Cold War. A strong defense will be worth more than a strong offense in this situation. In order for you to do this right, you need to have both a cohabitation agreement (discussed previously) and a prenuptial agreement.

Getting Married Yet Again (Remarriage)

You know what they say: The first time is for love; the second time is for money; the third time you require cash in advance!

If you do decide to remarry and you didn't prepare a prenuptial agreement, then you should tell the organist to play the following song from the group Queen as you are walking down the aisle: "Another One Bites the Dust," because that's what will happen if you are not prepared.

According to noted sociologist Constance Ahrons, approximately 85 percent of divorced men and 75 percent of divorced women get remarried within the first three years after divorce. These numbers suggest that most people are not turned off to marriage nor are they bitter about the experiences they have encountered. Most people, as per my interviewees, want to learn from the process so it will be a better experience the next time around.

If you do remarry within a year after the divorce, expect your ex to become furious. That's because your ex (and possibly even you) may harbor the hope of getting back together despite the reality of the divorce, the difficulty of being married to each other, and the damage that was created when you split.

The flip side is that if you remarry, the spouse may interpret this as a message from you that "The divorce was really your fault— I told you that I am capable of being part of a happy, peaceful, successful, and loving relationship for the rest of my life, and you will be alone, miserable and bitter the rest of your life." Indirectly you are saying that although you didn't get marriage right the first time, you did find a way to make it work the second time around. Certainly, this is not true, as I have quoted the 65 percent divorce rate among remarried spouses.

Interestingly, one of the more common triggers for post-divorce lawsuits involves stepparents who assume traditional roles, stepping into the role of the natural parent. This includes stepparents physically disciplining your children, verbally or sexually abusing them, or posing such harsh sanctions that they are not viewed as realistic (i.e., you can't play sports in high school, or you can't partake in an activity until your grades improve). The nonmarried spouse may feel threatened and feel that the new stepparent has crossed the line. The other birth parent, in turn, can file a motion that can lead to the start of a new custody trial. For this reason, you should set parenting boundaries with your new spouse.

As I've stated in my workshops, once an irrational ex, always an irrational ex! Therefore, you may want to delay remarriage if you are concerned about starting the divorce wars all over again. But, remember, your happiness and serenity need to come first.

Don't let your remarriage in any way affect the relationship you already have with your kids. You'll need to work both scenarios really well.

Mix and Match with the New Extended Family: Your Version of the Brady Bunch

If you do end up remarried, working all the new players into the fold will become a difficult task. If each of you has children, then blending the families will make things more challenging because each family was used to doing things in a particular way with the one parent.

There are many factors and new issues to take care of, including the possibility of any child in the blended family stating that your new partner is favoring their own kids over him and his siblings, and all the perceived inequities that will follow the newly formed family may create a huge rift.

The most important thing you both can do initially is to set the expectations as realistically as possible. The children need to know coming into the relationship what to expect. Many times disagreements and issues develop between stepchildren of close ages. You need to minimize those challenges before they occur.

Anything against the grain needs to be nipped in the bud. Approach this through entire family meetings and discuss what the ground rules should be for all future discussions. Let each child have their say as to how things should work if they had to design the new family from scratch themselves. Let them discuss the pros and cons of what will make the family function better, certainly like a real family. Activities should be done together with everyone involved, and a sense of closeness and camaraderie should develop. Change should be minimized and ultimatums avoided. Inclusion, not exclusion, wins the war.

With new family members come new traditions. Consider using a threefold approach: (1) taking care of people, (2) values, and (3) setting up an event or day in which the same activities take place each year. Families like routines and making things more predictable, rather than less predictable. This gives a huge sigh of relief to each family member and doesn't allow things important to the children's past to get swept under the rug and perhaps lost forever.

The number of people attending these future-blended-family functions is less important that making sure all the new members of your extended family are taken care of. The values expressed indicate what your family wants to continue to happen, such as helping out the needy, spending time with extended family, enjoying music with loved ones, or traveling and learning something new in the process. Don't wipe away traditions from each former family. Many times continuing those traditions and encouraging the new family members to become involved makes it even more enjoyable for all.

Stepparents with no children need time to develop and understand the rules of parenting. An entire new skill set needs to be learned for the first time. Stepparents should approach issues with genuine care, concern, and humor. They should look to share common ground. They should not overreact or put forth their demands as "my way or the highway." As is often said, don't sweat the small stuff.

Stepparents should respect the private time needed for bonding between the birth parent and child. On the flip side, children should respect the private time of stepparents.

The stepparents probably should be called by their first name, certainly in the beginning of the relationship. The children may feel uncomfortable calling anyone else something like Mom and Dad, especially when both birth parents are still alive. Stepparents should never try to take the place or play the role of the biological parent. They should just supplement it.

Caring relationships take time to develop, especially since all the children are thrown into a situation that they didn't ask for and may not accept initially. Stepfamily relationships take time to nurture so that a true, caring parent enters the picture.

Support Groups and Persons

If you are having a hard time emotionally, then joining a support group would probably make sense. If you can share your experiences and your feelings with others in a group setting who have gone through the same issues and the same process, it can be very rewarding since everyone in the room has essentially been there, done that. Some of these support groups may be covered through your health insurance so check your insurance policy.

On the one-on-one side, you can also discuss your feelings about divorce through Internet chat room sites or seek spiritual guidance through your family clergy. For individual counseling, you may decide to go to a therapist or psychologist or visit with a life coach who can help you get your life back on track. Again, seek referrals for any of these activities. Some of these sessions could also be covered through your health insurance.

The Bottom Line: Take Care of yourself

As I learned from many people over the years, only you can take care of yourself. You are responsible for your own actions, always. And that's because everyone has choices. People come and go from your life regularly, but you are always there to deal with whatever is left behind. There is some divine reason why people are brought into or taken out of your life. You need to take the necessary steps to ensure that you don't lose perspective, lose your cool, handle the situation wrong, or worse yet, get sick over the experience. You need to be functional in every aspect of your daily life.

You also mustn't feel sorry for yourself. It is hard, emotionally draining, and unpleasant all the way around. Watch what you eat, and get plenty of rest and exercise. Get involved in the community. Join clubs, play sports, participate in your religious organization and community boards, volunteer, take up a hobby that you've been dying to do for a long time, and become socially active.

You need to proactively force yourself into your regular routine again. It's too easy to do nothing and become depressed. You have to turn yourself back into the person you knew in a prior life. You need to rebound, and the sooner the better.

When you do bring yourself back to the level you were operating at beforehand, you'll feel better about life. As I stated in Chapter 1, you won't do anybody any good if you can't take care of yourself. You still have others who are dependent on you and you can't let them down. Be strong and move forward the right way by taking the high road all the way around. As my mother often says, this too shall pass!

Rattiner's Planning Tips

1. When it's time to recap the events, you will have learned much from the process. It would have been easier, cheaper, and healthier to work out the differences and the divorce during the process with minimal input from the lawyers.

2. Chapter two of your life states that you've been through the worst already and now it's your time to take care of yourself going forward. Remember, if you don't, no one else will, and there are a lot of people counting on you.

3. Read the divorce decree carefully. If you don't agree with the conclusions, you need to correct it as soon as possible. Once the ink dries, it's too late.

4. Obtain certified copies of the divorce decree because there are many documents and many instances where it is a necessity. Most entities you'll need to deal with won't accept unofficial legal copies.

5. Change the deed on real estate to your own name so you can apply for financing to buy your spouse out of his or her share of the housing interest. No tax liability is included in this transaction.

6. Transfer the car titles to the spouse who ends up with the car. Make sure you have all documentation for paperwork regarding paid-off loans or other liens.

7. Update all your insurance policy beneficiary designations. Remember, insurance passes by contract of law and that will always supersede a will. If you don't change them, then the person you want to get the benefits may not be legally entitled to them.

8. Go on COBRA health insurance if you are the nonworking spouse who is in between jobs. Coverage can be extended for up to 36 months.

9. Update your retirement plan beneficiary designations. Look at the list you prepared for the court disclosing all the different types of retirement plans so you don't forget any during the process.

10. Make sure you have completed a QDRO to actually split the money from a qualified retirement plan. The spouse who is likely to benefit from receiving those monies needs to be the one to pursue this. A QDRO isn't needed for an IRA.

11. Updating your will and other estate planning documents is important. The most current will is the one that is relied upon because it supersedes all previous wills. Make sure that it states that you are not married. Also change your health care proxies and powers of attorney so your ex can't control any of your decisions going forward.

12. Confirm that all your bank and brokerage accounts have been separated into your name only. Pass along a certified copy of the divorce decree to show that joint ownership is not to be applied in any circumstance.

13. Make sure your ex is off any joint credit cards. Debts that he or she rings up could become your responsibility if you don't follow through. Again, a copy of the certified divorce decree should be filed.

14. Keep meticulous records of all transactions involving the ex-spouse. You may need them in court later on.

15. Remove all personal assets from your prior residence before the divorce becomes final. After that, it could turn into a "he said, she said" contest as to what belongs to whom.

16. Update various organizations relating to name, address, and work-related changes, including notifying the IRS of an address change.

17. It's always about the kids. Need I say more?

18. If you are the custodial parent and are moving away, you'd better have good reason to do so. The noncustodial parent will take exception to that and make your life a living misery.

19. If you need to modify child support, perhaps start by discussing it with your ex. If that doesn't work, go to mediation or back to court only as a last resort.

20. Your children may never ultimately accept the divorce. It is your role to help them through the process, no matter how long it takes, so they can gain closure on the issue. Be persistent.

21. You can try to modify spousal support. Good luck.

22. After the divorce you need to be focusing on your new life. Dating is a starting point. How you work it in with your kids is the tricky issue. Don't involve the kids early in the process. Only involve them when it becomes serious. One year is probably a good time frame before introducing your kids to your new love interest.

23. If you are living with this new person, have all your issues stated in writing to prevent any future misunderstandings either while alive or at death, through the use of a cohabitation agreement and/or prenuptial agreement.

24. Prenuptial agreements are a necessity. They set the expectations from the beginning so everyone knows the deal ahead of time. You always must manage the other side's expectations both before and after the process, if there is an afterwards.

25. Remarriage is tricky business. Make sure your kids and even your ex are ready for it. Protect yourself before it happens.

26. *The Brady Bunch* may have been shown on TV in the 1970s but variations of it exist more today than during any prior time period. Blending the families will be a constant challenge, so setting the ground rules in advance, managing expectations,

and retaining important traditions and values will go a long way in helping everyone make this transition.

27. Support groups and individual counseling can help you get over the hump regarding the divorce and put you in a better place to succeed the next time around.

28. When push comes to shove, you need to protect yourself and take care of your main asset—you! Nothing else matters if you can't walk away from this grueling process happy, healthy, and focused.

CHAPTER

11

Planning for Same-Sex Couple Divorces

ISSUES SPECIFIC TO THESE COUPLES

B y getting married, couples are in essence signing a legal contract and agreeing to abide by the rules implicit in that marriage
contract. Those rules cover everything from ownership and division
of property while both are living and when either dies, to financial
support in the event of a relationship ending through separation
or divorce.

Unmarried couples, however, don't share their relationship
within the context of an automatic legal contract. When you can't
get married, you can't get divorced. Same-sex couples in America
do not have the right to legally marry in all states, nor do they have
the hassles or the protections provided by divorce law.

You've likely heard of cases where a same-sex partner of a very
famous and wealthy person threatened a lawsuit in an attempt to
obtain what they deemed their fair share of the assets or *palimony*
(think alimony for a pal), but most of the time these lawsuits are
dismissed due to lack of any written or implied contact, or settled
out of court to maintain as much privacy as possible for the wealthy,
famous partner.

Whatever your understanding or written agreement with your
former partner, because the relationship is nonmarital, the family
courts have no jurisdiction. Disputes over contract terms are civil
cases and enforcement is left to trial courts. The courts may get

involved if you are unable to reach a compromise, but that is a very expensive and time-consuming process that you'll likely want to avoid if at all possible.

Many people think that parting company without having to go through divorce sounds like a relief. In reality, we see many same-sex couples separate, and the dissolution of the partnership is far from easy or equitable.

Whenever two individuals commit to each other as a long-term couple, the partnership should establish up front each partner's rights, obligations, and responsibilities to their relationship and living situation. The best legal document to outline these details is a *domestic partnership agreement*, also known as a *cohabitation* agreement.

In reality, the majority of same-sex couples do not have a legally binding domestic partnership agreement. Most couples explore living together before spending a lot of money on lawyers drafting domestic partnership agreements, and sometimes couples never get around to drafting these documents but one day wake up and recognize that their partnership is over.

So how should same-sex couples approach the subject of divorce and separation of assets, living quarters, responsibilities, and so on?

In so many instances one partner happens to be significantly more financially savvy and/or a stronger personality and able to sway their influence over the situation for their own financial benefit and conveniences. Because there are no official legal guidelines that an unmarried couple must follow equivalent to their legally married counterparts, it is up to the parties of the dissolving couple to do the best that they can to achieve an equitable dissolution of the partnership. A financial adviser with experience working with same-sex couples can be of great assistance in helping to determine the best approach to untangle the financial implications of the relationship. At times it is extremely wise for each individual to hire their own legal counsel. The more assets involved or the more complex the situation, the more likely it is that you'll want to have professional legal counsel representing you in this separation.

I have known of many instances where couples broke up and one party of the couple was clearly relinquishing substantial assets or taking on significant debt just because they wanted to exit the relationship as peacefully and uneventfully as possible. Too many of us want to avoid a fight at any cost. When it comes to breaking up it's so much easier to walk away from your equity in the home or your desire to participate in your ex-partner's children's lives—initially; but in retrospect this quick and easy exit can be financially and emotionally devastating. See Exhibit 11.1 for a summary of important tips when dealing with same-sex couple divorces.

I encourage all unmarried couples to go through the same steps that we recommend in this book for married couples. You may also want a legal document to protect yourself. A cohabitation agreement and will are discussed in this chapter.

Domestic Partnership Agreement/Cohabitation Agreement

A cohabitation agreement is a useful document for any unmarried couple if they are living together and have any joint assets or if they just want to clarify their living arrangements and any possible financial matters going forward. The agreement can be extremely detailed or very basic. It should be properly signed, witnessed, and notarized to make it legally binding. It is important to remember that any such agreement must be mutually agreed to. If both parties do not agree and sign off on the document, there is no legal remedy, except perhaps a lengthy and costly civil trial as mentioned earlier.

Some of the items which may be addressed in the document are:

> *Current financial arrangements.* This section can be used to specify who will pay what. It may be a 50/50 split or it may be some other figure that is dependent on the income of both parties.
>
> *Assets.* This may read more like a prenuptial agreement in which each party outlines their individual assets obtained prior to their partnership arrangement as well as items obtained together during the partnership and describes what will happen with those assets upon the dissolution of the partnership, disability, or death. Keep in mind that a last will and testament may override this document. I discuss this in more detail shortly.
>
> *Support.* As mentioned earlier, in many same-sex couples there is often one major wage earner. This section can address the issue of what will happen should one of the partners

become disabled or lose their job, or if the partnership should be dissolved.

Children. If the couple has adopted children or become attached to the children of one or both partners, you may wish to provide for some kind of visitation or contact in the event of dissolution of the partnership.

Last Will and Testament

Because same-sex relationships have no legal remedy in most states, it is especially important to protect your partner with a last will and testament, properly signed, witnessed, and notarized as required by

The Personal Financial Planning Process

Step 1

First obtain copies of all of your and your partner's financial information—assets, liabilities, and income. You may have to focus on just compiling yours and then exchange it with your ex-partner since you likely have no legal access to their financial records.

Step 2

Compile your financial information into a net worth statement. On the left-hand side of the page list all of your assets. On the right-hand side of the page list all of your liabilities.

These should be divided into assets and liabilities held in your name alone, your ex-partner's name alone, and jointly held. Indicate whether you came into the relationship with this asset or liability. If possible indicate any additions or subtractions that have occurred during your relationship for each asset or liability.

Step 3

Gather information regarding the income both you and your partner were making at the time of your long-term commitment. Also list changes to income for either party, changes to pursuit or attainment of education, or career advancements that were made to benefit the partnership. And list the income each of you were making at the time of dissolution, plus a note regarding the earning potential of each party.

your state of residence. See the accompanying box for a summary of how to utilize the personal financial planning process for the divorce of a same-sex couple.

Let's run through an example to illustrate. Jean and Kathy had been together eight years at the time Jean decided that she needed to end the relationship. During their relationship Kathy made substantially more money than Jean. Kathy had no reservations about paying for the majority of the couple's lifestyle. Jean made approximately one-third of the total household income and contributed about one-third of the household expenditures. For the first time Jean was also able to make a maximum 401(k) retirement plan contribution because Kathy's income made up for any shortfall. Kathy had always contributed the maximum amount to her own company-sponsored retirement account.

The couple lived a somewhat lavish lifestyle, traveled extensively, and jointly owned a primary residence as well as a vacation home, with rights of survivorship. The primary residence had a mortgage in both of their names; the vacation home was paid in full. Other assets and liabilities are shown in Exhibit 11.1.

From a purely financial standpoint the couple's situation looked much like that of most legally married couples. They bought assets in joint ownership; they borrowed money together, and made use of joint or household checking and money market accounts for convenience. Neither party put her career on hold nor postponed or failed to take advantage of any financial or career advancement opportunities because of their relationship.

However, upon the dissolution of this relationship, Jean was unable to maintain the lifestyle that she had grown accustomed to with Kathy. Both parties recognized that they had significant financial entanglements, they had hurt feelings, and they were unable to arrive at a settlement agreement on their own. Subsequently they hired individual legal representation to help them through the division of assets.

Jean and Kathy concluded that Kathy had earned approximately two-thirds of the household income all throughout their relationship but Jean had single-handedly done a significant amount of work on both the couple's primary residence and the vacation home.

Jean also recognized that she could not afford to maintain the primary residence by herself. However, she did have strong convictions regarding keeping the vacation home as well as the contents

Assets		Liabilities	
Joint			
Primary residence*	$375,000	Residential mortgage	$165,000
Vacation home*	$170,000		
Home furnishings*	$45,000		
Vacation home furnishings*	$18,000		
Boat and jet skis*	$25,000		
Joint checking account*	$5,000		
Joint money market account*	$15,000		
Jean's Individual			
Checking account	$3,000		
Roth IRA	$22,000		
401(k) Profit Sharing Plan	$135,000		
Vehicle*	$12,000	Vehicle loan balance*	$8,000
Kathy's Individual			
Checking account	$11,000		
Traditional IRA	$148,000		
401(k) Profit Sharing Plan	$286,000		
Vehicle*	$28,000	Vehicle loan balance*	$24,000
Total Combined Assets	$1,298,000	Total Combined Liabilities	$197,000
Total of joint assets	$653,000	Total joint liabilities	$165,000

Exhibit 11.1   Jean and Kathy's Net Worth Statement

Total of Jean's assets	$172,000	Total of Jean's personal debts	$8,000
Total of Kathy's assets	$473,000	Total of Kathy's personal debts	$24,000

*Acquired after couple got together. All joint assets are titled 50/50 joint with rights of survivorship.
Vehicles are owned individually and each individual has been solely responsible for her vehicle debt.

Exhibit 11.1   (Continued)

of the vacation home. Through the guidance of their legal counsel Kathy and Jean were able to reach a compromise where both individuals felt that they had walked away from their financial partnership in the most equitable fashion possible.

The couple agreed that Jean would keep the vacation home, the vacation home furnishings, the boat, and one of the jet skis, plus she would receive $2,000 from the joint checking account and $5,000 from the couple's money market account. The combined total of these assets equaled slightly more than one-third of the couple's jointly owned property. The couple determined that from a financial standpoint one-third of the assets going to Jean made sense; however, because Jean did a significant amount of labor, she should also receive some benefit for that contribution.

The only jointly held liability this couple had prior to their parting was the primary residence mortgage. Fortunately, Kathy had the income and creditworthiness to be able to refinance the mortgage in her name individually. Jean signed a quitclaim deed transferring her share of the ownership in the primary residence to Kathy. Kathy did the same for Jean regarding the vacation home. Be very careful that this type of transfer of assets and liability be well documented. Unmarried couples cannot transfer assets or forgive debt without this being considered by the IRS as a gift. You may find it appropriate to engage the services of a qualified CPA financial planner to make sure this transfer occurs as it was intended.

Once the settlement agreement was reached, Kathy and Jean canceled their joint checking and money market accounts and distributed the proceeds to their individual accounts.

They also needed to change their beneficiary designations on their retirement plans, IRA accounts, and life insurance policies. Lastly, they both had to update their estate planning documents, which had named each other as successor trustee and health care agent and given each other power of attorney.

In this example, our separating couple had substantial assets and minimal debt. Conveniently, each of the women wanted to retain a home that made the asset split work out.

They may have substantial retirement plan assets; however, there are no qualified domestic relations orders (QDROs) in same-sex breakups because it takes a divorce court to issue these orders. If a same-sex couple has to divvy up assets from a qualified retirement plan or IRA, that may not be possible, and it's definitely not attractive from a tax and retirement planning angle. You'll want to consult with a qualified professional before messing with your retirement accounts.

Unlike our example, most often a couple has one home, bringing up other issues: Can one party afford to buy out the other? Where will the assets come from? When must the exiting party vacate? What if they can't agree or come up with the money to buy out the other party? With few assets, many couples have little choice but to sell the home that they shared and both make other housing arrangements.

The moral of the story is, breaking up is hard to do. Whether you have the hassles and rules of divorce law or have the freedom to try to achieve equitable settlement on your own, it's never easy. Make sure you get the professional guidance you need to protect yourself.

I will leave you with the following thoughts: In a recent poll, American men and women were asked if they would marry the same person if they had to do it all over again. Eighty percent of the men responded that they would marry the same woman. Fifty percent of the women responded that they would marry the same man. This confirms what the legendary Henny Youngman said about marriage: "The secret of a happy marriage remains a secret!"

Rattiner's Planning Tips

1. Same-sex couples do not enjoy the same favorable legal remedies that traditional couples do. Therefore added protection is necessary.

2. A cohabitation agreement can legally spell out in advance the issues that could arise in a divorcing same-sex couple relationship.
3. A will can also provide legal guidance for same-sex couples.
4. Qualified domestic relations orders (QDROs) do not exist for same-sex couples because it takes a divorce court to issue these orders.
5. Make sure that all beneficiary designations for retirement, life insurance, and IRA accounts are changed upon the dissolution of the partnership.
6. There are many financial advisers who specialize in same-sex couple divorces.

Appendix

CHARTS AND FORMS

The following charts from the American Bar Association summarize different state requirements regarding matters that arise in many divorce cases. Included here are:

Chart 1—Alimony/Spousal Support Factors

Chart 2—Custody Criteria

Chart 3—Child Support Guidelines

Chart 4—Grounds for Divorce and Residency Requirements

Chart 5—Property Division

Chart 6—Third-Party Visitation

The following forms from the Department of the Treasury, Internal Revenue Service, are also included in this Appendix:

Form 8332—Release/Revocation of Release of Claim to Exemption for Child by Custodial Parent

Form 8379—Injured Spouse Allocation

Form 8857—Request for Innocent Spouse Relief

STATE	Statutory List*	Marital Fault Not Considered	Marital Fault Relevant	Standard of Living	Status as Custodial Parent Considered
Alabama			x	x	
Alaska	x	x		x	x
Arizona	x	x		x	x
Arkansas		x			
California	x	x		x	
Colorado	x	x		x	x
Connecticut	x		x	x	x
Delaware	x	x		x	x
District of Columbia			x	x	
Florida	x		x	x	
Georgia	x		x	x	
Hawaii	x	x		x	x
Idaho	x		x	x	x
Illinois	x	x		x	x
Indiana	x	x			
Iowa	x	x		x	x
Kansas		x			
Kentucky			x^1	x	
Louisiana	x		x		x
Maine	x	x			
Maryland	x		x	x	
Massachusetts	x		x	x	
Michigan			x	x	
Minnesota	x	x		x	x
Mississippi			x		
Missouri			x	x	x
Montana	x	x		x	x
Nebraska	x	x		x	x
Nevada		x		x	x
New Hampshire	x		x	x	x
New Jersey	x		x	x	x
New Mexico	x	x		x	
New York	x		x	x	x
North Carolina	x		x	x	
North Dakota			x	x	
Ohio	x	x		x	x
Oklahoma		x		x	x
Oregon	x	x		x	x
Pennsylvania	x		x	x	
Rhode Island	x		x	x	x
South Carolina	x		x	x	x
South Dakota	x		x	x	
Tennessee	x		x	x	x
Texas	x		x	x	x
Utah	x		x	x	x
Vermont	x	x		x	x
Virginia	x		x	x	
Washington	x	x		x	
West Virginia	x		x		x
Wisconsin	x	x		x	x
Wyoming			x		

* Although there is a statutory list of factors, the court may in its discretion consider other factors under the particular circumstances of the case.

1. Only fault on the part of the party seeking alimony.

Chart 1 Alimony/Spousal Support Factors

Source: American Bar Association, *Family Law Quarterly* 41 (4): 709. Reprinted with permission.

STATE	Statutory Factors*	Child's Wishes	Joint Custody Authorized	Presumption in Favor of Joint Custody	Cooperative Parent	Domestic Violence**	Attorney or GAL***
Alabama		x^3	x		x	x	
Alaska	x	x	x		x	x	x
Arizona	x	x	x		x	x	x
Arkansas		x	x			x	
California		x^4	x	x^7	x	x	x
Colorado	x	x	x^1		x	x	x
Connecticut	x	x	x	x^7	x	x	x
Delaware	x	x	x			x	x
District of Columbia	x	x		x	x	x	x
Florida	x	x		x^1	x	x	x
Georgia	x	x^4	x			x	x
Hawaii		x^4	x			x	x
Idaho	x	x		x	x	x	
Illinois	x	x	x		x	x	x
Indiana	x	x	x		x	x	x
Iowa	x	x	x		x	x	x
Kansas	x	x	x		x	x	
Kentucky	x	x	x			x	
Louisiana	x	x	x		x	x	x
Maine	x	x	x^1		x	x	x
Maryland		x^3	x		x^3	x	x
Massachusetts			x		x	x	x
Michigan		x	x		x	x	x
Minnesota	x	x		x	x	x	x
Mississippi		x^3	x			x	x
Missouri	x	x	x		x	x	x
Montana	x	x	x^1			x	x
Nebraska⁸		x	x^1			x	x
Nevada⁸	x	x^4	x		x	x	
New Hampshire⁸	x	x		$x^{1,7}$	x	x	x
New Jersey	x	x	x		x	x	x
New Mexico	x	x^2		x	x	x	x
New York		x			x	x	x
North Carolina		x^3	x			x	
North Dakota	x	x	x		x^3	x	x
Ohio	x	x	x^1			x	x
Oklahoma		x^4	x		x	x	x
Oregon	x	x^3	x	x^7	x	x	
Pennsylvania		x^4	x		x	x	x
Puerto Rico						x	x
Rhode Island		x^3	x^3			x	
South Carolina		x^4	x^3			x	
South Dakota		x	x				
Tennessee	x	x	x^3		x	x	x
Texas		x	x^3		x	x	x
Utah	x	x	x		x		x
Vermont	x		x^1		x	x^6	x
Virginia	x	x	x		x	x	

Chart 2 Custody Criteria

Source: American Bar Association, *Family Law Quarterly* 41 (4): 710. Reprinted with permission.

Washington	x	x	x[1]			x	x
West Virginia	x	x	x[1]			x	x
Wisconsin	x	x	x		x	x	x
Wyoming	x	x[3]	x		x	x	

   * Although there is a statutory list of factors, the court may in its discretion consider other factors under the particular circumstances of the case.

   ** The jurisdiction has enacted a statute permitting consideration of domestic violence in conjunction with child custody. The statutes vary from making domestic violence a factor in custody determinations to imposing presumptions against custody in batterers or imposing special procedural considerations in cases involving domestic violence.

   *** This column indicates whether a state has statutory authority for appointment of a Guardian ad litem or attorney for a child, specifically in child custody cases.

   1. Does not use the term "child custody" but instead uses "parental responsibilities and rights" or similar terminology.

   2. The wishes of children under age fourteen are a factor to be considered; the court must consider the wishes of a child fourteen years of age or older.

   3. By case law.

   4. Court must consider the wishes of a child of sufficient maturity to express them.

   5. Uses the terminology "managing conservator" of the child to describe a custodial parent.

   6. The presence of domestic violence may be a defense for a parent who refuses to comply with a visitation order.

   7. Presumption in favor of joint custody if the parents agree to it.

   8. Comprehensive legislative revision recently effective.

Chart 2 *(Continued)*

STATE	Income Share	Percent of Income	Extraordinary Medical Deduction	Child-Care Deduction	College Support	Shared Parenting Time Offset
Alabama ALA. CODE § 30-3-1	x	x	x p	x m	x	
Alaska ALASKA STAT. § 25.27.060		x	x m	x	x	x
Arizona ARIZ. REV. STAT. ANN. § 25-320	x		x m	x p		
Arkansas ARK. CODE ANN. § 9-12-312		x	x d	x d		
California CAL. FAM. CODE § 4001 CAL. FAM. CODE § 3585	x		x m	x m		x
Colorado COLO. REV. STAT. § 14-10-115	x		x m	x m		x
Connecticut CONN. GEN. STAT. § 466-81	x		x d		x	
Delaware DEL. CODE ANN. tit. 13 § 1513			x m	x m		x*
District of Columbia D.C. CODE § 16-916.01		x	x d	x	x	x
Florida FLA. STAT. § 61.30	x		x p	x m		
Georgia GA. CODE ANN. § 19-6-15		x	x p	x m		
Hawaii HAW. REV. STAT. § 5760-7	x	x	x m^3	x	x	x
Idaho IDAHO CODE ANN. § 32-706	x		x m	x p		x
Illinois 750 ILL. COMP. STAT. 5/505		x			x	
Indiana IND. CODE § 31-16-6-1	x		x p	x m	x	x
Iowa IOWA CODE § 598.21		x		x m	x	x
Kansas KAN. STAT. ANN. § 38-1595	x			x m		x
Kentucky KY. REV. STAT. ANN. § 403.212	x		x m	x p		
Louisiana	x		x m	x m		
Maine ME. REV. STAT. ANN. tit. 19, § 2007	x		x m	x m		
Maryland MD. CODE ANN., FAM. L. § 12-204	x		x m	x m		x
Massachusetts MASS. GEN. LAWS. ch. 208, § 28		x	x m	x	x	
Michigan MICH. COMP. LAW § 722.27	x		x m	x m	x	x
Minnesota MINN. STAT. § 518.17		x		x m		x
Mississippi MISS. CODE ANN. § 43-19-101		x	x d	x d		
Missouri MO. REV. STAT. § 452.340	x		x	x	x	x
Montana MONT. CODE ANN. § 40-4-204			x m	x m		
Nebraska NEB. REV. STAT. § 42-364	x		x d	x m		x
Nevada		x	x m	x d		x

Chart 3 Child Support Guidelines

Source: American Bar Association, Family Law Quarterly 41 (4): 711. Reprinted with permission.

STATE	Income Share	Percent of Income	Extraordinary Medical Deduction	Child-Care Deduction	College Support	Shared Parenting Time Offset
New Hampshire N.H. REV. STAT. ANN. § 458:4		x	x d		x	
New Jersey N.J. STAT. ANN. § 2A:17-56.23a	x		x m	x m	x	x
New Mexico N.M. STAT. § 40-4-11.1	x		x p	x m		x
New York N.Y. DOM REL. § 240	x		x m	x m	x	
North Carolina N.C. GEN. STAT. § 52C-2.201	x		x p	x m		x
North Dakota N.D. CENT. CODE § 14-09-09.7		x		x d		
Ohio OHIO REV. CODE ANN. § 3109.05	x		x p	x m		x p
Oklahoma OKLA. STAT. tit. 43, § 119	x		x a	x m		x
Oregon OR. REV. STAT. § 107.108	x		x p	x m	x	x
Pennsylvania 23 PA. CONS. STAT. ANN. § 4322	x		x m/d	x m		
Rhode Island R.I. GEN. LAWS § 15-5-16.2	x		x d	x m		
South Carolina S.C. CODE ANN. § 20-3-160	x		x d	x m	x	
South Dakota S.D. CODIFIED LAW § 25-7-6.2	x		x d	x d		
Tennessee TENN. CODE ANN. § 36-5-101		x	x m		x[1]	x[2]
Texas TEX. FAM. CODE ANN. § 154.121		x	x m	x d		
Utah UTAH CODE ANN. § 30-3-5	x		x m	x m/p		x
Vermont VT. STAT. ANN. tit. 15, § 654	x		x m	x m		x
Virginia VA. CODE ANN. § 20-108.2	x		x a	x a		x
Washington WASH. REV. CODE § 26.09.170	x		x m	x m	x	
West Virginia W. VA. CODE § 48-6-301	x		x m	x m		x
Wisconsin WIS. STAT. § 767.57		x	x m	x d		
Wyoming WYO. STAT. ANN. § 20-2-307	x		x d	x d		x

* Chart prepared by Laura W. Morgan from her treatise, *Child Support Guidelines: Interpretation and Application.*

** = by case law

a = mandatory add-ons

m = mandatory deduction

p = permissive deduction

d = deviation factor

1. May be voluntarily agreed by the parties, in which case it is contractually enforceable thereafter, but otherwise may not be imposed by the court. However, an obligor parent may be required to contribute during a child's minority to an educational trust fund, which would be used for college costs postminority.

2. Support may be increased or decreased it the obligor spends more or less than 80 days (the putative normal amount of time) with a child.

3. Credit given for actual cost of health care insurance premium paid for children.

Chart 3 *(Continued)*

STATE	No Fault Sole Ground	No Fault Added to Traditional	Incompatibility Irreconcilable Differences, or Similar Ground	Living Separate and Apart	Judicial Separation	Durational Requirements
Alabama		x	x	2 years	x	6 months
Alaska		x	x		x	none
Arizona	x	x^2	x			90 days
Arkansas		x^2		18 months	x	60 days
California	x		x		x	6 months[1]
Colorado	x		x		x	90 days
Connecticut		x	x	18 months	x	1 year
Delaware		x	x	6 months	x	6 months
District of Columbia	x			6 months[4]; 1 year	x	6 months
Florida	x		x			6 months
Georgia		x	x			6 months
Hawaii	x		x	2 years	x	6 months
Idaho		x	x	5 years		6 weeks
Illinois		x		2 years	x	90 days
Indiana	x		x		x	6 months
Iowa	x		x		x	1 year
Kansas	x		x		x	60 days
Kentucky	x		x		x	180 days
Louisiana		x^2		6 months[3]	x	6 months
Maine		x	x		x	6 months
Maryland		x		12 months	x	1 year
Massachusetts		x	x		x	none
Michigan	x		x		x	180 days
Minnesota	x		x		x	180 days
Mississippi		x	x^4			6 months
Missouri	x		x		x	90 days
Montana	x		x	180 days	x	90 days
Nebraska	x		x		x	1 year
Nevada	x		x	1 year	x	6 weeks
New Hampshire		x	x		x	1 year
New Jersey		x	x^7	18 months	x	1 year
New Mexico		x	x			6 months
New York		x		1 year[5]	x	1 year
North Carolina		x		1 year	x	6 months
North Dakota		x	x		x	6 months
Ohio		x	x	1 year		6 months
Oklahoma		x	x		x	6 months
Oregon	x		x		x	6 months
Pennsylvania		x	x^4	2 years		6 months
Rhode Island		x	x	3 years	x	1 year
South Carolina		x		1 year	x	1 year[6]
South Dakota		x	x		x	none
Tennessee		x	x	2 years	x	6 months
Texas		x	x	3 years		6 months
Utah		x	x	3 years	x	3 months
Vermont		x		6 months		6 months
Virginia		x		1 year	x	6 months
Washington	x		x^4	12 months		none
West Virginia		x	x	1 year	x	1 year
Wisconsin	x			12 months	x	6 months
Wyoming		x			x	60 days

1. California requires domicile as distinguished from residency for jurisdictional purposes.
2. Covenant marriage statutes establish specific grounds for divorce for covenant marriages.
3. Two years for covenant marriages.
4. Available in a jointly filed petition.
5. New York requires that the parties live separate and apart after the execution of a written separation agreement.
6. South Carolina's one-year residency requirement only applies where the Plaintiff is a resident of the state but the defendant is not. If both parties are residents of South Carolina, the durational requirement is three months.
7. New Jersey requires that irreconcilable differences cause the breakdown of the marriage for six months.

Chart 4 Grounds for Divorce and Residency Requirements

Source: American Bar Association, *Family Law Quarterly* 41 (4): 713. Reprinted with permission.

STATE	Community Property	Only Marital/Community Property Divided	Statutory List of Factors	Nonmonetary Contributions	Economic Misconduct	Contribution to Education
Alabama		x		x		x
Alaska	x^1		x	x	x	
Arizona	x	x			x	x
Arkansas		x	x	x	x	
California	x	x^2			x	x
Colorado		x	x	x	x	
Connecticut			x	x	x	x
Delaware		x	x	x	x	x
District of Columbia		x	x	x	x	
Florida		x	x	x	x	x
Georgia		x				
Hawaii		x	x	x^3	x^4	
Idaho	x	x	x			
Illinois		x	x	x	x	
Indiana			x	x	x	
Iowa			x	x	x	x
Kansas			x		x	
Kentucky		x	x	x	x	x
Louisiana	x	x^2				
Maine		x	x	x	x	
Maryland		x	x	x	x	
Massachusetts			x	x	x	x
Michigan		x		x	x	x
Minnesota		x	x	x	x	
Mississippi				x	x	
Missouri		x	x	x	x	x
Montana			x	x	x	
Nebraska			x	x		
Nevada	x	x		x	x	x
New Hampshire			x	x	x	x
New Jersey						
New Mexico	x	x				
New York		x	x	x	x	x
North Carolina		x	x	x	x	x
North Dakota				x	x	x
Ohio		x	x	x	x	x
Oklahoma		x		x	x	
Oregon				x	x	x
Pennsylvania		x	x	x	x	x
Rhode Island		x	x	x	x	x
South Carolina		x	x	x	x	x
South Dakota				x	x	
Tennessee		x	x	x	x	x
Texas	x	x			x	
Utah						
Vermont			x	x	x	x
Virginia		x	x	x	x	x
Washington	x		x			
West Virginia		x	x	x	x	x
Wisconsin	x	x	x	x	x	x
Wyoming			x	x	x	x

1. The parties may contract to make some or all of their marital property community property.
2. Community property must be divided equally.
3. Nonmonetary contributions during marriage do not affect property division nor does the lack of them.
4. No statutory provision; case law is mixed.

Chart 5 Property Division

Source: American Bar Association, *Family Law Quarterly* 41 (4): 714. Reprinted with permission.

STATE	Stepparents	Grandparents, Generally*	Grandparents—Death of Their Child	Grandparents—Child Divorce	Grandparents—Parents Never Married	Any Interested Party	After Termination of Parental Rights or Adoption
Alabama		x	x	x	x		x
Alaska		x					x
Arizona			x^9	x^9	x^9	x^2	
Arkansas	x		x	x	x	$x^{2,4}$	
California	x^1		x^1	x^1		$x^{2,4}$	
Colorado			x^1	x^1	x^1	x^2	
Connecticut						x^1	
Delaware	x	x^{10}				$x^{2,4}$	
District of Columbia							
Florida			x^1	x^1	x^1		
Georgia		x^6					
Hawaii						$x^{1,2}$	
Idaho	$x^{2,4}$	x					
Illinois	x^1		x	x	x		
Indiana			x	x	x		
Iowa		x					
Kansas	x	$x^{1,6}$					
Kentucky		x					x
Louisiana	$x^{2,4}$		x	x			x
Maine		x	x			$x^{2,4}$	
Maryland	$x^{2,4}$	x^1					
Massachusetts		x	x	x		$x^{2,4}$	
Michigan		x	x	x			
Minnesota			x^6	x^6	x^6	$x^{1,2}$	
Mississippi		$x^{2,9}$	x	x		$x^{2,4}$	
Missouri		$x^{2,9}$	x	x			
Montana		x					
Nebraska			x	x	x		
Nevada			x	x	x	x^2	
New Hampshire		x					
New Jersey		x^1				$x^{2,4,7}$	
New Mexico		$x^{2,6}$	x	x			
New York		x^2	x			$x^{2,4}$	
North Carolina		x^5		x			
North Dakota		x				$x^{2,4}$	
Ohio			$x^{1,6}$	x^1	x^1		
Oklahoma			x	x	x		
Oregon		x^6				x^2	
Pennsylvania	$x^{2,4}$	x^2	x	x		$x^{2,4,7}$	
Puerto Rico		x	x	x			
Rhode Island		x^9	x	x		$x^{2,4}$	
South Carolina							
South Dakota		x^9				x^2	
Tennessee	x	x^9	x	x			
Texas			x	x		$x^{2,4}$	
Utah		x^6					

Chart 6 Third-Party Visitation

Source: American Bar Association, Family Law Quarterly 41 (4): 715. Reprinted with permission.

Vermont		x^6	x			$x^{2,4}$	
Virginia						x	
Washington						x^8	
West Virginia		x					
Wisconsin	x^3			x		x^{10}	$x^{2,4}$	
Wyoming		x					

* Grandparents may obtain visitation when the parents are alive and regardless of their marital status. Many of these statutes contain requirements, such as the establishment of a substantial relationship, the best interests of the child, the existence of a residential relationship, the parent's unreasonable denial of visitation, or a combination of these.

1. A court of the state has declared the statute unconstitutional either on its face or as applied.

2. A person who stands "in loco parentis," who is a "de facto," "equitable" or "psychological parent," or who has a substantial residential relationship with a child may seek visitation or custody without showing that a parent is unfit or other extraordinary circumstances. Some statutes impose a time requirement for the duration of the relationship before visitation or custody may be sought. New York requires proof of "extraordinary circumstances."

3. Stepparent may seek visitation only when s/he is the surviving spouse of a deceased parent.

4. Case law permits stepparents to seek custody as de facto parents.

5. An independent action for visitation may be maintained only when child has been adopted by a stepparent.

6. Grandparent may petition for visitation in stepparent adoption situations.

7. Case law is mixed.

8. Washington's third-party visitation statute has been declared unconstitutional, but its supreme court has recognized that de facto parents have custody & visitation rights.

9. Third-party petitioning for visitation must show that visitation was denied not merely limited.

10. Visitation cannot be ordered over the objection of one of the natural parents if they are married.

Chart 6 *(Continued)*

Form **8332**
(Rev. February 2009)
Department of the Treasury
Internal Revenue Service

Release/Revocation of Release of Claim to Exemption for Child by Custodial Parent

▶ Attach a separate form for each child.

OMB No. 1545-0074

Attachment
Sequence No. **115**

Name of noncustodial parent

Noncustodial parent's social security number (SSN) ▶

Part I   Release of Claim to Exemption for Current Year

I agree not to claim an exemption for _____
                                                      Name of child

for the tax year 20____ .

_____   _____   _____
Signature of custodial parent releasing claim to exemption   Custodial parent's SSN   Date

Note. If you choose not to claim an exemption for this child for future tax years, also complete Part II.

Part II   Release of Claim to Exemption for Future Years (If completed, see **Noncustodial parent** on page 2.)

I agree not to claim an exemption for _____
                                                      Name of child

for the tax year(s)_____ .
             (Specify. See instructions.)

_____   _____   _____
Signature of custodial parent releasing claim to exemption   Custodial parent's SSN   Date

---

Part III   Revocation of Release of Claim to Exemption for Future Year(s)

I revoke the release of claim to an exemption for _____
                                                      Name of child

for the tax year(s)_____ .
             (Specify. See instructions.)

_____   _____   _____
Signature of custodial parent revoking the release of claim to exemption   Custodial parent's SSN   Date

---

General Instructions

What's New

New rules apply to allow the custodial parent to revoke a previous release of claim to exemption. For details, see *Revocation of release of claim to exemption* on this page.

Purpose of Form

If you are the custodial parent, you can use this form to do the following.

● Release a claim to exemption for your child so that the noncustodial parent can claim an exemption for the child.

● Revoke a previous release of claim to exemption for your child.

Release of claim to exemption. This release of the exemption will also allow the noncustodial parent to claim the child tax credit and the additional child tax credit (if either applies). Complete this form (or sign a similar statement containing the same information required by this form) and give it to the noncustodial parent. The noncustodial parent must attach this form or similar

statement to his or her tax return each year the exemption is claimed. Use Part I to release a claim to the exemption for the current year. Use Part II if you choose to release a claim to exemption for any future year(s).

Revocation of release of claim to exemption. Use Part III to revoke a previous release of claim to an exemption. The revocation will be effective no earlier than the tax year following the year in which you provide the noncustodial parent with a copy of the revocation or make a reasonable effort to provide the noncustodial parent with a copy of the revocation. Therefore, if you revoke a release on Form 8332 and provide a copy of the form to the noncustodial parent in 2009, the earliest tax year the revocation can be effective is 2010. You must attach a copy of the revocation to your tax return each year the exemption is claimed as a result of the revocation. You must also keep for your records a copy of the revocation and evidence of delivery of the notice to the noncustodial parent, or of reasonable efforts to provide actual notice.

Custodial Parent and Noncustodial Parent

The custodial parent is the parent with whom the child lived for the greater part of the year. The other parent is the noncustodial parent.

If the parents divorced or separated during the year and the child lived with both parents before the separation, the custodial parent is the one with whom the child lived for the greater part of the rest of the year.

See Regulations section 1.152-4 for more details on determining custody.

Exemption for a Dependent Child

A dependent is either a qualifying child or a qualifying relative. See your tax return instruction booklet for the definition of these terms. Generally, a child of divorced or separated parents will be a qualifying child of the custodial parent. However, if the special rule on page 2 applies, then the child will be treated as the qualifying child or qualifying relative of the noncustodial parent for purposes of the dependency exemption, the child tax credit, and the additional child tax credit.

For Paperwork Reduction Act Notice, see back of form.   Cat. No. 13910F   Form **8332** (Rev. 2-2009)

Form 8332 Release/Revocation of Release of Claim to Exemption for Child by Custodial Parent

304   Appendix

Form 8332 (Rev. 2-2009)

Page **2**

Special Rule for Children of Divorced or Separated Parents

A child is treated as a qualifying child or a qualifying relative of the noncustodial parent if all of the following apply.

1. The child received over half of his or her support for the year from one or both of the parents (see the *Exception* below). Public assistance payments, such as Temporary Assistance for Needy Families (TANF), are not support provided by the parents.

2. The child was in the custody of one or both of the parents for more than half of the year.

3. Either of the following applies.

a. The custodial parent agrees not to claim an exemption for the child by signing this form or a similar statement. If the decree or agreement went into effect after 1984, see *Post-1984 decree or agreement* below.

b. A pre-1985 decree of divorce or separate maintenance or written separation agreement states that the noncustodial parent can claim the child as a dependent. But the noncustodial parent must provide at least $600 for the child's support during the year. This rule does not apply if the decree or agreement was changed after 1984 to say that the noncustodial parent cannot claim the child as a dependent.

For this rule to apply, the parents must be one of the following.

● Divorced or legally separated under a decree of divorce or separate maintenance.

● Separated under a written separation agreement.

● Living apart at all times during the last 6 months of the year.

If this rule applies, and the other dependency tests in your tax return instruction booklet are also met, the noncustodial parent can claim the exemption for the child.

Exception. If the support of the child is determined under a multiple support agreement, this special rule does not apply and this form should not be used.

Post-1984 decree or agreement. If the divorce decree or separation agreement went into effect after 1984 and before 2009, the noncustodial parent can attach certain pages from the decree or agreement instead of Form 8332. To be able to do this, the decree or agreement must state all three of the following.

1. The noncustodial parent can claim the child as a dependent without regard to any condition (such as payment of support).

2. The other parent will not claim the child as a dependent.

3. The years for which the claim is released.

The noncustodial parent must attach all of the following pages from the decree or agreement.

● Cover page (include the other parent's SSN on that page).

● The pages that include all of the information identified in (1) through (3) above.

● Signature page with the other parent's signature and date of agreement.

 The noncustodial parent must attach the required information even if it was filed with a return in an earlier year.

The noncustodial parent can no longer attach certain pages from a divorce decree or separation agreement instead of Form 8332 if the decree or agreement was executed after 2008. If the decree or separation agreement was executed before 2009, the noncustodial parent can continue to attach certain pages from the decree or agreement as discussed above.

Specific Instructions

Custodial Parent

Part I. Complete Part I to release a claim to exemption for your child for the current tax year.

Part II. Complete Part II to release a claim to exemption for your child for one or more future years. Write the specific future year(s) or "all future years" in the space provided in Part II.

 To help ensure future support, you may not want to release your claim to the exemption for the child for future years.

Part III. Complete Part III if you are revoking a previous release of claim to exemption for your child. Write the specific future year(s) or "all future years" in the space provided in Part III.

The revocation will be effective no earlier than the tax year following the year you provide the noncustodial parent with a copy of the revocation or make a reasonable effort to provide the noncustodial parent with a copy of the revocation. Also, you must attach a copy of the revocation to your tax return for

each year you are claiming the exemption as a result of the revocation. You must also keep for your records a copy of the revocation and evidence of delivery of the notice to the noncustodial parent, or of reasonable efforts to provide actual notice.

Example. In 2007, you released a claim to exemption for your child on Form 8332 for the years 2008 through 2010. You would now like to revoke the previous release of exemption. If you complete Part III of Form 8332 and provide a copy of the form to the noncustodial parent in 2009, the revocation will be effective for 2010.

Noncustodial Parent

Attach this form or similar statement to your tax return for each year you claim the exemption for your child. You can claim the exemption only if the other dependency tests in your tax return instruction booklet are met.

 If the custodial parent released his or her claim to the exemption for the child for any future year, you must attach a copy of this form or similar statement to your tax return for each future year that you claim the exemption. Keep a copy for your records.

Paperwork Reduction Act Notice. We ask for the information on this form to carry out the Internal Revenue laws of the United States. You are required to give us the information. We need it to ensure that you are complying with these laws and to allow us to figure and collect the right amount of tax.

You are not required to provide the information requested on a form that is subject to the Paperwork Reduction Act unless the form displays a valid OMB control number. Books or records relating to a form or its instructions must be retained as long as their contents may become material in the administration of any Internal Revenue law. Generally, tax returns and return information are confidential, as required by Internal Revenue Code section 6103.

The average time and expenses required to complete and file this form will vary depending on individual circumstances. For the estimated averages, see the instructions for your income tax return.

If you have suggestions for making this form simpler, we would be happy to hear from you. See the instructions for your income tax return.

Form 8332 *(Continued)*

Form **8379** (Rev. January 2009) Department of the Treasury Internal Revenue Service	**Injured Spouse Allocation** ▶ **See instructions.**	OMB No. 1545-0074 Attachment Sequence No. **104**

Part I   Should you file this form? You must complete this part.

1 Enter the tax year for which you are filing this form. ▶ _____ Answer the following questions for that year.

2 Did you (or will you) file a joint return?
   ☐ **Yes.** Go to line 3.
   ☐ **No. Stop here.** Do not file this form. You are not an injured spouse.

3 Did (or will) the IRS use the joint overpayment to pay any of the following legally enforceable past-due debt(s) owed only by your spouse? (see instructions)
   ● Federal tax ● State income tax ● Child support ● Spousal support ● Federal nontax debt (such as a student loan)
   ☐ **Yes.** Go to line 4.
   ☐ **No. Stop here.** Do not file this form. You are not an injured spouse.
   Note. If the past-due amount is for a joint federal tax, you may qualify for innocent spouse relief for the year to which the overpayment was applied. See *Innocent Spouse Relief,* on page 2 for more information.

4 Are you legally obligated to pay this past-due amount?
   ☐ **Yes. Stop here.** Do not file this form. You are not an injured spouse.
   Note. If the past-due amount is for a joint federal tax, you may qualify for innocent spouse relief for the year to which the overpayment was applied. See *Innocent Spouse Relief,* on page 2 for more information.
   ☐ **No.** Go to line 5.

5 Were you a resident of a community property state (Arizona, California, Idaho, Louisiana, Nevada, New Mexico, Texas, Washington, or Wisconsin) at any time during the tax year entered on line 1? (see instructions)
   ☐ **Yes.** Enter name(s) of community property state(s) _____ .
   Skip lines 6 through 9 and **go to Part II** and complete the rest of this form.
   ☐ **No.** Go to line 6.

6 Did you make and report payments, such as federal income tax withholding or estimated tax payments?
   ☐ **Yes.** Skip lines 7 through 9 and **go to Part II** and complete the rest of this form.
   ☐ **No.** Go to line 7.

7 Did you have earned income, such as wages, salaries, or self-employment income?
   ☐ **Yes.** Go to line 8.
   ☐ **No.** Skip line 8 and go to line 9.

8 Did (or will) you claim the earned income credit or additional child tax credit?
   ☐ **Yes.** Skip line 9 and **go to Part II** and complete the rest of this form.
   ☐ **No.** Go to line 9.

9 Did (or will) you claim a refundable tax credit, such as the health coverage tax credit or refundable credit for prior year minimum tax?
   ☐ **Yes.** Go to Part II and complete the rest of this form.
   ☐ **No. Stop here.** Do not file this form. You are not an injured spouse.

Part II   Information About the Joint Tax Return for Which This Form Is Filed

10 Enter the following information exactly as it is shown on the tax return for which you are filing this form.
    The spouse's name and social security number shown first on that tax return must also be shown first below.

First name, initial, and last name shown first on the return	Social security number shown first	If Injured Spouse, check here ▶ ☐
First name, initial, and last name shown second on the return	Social security number shown second	If Injured Spouse, check here ▶ ☐

11 Check this box only if you are divorced or legally separated from the spouse with whom you filed the joint return and you want your refund issued in your name only .   .   .   .   ☐

12 Do you want any injured spouse refund mailed to an address different from the one on your joint return? ☐ **Yes** ☐ **No**
    If "Yes," enter the address. _____
    Number and street   City, town, or post office, state, and ZIP code

For Privacy Act and Paperwork Reduction Act Notice, see page 4.   Cat. No. 62474Q   Form **8379** (Rev. 1-2009)

Form 8379 Injured Spouse Allocation

Form 8379 (Rev. 1-2009)   Page **2**

Part III   Allocation Between Spouses of Items on the Joint Tax Return (see instructions)

Allocated Items	(a) Amount shown on joint return	(b) Allocated to injured spouse	(c) Allocated to other spouse
13 Income: **a.** Wages			
b. All other income			
14 Adjustments to income			
15 Standard deduction or Itemized deductions			
16 Number of exemptions			
17 Credits (**do not** include any earned income credit)			
18 Other taxes			
19 Federal income tax withheld			
20 Payments			

Part IV   Signature. Complete this part only if you are filing Form 8379 by itself and not with your tax return.

Under penalties of perjury, I declare that I have examined this form and any accompanying schedules or statements and to the best of my knowledge and belief, they are true, correct, and complete. Declaration of preparer (other than taxpayer) is based on all information of which preparer has any knowledge.

Keep a copy of this form for your records	Injured spouse's signature		Date	Phone number (optional) ( )
Paid Preparer's Use Only	Preparer's signature ▶	Date	Check if self-employed ☐	Preparer's SSN or PTIN
	Firm's name (or yours if self-employed), address, and ZIP code ▶		EIN	
			Phone no. ( )	

General Instructions

Purpose of Form

Form 8379 is filed by one spouse (the injured spouse) on a jointly filed tax return when the joint overpayment was (or is expected to be) applied (offset) to a past-due obligation of the other spouse. By filing Form 8379, the injured spouse may be able to get back his or her share of the joint refund.

Are You an Injured Spouse?

You may be an injured spouse if you file a joint tax return and all or part of your portion of the overpayment was, or is expected to be, applied (offset) to your spouse's legally enforceable past-due federal tax, state income tax, child or spousal support, or a federal nontax debt, such as a student loan.

Complete Part I to determine if you are an injured spouse.

Innocent Spouse Relief

Do not file Form 8379 if you are claiming innocent spouse relief. Instead, file Form 8857. Generally, both spouses are responsible for paying the full amount of tax, interest, and penalties due on your joint return. However, if you qualify for innocent spouse relief, you may be relieved of part or all of the joint liability. You may qualify for relief from the joint tax liability if (a) there is an understatement of tax because your spouse omitted income or claimed false deductions or credits, and you did not know or have reason to know of the understatement, (b) there is an understatement of tax and you are divorced, separated, or no longer living with your spouse, or (c) given all the facts and circumstances, it would not be fair to hold you liable for the tax. See Pub. 971 for more details.

When To File

File Form 8379 when you become aware that all or part of your share of an overpayment was, or is expected to be, applied (offset) against your spouse's legally enforceable past-due obligations. You must file Form 8379 for each year you meet this condition and want your portion of any offset refunded.

A Notice of Offset for federal tax debts is issued by the IRS. A Notice of Offset for past-due state income tax, child or spousal support, or federal nontax debts (such as a student loan) is issued by the U.S. Treasury Department's Financial Management Service (FMS).

 Visit www.irs.gov/taxtopics/tc203.html and www.fms.treas.gov/faq/offsets.html, for more information about refund offsets and debts.

Form **8379** (Rev. 1-2009)

Form 8379 (Continued)

Where To File

See the chart below to determine where to file your Form 8379.

IF you file Form 8379...	THEN mail Form 8379...
with your joint return	and your joint return to the Internal Revenue Service Center for the area where you live.*
by itself after you filed your original joint return on paper	to the same Internal Revenue Service Center where you filed your original return.*
by itself after you filed your original joint return electronically	to the Internal Revenue Service Center for the area where you live.*
with an amended return (Form 1040X) or other subsequent return	to the Internal Revenue Service Center for the area where you live.*

*See your tax return instructions for the mailing address.

How To File

You can file Form 8379 with your joint tax return or amended joint tax return (Form 1040X), or you can file it afterwards by itself. File Form 8379 with Form 1040X only if you are amending your original return to claim a joint refund.

If you file Form 8379 with your joint return, attach it to your return in the order of the attachment sequence number (located in the upper right corner of the tax form). Enter "Injured Spouse" in the upper left corner of page 1 of the joint return.

If you file Form 8379 separately, please be sure to attach a copy of all Forms W-2 and W-2G for both spouses, and any Forms 1099 showing federal income tax withholding, to Form 8379. The processing of Form 8379 may be delayed if these forms are not attached, or if the form is incomplete when filed.

Amending Your Tax Return

If you file an amended joint tax return (Form 1040X) to claim an additional refund and you do not want your portion of the overpayment to be applied (offset) against your spouse's legally enforceable past-due obligation(s), then you will need to complete and attach another Form 8379 to allocate the additional refund.

Time Needed To Process Form 8379

Generally, if you file Form 8379 with a joint return on paper, the time needed to process it is about 14 weeks (11 weeks if filed electronically). If you file Form 8379 by itself after a joint return has been processed, the time needed is about 8 weeks.

Specific Instructions

Part I

Line 3. Not all debts are subject to a tax refund offset. To determine if a debt is owed (other than federal tax), and whether an offset will occur, contact FMS at 1-800-304-3107 (for TTY/TDD help, call 1-866-297-0517).

 Filing Form 8379 when no past-due obligation exists will delay your refund.

Line 5. If you live in a community property state, special rules will apply to the calculation of your injured spouse refund. Enter the community property state(s) where, at any time during the year, you and your spouse resided and intended to

establish a permanent home. For more information about the factors used to determine whether you are subject to community property laws, see Pub. 555.

In community property states, overpayments are considered joint property and are generally applied (offset) to legally owed past-due obligations of either spouse. However, there are exceptions. The IRS will use each state's rules to determine the amount, if any, that would be refundable to the injured spouse. Under state community property laws, 50% of a joint overpayment (except the earned income credit) is applied to non-federal tax debts such as child or spousal support, student loans, or state income tax. However, state laws differ on the amount of a joint overpayment that can be applied to a federal tax debt. The earned income credit is allocated to each spouse based on each spouse's earned income.

For more guidance regarding the amount of an overpayment from a joint tax return that the IRS may offset against a spouse's separate tax liability, see the revenue ruling for your state below.

IF you live in . . .	THEN use . . .
Arizona, or Wisconsin	Rev. Rul. 2004-71 available at: http://www.irs.gov/irb/2004-30_IRB/ar10.html
California, Idaho, or Louisiana	Rev. Rul. 2004-72 available at: http://www.irs.gov/irb/2004-30_IRB/ar11.html
New Mexico, Nevada, or Washington	Rev. Rul. 2004-73 available at: http://www.irs.gov/irb/2004-30_IRB/ar12.html
Texas	Rev. Rul. 2004-74 available at: http://www.irs.gov/irb/2004-30_IRB/ar13.html

Part III

To properly determine the amount of tax owed and overpayment due to each spouse, an allocation must be made as if each spouse filed a separate tax return instead of a joint tax return. So, each spouse must allocate his or her separate wages, self-employment income and expenses (and self-employment tax), and credits such as education credits, to the spouse who would have shown the item(s) on his or her separate return.

Other items that may not clearly belong to either spouse (for example, a penalty on early withdrawal of savings from a joint bank account) would be equally divided.

If you live in a community property state, follow the instructions below to allocate your income, expenses, and credits. The IRS will apply your state's community property laws based on your allocation.

The IRS will figure the amount of any refund due the injured spouse.

Line 13a. Enter only Form W-2 income on this line. Enter the separate income that each spouse earned.

Line 13b. Identify the type and amount. Allocate joint income, such as interest earned on a joint bank account, as you determine. Be sure to allocate all income shown on the joint return.

Line 14. Enter each spouse's separate adjustments, such as an IRA deduction. Allocate other adjustments as you determine.

Line 15. If you used the standard deduction on your joint tax return, enter in both columns (b) and (c) one-half of the basic standard deduction shown in column (a). Also allocate any real estate taxes and any disaster loss as you determine.

Form 8379 *(Continued)*

However, if you checked the boxes for age or blindness at the top of page 2 of Form 1040 or 1040A, enter your total standard deduction on line 15, column (a). Allocate your basic standard deduction (including any real estate taxes or disaster loss) as explained earlier. Your basic standard deduction is as follows: 2004—$9,700; 2005—$10,000; 2006—$10,300; 2007—$10,700; 2008—$10,900; 2009—$11,400. If someone could claim you or your spouse as a dependent, your basic standard deduction is the amount on line 3a of the standard deduction worksheet (line 5a for 2004; line 4 for 2008). Then use the following worksheet to allocate the additional standard deduction (the difference between the total standard deduction and the basic standard deduction).

1. Enter here the total number of boxes checked for age or blindness **for yourself** at the top of page 2 of Form 1040 or 1040A _____

2. Enter the additional standard deduction for the year as shown below . . . . _____

2004	$950	2007	$1,050
2005	$1,000	2008	$1,050
2006	$1,000	2009	$1,100

3. Multiply line 2 by line 1. Include this amount on line 15, column (b) . . . . _____

4. Enter here the total number of boxes checked for age or blindness **for your spouse** at the top of page 2 of Form 1040 or 1040A . . _____

5. Multiply line 4 by line 2. Include this amount on line 15, column (c) . . . . _____

If you itemize your deductions, enter each spouse's separate deductions, such as employee business expenses. Allocate other deductions as you determine.

Line 16. Allocate the exemptions claimed on the joint return to the spouse who would have claimed them if separate returns had been filed. Enter whole numbers only. For example, you cannot allocate 3 exemptions by giving 1.5 exemptions to each spouse.

Line 17. Allocate any child tax credit, child and dependent care credit, and additional child tax credit to the spouse who was allocated the qualifying child's exemption. But if you attached Form 8901 to your tax return, allocate the child tax credit as you determine. Do not include any earned income credit here; the IRS will allocate it based on each spouse's income. Allocate business credits based on each spouse's interest in the business. Allocate any other credits as you determine.

Line 18. Allocate self-employment tax to the spouse who earned the self-employment income.

Line 19. Enter federal income tax withheld from each spouse's income as shown on Forms W-2, W-2G, and 1099. Be sure to attach copies of these forms to your tax return or to Form 8379 if you are filing it by itself. Also include on this line any excess social security or tier 1 RRTA tax withheld.

Line 20. You can allocate joint estimated tax payments in any way you choose as long as both you and your spouse agree. If you cannot agree, the estimated tax payments will be allocated according to the following formula:

$$\frac{\text{Each spouse's separate tax liability}}{\text{Both separate tax liabilities}} \times \text{Estimated tax payments}$$

Form 8379 *(Continued)*

Allocate each spouse's separate estimated tax payments to the spouse who made them.

How To Avoid Common Mistakes

Mistakes may delay your refund or result in notices being sent to you.

● Make sure to enclose copies of all Forms W-2 and W-2G for both spouses, and any Forms 1099 showing income tax withheld, to prevent a delay in processing your allocation.

● Enter "Injured Spouse" in the upper left corner of page 1 of your joint return.

● Any dependency exemptions must be entered in whole numbers. Do not use fractions.

● Items of income, expenses, credits and deductions must be allocated to the spouse who would have entered the item on his or her separate return.

● Make sure the debt is subject to offset (for example, a legally enforceable past-due federal tax, state income tax, child or spousal support, or other federal nontax debt, such as a student loan).

Form **8857**
(Rev. June 2007)
Department of the Treasury
Internal Revenue Service   (99)

Request for Innocent Spouse Relief

▶ Do not file with your tax return.   ▶ See separate instructions.

OMB No. 1545-1596

Important things you should know

- Answer all the questions on this form that apply, attach any necessary documentation, and sign on page 4. Do not delay filing this form because of missing documentation. See instructions.
- By law, the IRS must contact the person who was your spouse for the years you want relief. There are no exceptions, even for victims of spousal abuse or domestic violence. Your personal information (such as your current name, address, and employer) will be protected. However, if you petition the Tax Court, your personal information may be released. See instructions for details.
- If you need help, see *How To Get Help* in the instructions.

Part I   Should you file this form? You **must** complete this part for each tax year.

		Tax Year 1		Tax Year 2		Tax Year 3*	

1   Enter each tax year you want relief. It is important to enter the correct year. For example, if the IRS used your 2006 income tax refund to pay a 2004 tax amount you jointly owed, enter tax year 2004, not tax year 2006 . . . . ▶
    Caution. The IRS generally cannot collect the amount you owe until your request for each year is resolved. However, the time the IRS has to collect is extended. See *Collection Statute of Limitations* on page 3 of the instructions.

2   Check the box for each year you would like a refund if you qualify for relief. You may be required to provide proof of payment. See instructions . . . . ▶

	Yes	No	Yes	No	Yes	No

3   Did the IRS use your share of the joint refund to pay any of the following past-due debts of your spouse: federal tax, state income tax, child support, spousal support, or federal non-tax debt such as a student loan?
- If "Yes," **stop here**; do not file this form for that tax year. Instead, file Form 8379. See instructions.
- If "No," go to line 4 . . . .

4   Did you file a joint return for the tax year listed on line 1?
- If "Yes," skip line 5 and go to line 6.
- If "No," go to line 5 . . . .

5   If you did not file a joint return for that tax year, were you a resident of Arizona, California, Idaho, Louisiana, Nevada, New Mexico, Texas, Washington, or Wisconsin?
- If "Yes," see *Community Property Laws* on page 2 of the instructions.
- If "No" on both lines 4 and 5, **stop here**. Do not file this form for that tax year . .

*If you want relief for more than 3 years, fill out an additional form.

Part II   Tell us about yourself

6 Your current name (see instructions)	Your social security number
Your current home address (number and street). If a P.O. box, see instructions.	Apt. no. County
City, town or post office, state, and ZIP code. If a foreign address, see instructions.	Best daytime phone number ( )

Part III   Tell us about you and your spouse for the tax years you want relief

7   Who was your spouse for the tax years you want relief? File a separate Form 8857 for tax years involving different spouses or former spouses.

That person's current name	Social security number (if known)
Current home address (number and street) (if known). If a P.O. box, see instructions.	Apt. no.
City, town or post office, state, and ZIP code. If a foreign address, see instructions.	Best daytime phone number ( )

For Privacy Act and Paperwork Reduction Act Notice, see instructions.   Cat. No. 24647V   Form **8857** (Rev. 6-2007)

Form 8857 Request for Innocent Spouse Relief

Note. If you need more room to write your answer for any question, attach more pages. Be sure to write your name and social security number on the top of all pages you attach.

Part III   *(Continued)*

8   **What is the current marital status between you and the person on line 7?**

☐ Married and still living together

☐ Married and living apart since ___/___/___
                                    MM   DD   YYYY

☐ Widowed since ___/___/___   Attach a photocopy of the death certificate and will (if one exists).
                  MM   DD   YYYY

☐ Legally separated since ___/___/___   Attach a photocopy of your entire separation agreement.
                            MM   DD   YYYY

☐ Divorced since ___/___/___   Attach a photocopy of your entire divorce decree.
                   MM   DD   YYYY

Note. A divorce decree stating that your former spouse must pay all taxes does not necessarily mean you qualify for relief.

9   **What was the highest level of education you had completed when the return(s) were filed?** If the answers are **not** the same for all tax years, explain.

☐   High school diploma, equivalent, or less
☐   Some college
☐   College degree or higher. List any degrees you have ▶ _____
List any college-level business or tax-related courses you completed ▶ _____
_____

Explain ▶ _____
_____

10   **Were you a victim of spousal abuse or domestic violence during any of the tax years you want relief?** If the answers are **not** the same for all tax years, explain.

☐ Yes. **Attach a statement** to explain the situation and **when** it started. Provide photocopies of any documentation, such as police reports, a restraining order, a doctor's report or letter, or a notarized statement from someone who was aware of the situation.

☐ No.

11   **Did you sign the return(s)?** If the answers are **not** the same for all tax years, explain.

☐ Yes. If you were forced to sign under duress (threat of harm or other form of coercion), check here ▶ ☐. See instructions.

☐ No. Your signature was forged. See instructions.

12   **When any of the returns were signed, did you have a mental or physical health problem or do you have a mental or physical health problem now?** If the answers are **not** the same for all tax years, explain.

☐ Yes. **Attach a statement** to explain the problem and **when** it started. Provide photocopies of any documentation, such as medical bills or a doctor's report or letter.

☐ No.

Part IV   **Tell us how you were involved with finances and preparing returns for those tax years**

13   **How were you involved with preparing the returns?** Check all that apply and explain, if necessary. If the answers are **not** the same for all tax years, explain.

☐ You filled out or helped fill out the returns.
☐ You gathered receipts and cancelled checks.
☐ You gave tax documents (such as Forms W-2, 1099, etc.) to the person who prepared the returns.
☐ You reviewed the returns before they were signed.
☐ You did not review the returns before they were signed. Explain below.
☐ You were not involved in preparing the returns.
☐ Other ▶ _____
Explain how you were involved ▶ _____
_____
_____
_____

Form 8857 *(Continued)*

Form 8857 (Rev. 6-2007)   Page **3**

Note. If you need more room to write your answer for any question, attach more pages. Be sure to write your name and social security number on the top of all pages you attach.

Part IV   *(Continued)*

14   **When the returns were signed, were you concerned that any of the returns were incorrect or missing information?** Check all that apply and explain, if necessary. If the answers are **not** the same for all tax years, explain.

☐ You knew something was incorrect or missing, but you said nothing.
☐ You knew something was incorrect or missing and asked about it.
☐ You did not know anything was incorrect or missing.
Explain ▶ _____
_____

15   **When any of the returns were signed, what did you know about the income of the person on line 7?** If the answers are **not** the same for all tax years, explain.

☐ You knew that person had income.

List each type of income on a separate line. (Examples are wages, social security, gambling winnings, or self-employment business income.) Enter each tax year and the amount of income for each type you listed. If you do not know any details, enter "I don't know."

Type of income	Who paid it to that person	Tax Year 1	Tax Year 2	Tax Year 3
		$	$	$
		$	$	$
		$	$	$

☐ You knew that person was self-employed and you helped with the books and records.
☐ You knew that person was self-employed and you did not help with the books and records.
☐ You knew that person had no income.
☐ You did not know if that person had income.
Explain ▶ _____

16   **When the returns were signed, did you know any amount was owed to the IRS for those tax years?** If the answers are **not** the same for all tax years, explain.

☐ Yes. Explain when and how you thought the amount of tax reported on the return would be paid ▶ _____
_____
☐ No.
Explain ▶ _____

17   **When any of the returns were signed, were you having financial problems** (for example, bankruptcy or bills you could not pay)? If the answers are **not** the same for all tax years, explain.

☐ Yes. Explain ▶ _____
_____
☐ No.
☐ Did not know.
Explain ▶ _____

18   **For the years you want relief, how were you involved in the household finances?** Check all that apply. If the answers are **not** the same for all tax years, explain.

☐ You knew the person on line 7 had separate accounts.
☐ You had joint accounts but you had limited use of them or did not use them. Explain below.
☐ You used joint accounts. You made deposits, paid bills, balanced the checkbook, or reviewed the monthly bank statements.
☐ You made decisions about how money was spent. For example, you paid bills or made decisions about household purchases.
☐ You were not involved in handling money for the household.
☐ Other ▶ _____
Explain anything else you want to tell us about your household finances ▶ _____
_____

19   **Has the person on line 7 ever transferred assets (money or property) to you?** (Property includes real estate, stocks, bonds, or other property to which you have title.) See instructions.

☐ Yes. List the assets and the dates they were transferred. Explain why the assets were transferred ▶ _____
_____
☐ No.

Form **8857** (Rev. 6-2007)

Form 8857 *(Continued)*

Form 8857 (Rev. 6-2007)   Page **4**

Part V	Tell us about your current financial situation

20 Tell us the number of people currently in your household.   Adults _____   Children _____

21 Tell us your current average monthly income and expenses for your entire household. If family or friends are helping to support you, include the amount of support as gifts under **Monthly income**. Under **Monthly expenses**, enter all expenses, including expenses paid with income from gifts.

Monthly income	Amount	Monthly expenses	Amount
Gifts		Federal, state, and local taxes deducted from your paycheck	
Wages (Gross pay)		Rent or mortgage	
Pensions		Utilities	
Unemployment		Telephone	
Social security			
Government assistance, such as housing, food stamps, grants		Food	
Alimony		Car expenses, payments, insurance, etc.	
		Medical expenses, including medical insurance	
Child support		Life insurance	
Self-employment business income . .		Clothing	
Rental income		Child care	
Interest and dividends		Public transportation	
Other income, such as disability payments, gambling winnings, etc. List the type below:		Other expenses, such as real estate taxes, child support, etc. List the type below:	
Type _____		Type _____	
Type _____		Type _____	
Type _____		Type _____	
Total . . . . ▶		Total . . . . ▶	

22 Please provide any other information you want us to consider in determining whether it would be unfair to hold you liable for the tax. If you need more room, attach more pages. Be sure to write your name and social security number on the top of all pages you attach.

Caution
By signing this form, you understand that, by law, we must contact the person on line 7. See instructions for details.

Sign Here

Keep a copy for your records.

Under penalties of perjury, I declare that I have examined this form and any accompanying schedules and statements, and to the best of my knowledge and belief, they are true, correct, and complete. Declaration of preparer (other than taxpayer) is based on all information of which preparer has any knowledge.

Your signature ▶		Date

Paid Preparer's Use Only	Preparer's signature ▶		Date	Check if self-employed ☐	Preparer's SSN or PTIN
	Firm's name (or yours if self-employed), address, and ZIP code ▶			EIN	
				Phone no. ( )	

Form **8857** (Rev. 6-2007)

Form 8857 *(Continued)*

About the Author

Jeffrey H. Rattiner is president and chief executive officer of the JR Financial Group, Inc., which is a financial planning and information holding company with offices in the Denver and Phoenix metro areas serving consumers and financial services organizations. Mr. Rattiner earned his bachelor's degree in business administration with an emphasis in marketing management from Bernard M. Baruch College of the City University of New York in 1981; his MBA in certified public accounting from Hofstra University in 1983; and his certified financial planner education from New York University in 1992. He is a CERTIFIED FINANCIAL PLANNER® (CFP) and a certified public accountant (CPA) in New York, Colorado, and Arizona.

Mr. Rattiner's extensive Rattiner's Financial Planning Fast Track®(FPFT) boot camp program, which satisfies the CFP Board educational requirement in only seven months, trains professionals on how to become CFP licensees, and won critical acclaim as the cover story in the December 2001 issue of *Financial Planning Magazine*. Mr. Rattiner also informs and educates financial planners on how to become more successful in practice. He authored *Rattiner's Review for the CFP Certification Examination—Fast Track Study Guide* (now in its third edition) and *Rattiner's Financial Planner's Bible* for John Wiley & Sons, as well as *Getting Started as a Financial Planner* for Bloomberg Press (now in its second edition), *Financial Planning Answer Book* for CCH (annual release), *Adding Personal Financial Planning to Your Practice* for the American Management Association, and *Personal Financial Planning Library* for Harcourt Brace. He also co-authored *Practicing Financial Planning* for Mittra and Associates.

Mr. Rattiner is a frequently sought after speaker industry-wide, focusing on financial services organizations and consumer-related organizations, and has given presentations on personal financial planning, cash flow management, insurance planning, investment planning, income tax planning, employee benefit and retirement planning, Social Security, estate planning, small business owner planning, highly compensated employee issues, building and marketing a financial planning practice, and divorce planning.

He has been the director of professional development and corporate sponsorship for the Institute of Certified Financial Planners (ICFP); the director of technical standards for the Certified Financial Planner Board of Standards (CFP Board); and was previously employed as technical manager in the Personal Financial Planning (PFP) division of the American Institute of Certified Public Accountants (AICPA) in New York City.

Mr. Rattiner can be reached at jeff@financialgroup.com, www.jrfinancialgroup.com, or (720) 529-1888.

Index